Circuit Journeys

First published in 1888, thirty-four years after his death, Lord Cockburn's *Circuit Journeys* is a welcome addition to the Byways series of rediscoveries.

Henry Cockburn was born in the Parliament Close of old Edinburgh in 1779, the son of Archibald Cockburn and Janet Melville. He entered the High School in 1787 and the University of Edinburgh in 1793, spending "about nine years at two dead languages, which we did not learn." But the lectures of philosopher Dugald Stewart "were like the opening of the heavens," and a debating club brought him in contact with Jeffrey, Horner and Brougham, from whom he imbibed Whig opinions. Called to the Scottish Bar in 1800, in 1807 his uncle, the all-powerful Lord Melville, appointed him an advocate depute — a non-political post, from which, on political grounds, he "had the honour of being dismissed" in 1810. The following year he married Elizabeth Macdowall and made his home at Bonally Tower at the base of the Pentland Hills. Cockburn rose, with Jeffrey, to share the leadership of the Scottish Bar and with Jeffrey was counsel for three prisoners charged with sedition (1817-19). A zealous supporter, by pen as well as tongue, of parliamentary reform, he became Solicitor-General for Scotland under the Grey Ministry in 1830; had the chief hand in drafting the Scottish Reform Bill; in 1834 was made, as Lord Cockburn, a judge of the Court of Session; and in 1837 a lord of justiciary — which is where this volume starts. Henry Cockburn died in 1854 and is buried in the Dean Cemetery, Edinburgh, near Francis Jeffrey. Other works by Lord Cockburn are his *Life of Jeffrey* (1852), *Memorials of his Time* (1856), *Journal 1831-44* (2 vols. 1874) and *Trials for Sedition in Scotland* (2 vols. 1888).

Henry, Lord Cockburn

Circuit Journeys

Lord Cockburn

Byways

First Published 1983 by Byway Books
9 Maxton Court, Hawick, Roxburghshire TD9 7QN

© **Byway Books**

ISBN 0 907448 03 8

Phototypeset in Compugraphic English 18
and Printed in Scotland by Kelso Graphics,
The Knowes, Kelso, Roxburghshire

**This book is published with the financial assistance of
the Scottish Arts Council**

CONTENTS

Illustrations

Acknowledgements
The silhouette on page 1 by Edouart is published by courtesy of the Scottish National Portrait Gallery. Portraits of Lord Cockburn, Lord Moncrieff and Lord Braxfield are by Sir Henry Raeburn and the calotype of Lord Cockburn on p.250 is by D.O. Hill.

Erratum
Pages 193, 194, 195 and 196 should be read in the order 195, 196, 193 and 194.

Preface

BONALY, 28th March 1838

I have got this volume (prepared under the personal directions of Thomas Maitland, the first gentlemen binders) in order to record anything remarkable that may occur in my Circuits. It will be my fate to perform these journeys, being a Criminal Judge, as long as I am fit for anything, and it gives scenes, which repetition generally makes dull, an interest to have one's attention called, by the excitement of a diary, to occurrences which, however insignificant to strangers, are important to the individual engaged, and who always regrets to find that the impression of them is gone.

I wish that the Court of Justiciary had always had a Judge who left such a journal. The very uniformity of its subjects, implying a description from age to age of the same sort of occurrences and of the same parts of the country, and, of course, of their gradual changes, would have given it a value which detached records, though individually more curious, could not have possessed. If even Fountainhall, though not nearly far enough back, had imparted his observing and record-ing spirit to one of each series of his successors, what a curious picture would their continued memoranda have by this time given us of singular local men, of the changes of districts, of the progress of the law, of important trials, of strange manners, and of striking provincial events.

I did not think of keeping any note of my Circuit memorabilia till lately; so I must mention my two first expeditions from memory.

Circuit Journeys

WEST CIRCUIT
1837

30th March 1838. — My first Circuit was the West, which began at Stirling on Saturday the 16th of September 1837.

I went on the 14th, with my friend Sir Thomas Lauder, to Airthrie, to visit my cousin (by affinity), Lord Abercromby, and passed two delightful days at his hospitable house and most beautiful place. The whole of the forenoon of the 15th was passed with Sir Thomas and John Kirkpatrick, Esq., late Chief-Justice of the Ionian Islands, on Demyat Hill. The day was delightful; I can scarcely conceive nobler prospects than there are from that mountain. It is one of the many places which make us not at all afraid to boast of Scotland, even in comparison with Switzerland. Our solitude and elevation derived an additional charm from the distant view of the people sweltering below at the Stirling races. Nevertheless, having an excellent telescope, we could not resist the temptation of looking at a race, which we saw better and more minutely than many who were on the course.

Lord Moncreiff was my colleague. We finished the business on Saturday the 16th. On Sunday we went in procession to church, guarded by part of a regiment of the line, but without music, an omission which would have been deemed Jacobinical a few years ago, but which the modern notions of Sunday require. The pious have, within these six or eight years, taken his music even from his Majesty's Commissioner to the General Assembly.

We had a very pleasant party (for a Circuit) at dinner that day, including Mrs. Cockburn, my daughters Graham and Elizabeth, and my niece, Eliza Maitland, and sundry redcoats. The Provost was so charmed with my talk (I suppose) that he rose and proposed my health with all the honours. Moncreiff checked this compliment. But the chance of such an occurrence is one of the many things which show the inexpediency of these Circuit dinners.

On Monday the 18th Moncreiff and I parted. He went to Inverary, I to Renfrewshire. I got to my brother-in-law's at Barr, by Lochwinnoch, to dinner. Stayed there till Tuesday night, when I went to Glasgow, and tried civil causes from

Wednesday morning till Saturday evening, when I returned to Barr and remained there till Monday the 25th, when I went to Possil, near Glasgow, the residence of Archibald Alison, the Sheriff of Lanarkshire, where I met Moncreiff, and where we continued all night.

Next morning, Tuesday, 26th September 1837, we made a grand procession into the Court, the grandest I ever saw at a Scotch Circuit; there were four carriages and four, besides four or five with two horses, — plenty Lancers, in all their bravery of men and steeds, — rows of well-drilled police, — music, — gazers, etc. It took us till the evening of the next Tuesday to dispose of the criminal cases.

I am happy to say that there were unusually few pleas of guilty. These pleas are odious. They sometimes happen from genuine contrition, sometimes from despair, and sometimes from a desire to hide the atrocious features of the offence by preventing their disclosure in evidence. But confessions from these causes are very rare; the common cause is an idea that saving trouble will conciliate the Court. And accordingly it sometimes has this effect far too much, and a very few years ago it had to a shameful degree. It mitigated the sentence not merely truly, but avowedly. It was quite common to hear it stated from the Bench, as one of the reasons why peculiar leniency was shown, that the prisoner "had pleaded guilty, and thereby saved the Court all trouble." This was the phrase; and the judicial feeling occasionally assumed the still worse form of its being stated to the prisoner as an aggravation of his guilt, that, instead of acknowledging what he must have known to be true, he had gone to trial. There was a case within these last eight years, in which a prisoner's counsel advised and forwarded a petition for mercy to Government, founded on this sentiment having been uttered from the Bench at passing sentence. It is the principle of a great majority of the Court to let pleas of guilty have no effect whatever on the punishment. And indeed it is rare to find a case in which a sane man can dream of pleading guilty, unless it be to please the Court, and thereby to soften the sentence. By going to trial he has always the chance of escaping, and he can only be convicted at the worst. So what better — except with a view to the result — is he of confessing? Even a wish to conceal the aggravations of his guilt, which is the most rational motive for this course, is only a good one on the supposition that the Court in awarding the punishment goes beyond the facts asserted in the indictment, or lets itself be more inflamed by the witnesses' descriptions of the occurrences than by the prosecutor's. Pleas of guilty, therefore, are a bad sign of the Court.

There were two convictions for murder — one against a woman for drowning her child, and one against a man, a tobacco-spinner, who first married a woman who he knew had several illegitimate children, and then, from jealousy, killed her

3

by repeated stabs. They were both sentenced to be executed at Paisley on the same day. The woman's sentence was commuted into the strange substitute of imprisonment for four years, but the man's was carried into effect.

I tried his case, and consequently had to pronounce the sentence — the first capital one I ever pronounced, and I hope the last. It is a very painful duty.

There is a great art in pronouncing sentences. The old judges used generally to abuse the prisoner. The feelings of a later age would not tolerate this. But they have introduced a sermonising system which it requires some courage in any judge to avoid. Even in the slightest case — not extending beyond imprisonment — the prisoner must always be reminded of his latter end and of his immortal soul, and two of us very rarely ever fail to point out the way to salvation by actually naming Redemption and the Redeemer. There are others (inter quos ego) who think that more direct and practical expositions of the personal and immediate consequences of crime are more likely to operate on worldly audiences and worldly villains. The misfortune of the religious plan is, that as adherence to it is thought a duty, it is apt to lose its effect by being applied indiscriminately to every case. A proper mixture of the two would be the best thing.

Moncreiff, the most excellent of men, and one of the most admirable of judges, but whose piety and simplicity sometimes give him odd views, has signalised himself twice, in passing sentence, by principles which have greatly diverted his friends, and produced much speculation among English lawyers, as I heard his friend Brougham, when Chancellor, tell him.

Once was in dooming a man to die for murdering a female who lived with him. It was altogether a shocking case, but his Lordship found out, and debated upon this peculiar atrocity, that the woman he had killed was not his wife, but only his mistress, because, as he explained, if she had been your wife, there might possibly have been some apology for you, on account of the difficulty of getting quit of a wife in any other way. But this unfortunate woman being only your associate, you might have freed yourself from her whenever you chose. How Brougham revelled over this discovery, that it was a less crime to murder a wife than to murder a mistress!

His other view I had heard of before, but I actually heard it personally at this Circuit. Both were cases of bigamy; and his Lordship after explaining, as anybody else might have done, the usual atrocities of the offence, such as the perfidy and cruelty to both women, the confusion and destitution of families, etc., added, nearly in these words:- "All this is bad; but your true iniquity consists in this, that you degraded that holy ceremony which our blessed Saviour condescended to select as the type of the connection between him and his redeemed church." He put a strong emphasis upon the word condescended; why, I know not. I must do the public the justice to say that it did not

4

seem to sympathise with the statement that this was the chief guilt of bigamy.

If I were a culprit, I would rather be sentenced by Moncreiff than by any judge I have ever known. He is, in general, very sensible, and always very kind, and never dreams of making it an occasion for display, but addresses the prisoner almost as if he were an unfortunate friend, for whose temporal and eternal welfare he had a deep anxiety, to whom he pointed out penitence and the formation of better habits as the only means of reaching future happiness, and of whose reformation he rarely despaired.

GLASGOW CIRCUIT
1838

31st March 1838. — The Glasgow Winter Circuit began on Tuesday 9th January 1838, and closed on the evening of Friday the 12th. I was engaged with the famous case of the cotton-spinners at Edinburgh, and only got to Glasgow on the evening of the 9th. Lord Medwyn took the first day at Glasgow alone.

Nothing particular took place at this Circuit, except that everybody was under the deepest anxiety about the result of the cotton-spinners' case which I had left unfinished; and so all our thoughts were of Trades Unions and the guilt that is apt to adhere to combinations. There was indeed a trial of a man called Thomas Riddle for the offence of compelling a workman by violence to give over working. This case fell to me. He pleaded guilty, but got no reward, for he was transported for seven years, being the full measure that would have been dealt to him after the toughest resistance. I had no warning, and consequently no premeditation, but on the spot gave him an address which has had its full crop of undeserved praise. It was not only circulated extensively both here and in England, but was applauded in the House of Commons (about a month ago) when the case of the cotton-spinners was under discussion. And all this solely because while it pointed out the criminality of violence, it judicially acknowledged the innocence of mere combination, and thus removed the imputation that Courts did not do justice to workmen.

Medwyn, in addressing the sheriffs and magistrates gave a lecture, and a good one, on the same subject, to which the Sheriff of Lanarkshire, Alison, took occasion to add a long discourse, giving a view of the morals and statistics of strikes and unions.

These three addresses may be found in Swinton's report of the trial of the cotton-spinners. Alison's has been expanded into an article in the forthcoming number of the Edinburgh Review, written by himself.

This is the second time that my friend Alison has made a long speech after the judge, a very dangerous and unusual practice, which he probably won't be allowed to repeat. The first time he tried it, a bailie attempted to compel the Court to let him answer, as he said that the Sheriff had attacked the Town Council, which shows the inexpediency of tolerating such harangues.

NORTH CIRCUIT

Aviemore, Thursday, 12th April 1838. — I am here upon the North Circuit, which begins at Inverness on Saturday the 14th.

I left Edinburgh on Monday last, the 9th, with my daughters Jane and Graham. Jane not being strong, we resolved to take it leisurely. So we slept the first night at Perth. I walked nearly two hours along the water side on the North Inch, and watched the fishers toiling very fruitlessly for salmon. The watcher at the bridge told me next morning that in the last twenty-four hours they had only killed one fish.

Next day we went to Dunkeld, — to Pitlochrie — to Kindrogan, the residence of my old friend Patrick Small Keir, where we stayed till this morning.

The whole of this country, from Edinburgh to Kindrogan, except that constantly wet, cold, and dull region of Kinross, is beautiful. But this is not the season to see it in. I used to think that Scotch scenery depended so much on rock, hill, water, and fir, that the foliage of deciduous wood was of less importance to it than to most other scenery. There are some parts of the Highlands where this is true, — where leaves do little for the dark mountain, the perpetual pine, the gleaming cataract, and the blue loch. But in general it is not true. I could scarcely have conceived that a tract of country which has so many noble fixed features could suffer so much in its appearance from the foliage being still dead. It has a great deal of good moderate forest trees, and is everywhere richly sprinkled with birch. I have often seen it at this season, but I had forgotten the bareness and coldness of the leafless stems; the want of colour over the wooded surface; the exposure of everything; the disproportioned bringing out of the evergreen firs, and the general deadness. Even Dunkeld seemed chill and unsettled, with its picturesque slate quarries brought too near, its long wintry reaches of cold, steelly water, and its cathedral, apparently rising and staring over the country. It is grievous to see how the last savage winter has desolated the ornamental evergreens. There are few sorts that have not suffered, but the Arbutus and Laurustinus seem, in general, to be destroyed.

Kindrogan, which I never saw before, is a very nice little Highland place. A sensible house, picturesque rocks, good hills, and an excellent stream. We were most kindly treated, and very happy.

Killiecrankie looked worse, from its nakedness, than even Dunkeld. It is common to abuse the country from the Pass to this. I have always thought it magnificent. Even the solitude and desolation of Dalwhinnie is sublime. The approach to Aviemore becomes interesting soon after the waters begin to flow Spey-ward, till at last the full prospect of these glorious Cairngorms, with their forests and peaks and valleys, exhibits one of the finest pieces of mountain scenery in Britain. To-day they were covered with snow, which had to be cut several feet deep in four places on the road.

The first time I was in this inn was in 1797 or 1798, when, with two other boys, I made a tour in a gig to Inverness, and home by Fort Augustus, and over Corryarrick.

My studies in the chaise have hitherto been the new number of the Edinburgh Review, and the last volume of Lockhart's Life of Scott. The review is not just yet published (No. 135). The striking article is the first, on the abuses of the press, by Brougham. It is a curious performance, and will produce much discussion. The portraits of his contemporaries are worthy of Clarendon. They are all too favourably drawn. Lockhart mentions Scott as having gone to see my old client, Mrs. Smith, who was guilty, but acquitted, of murder by poison. The case made a great noise. Scott's description of the woman is very correct. She was like a vindictive masculine witch. I remember him sitting within the bar, looking at her. Lockhart should have been told that as we were moving out, Sir Walter's remark upon the acquittal was: "Well, sirs! all I can say is, that if that woman was my wife, I should take good care to be my own cook."

Inverness, Friday Night, 13th April 1838. — We left Avie-more to-day at eleven, and got here about three. A beautiful day. There are three interesting things in this part of the road, — the wood of Scotch firs (I forget its name) near the Bridge of Carr, the branches being more gnarled and tossed about like those of forest trees, than any fir branches I ever saw, — the long, deep, pastoral descents and rises of the road; and the glorious bursts of the Moray Firth, and the Ross-shire and other hills when the height, about five miles from Inverness, is gained. Yet some monsters are improving the country (as they no doubt call it) by planting out these magnificent prospects, by lining the road with abominable stripes of wretched larch trees. Our only hope is in the boys and the cattle.

My heart will ever warm at the mention of the Bridge of Carr. The first I was ever at Relugas, the Paradise formerly possessed by my friend Sir Thomas Dick Lauder, now above twenty years ago, he joined the late excellent Dr. Gordon, Mr. Macbean, and me, who had come from Edinburgh there; and what a day! and how many happy days! succeeded that meeting! After an alarming breakfast — alarming both from its magnitude and its mirth, we rolled along in two gigs, on a splendid autumnal day, till we annihilated the twenty-two miles between us and Eden; where began the first of a course of almost annual visits, hallowed in my memory by scenery and friendship, by the society and progress of a happy family, and, above all, by the recollection of Gordon. The Bridge of Carr brings them all to my eye, and to my heart.

Huntly, Tuesday, 17th April 1838, Night. — On Saturday the 14th, I was in Court till midnight.

The only curious case was that of Malcolm McLean, a fisherman from Lewis, who is doomed to die upon the 11th of May, for the murder of his wife. He admitted that he killed her, and intentionally, but the defence by his counsel was that he was mad at the time. There was not the slightest foundation for this, for though he was often under the influence of an odd mixture of wild religious speculation, and of terrified superstition, he had no illusion, and in all the affairs of life, including all his own feelings and concerns, was always dealt with as a sound practical man. One part of his pretended craziness was said to consist in his making machinery to attain the perpetual motion, and his believing that he had succeeded. This shows that this famous problem is not in such vogue as it once was. But the thing that seemed to me to be the oddest in the matter, was the perfect familiarity with which the common Celts of Lewis talked and thought of the thing called the perpetual motion, whatever they fancied it. Their word for it, according to the common process of borrowing terms with ideas, was, "Perpetual Motion", pronounced and treated by them as a Gaelic expression. The words "Perpetual motion," were used in the middle of Gaelic sentences without stop or surprise, exactly as we use any Anglified French term.

This man's declaration, which told the whole truth with anxious candour, contained a curious and fearful description of the feelings of a man about to commit a deliberate murder. He had taken it into his head that his wafe was unkind, and perhaps faithless to him, and even meant to kill him, and therefore he thought it better, upon the whole, to prevent this by killing her, which accordingly, on a particular day, he was determined to do. He went to work on a piece of ground in the morning, thinking, all the time he was working, of going into the house and doing the deed, but was unwilling and infirm. However, he at last resolved, went in, sat down, she at the opposite side of the fire, the children in and out, but still he could not, and went to work again. After reasoning and dreaming of the great deed of the day, he went to the house again, but still could not, and came out; and this alternate resolving and wavering, this impulse of passion, and this recoiling of nature recurred most part of the day, till at last, sitting opposite to her again, he made a sudden plunge at her throat, and scientifically Burked her by compressing the mouth and nose, after which a sore fit of sated fury succeeded, which gave way, when people began to come in, to an access of terror and cunning, which made him do everything possible for his own safety, till tired of wandering about, and haunted by some of his religious notions, he went towards Stornoway to redeliver himself (for he had been previously taken, but escaped), when he was discovered. He is now low and resigned, and says he has not been so comfortable for years, because he has got the better of the Devil at last, and is sure of defying him on the 11th of May.

I never left home for ten days without finding an acquaintance gone before I returned. One letter, received yesterday, informs me of the death of Sir James Fergusson of Kilkerran, of my old schoolfellow McDonald of Staffa, and of William Murray, a boy, the son of the Lord Advocate. This last is the saddest possible death. He was a nice clever boy; the only child of his parents; and the only hope of the House of Henderland. I fear it will extinguish his mother, his father, and his uncle, the head of the family.

I went officially to church on Sunday, and was again in Court yesterday till twelve at night. To-day we came here, amidst a strong bitter wind, loaded with driving snow, which has been our fare since Tuesday morning, this being the end of our last vernal month.

I refreshed myself again with a walk over the ruins of Elgin Cathedral, along with my daughter Graham. What a pile! And what fragments! It is now in very tolerable order; certainly by far the best kept old ruin, public or private, in Scotland; a country which disgraces itself by its disregard of its ancient buildings, and the base uses to which it lets them be turned. The merit of putting Elgin in order belongs partly to the Crown, but still more to an old man who for above forty years has had the charge of showing the Cathedral and has spent his life in clearing away rubbish, disclosing parts of the building, and preserving fragments, — all literally with his own hands. The name of this combatant of time is John Shanks. The rubbish, he says, "has made an auld man o' me," which, with the help of seventy years, it no doubt has. He used to have a strong taste for whisky, but always a stronger one for antiquities and relics of the cathedral. He is now a worthy garrulous body, who can only speak however about the tombs and ruins, and recites all the inscriptions as if he could not help it, and is more at home with the statues of the old bishops and soldiers than with his own living family.

Perth, Monday, 23rd April 1838. — We reached Aberdeen on the 18th, through clouds of snow and bitter blasts. There were three wreaths between Huntly and Pitmachie, which really alarmed me.

I know no part of Scotland so much, and so visibly, improved within thirty years as Aberdeenshire. At the beginning of that time, the country between Keith and Stonehaven was little else than a hopeless region of stones and moss. There were places of many miles where literally there was nothing but large white stones of from half a ton to ten tons in weight, to be seen. A stranger to the character of the people would have supposed that despair would have held back their hands from even attempting to remove them. However, they began, and year after year have been going on making dikes and drains, and filling up holes with these materials, till at last they have created a country which, when the rain happens to cease, and the sun to shine, is really very endurable.

Moncreiff joined me at Aberdeen, and we were three days in Court there, from morning till past midnight. There was nothing curious in any of the cases. The weather was so bad that we had no public procession, but went to Court privately and respectably. The dignity of justice would be increased if it always rained. Yet there are some of us who like the procession, though it can never be anything but mean and ludicrous, and who fancy that a line of soldiers, or the more civic array of paltry police-officers, or of doited special constables, protecting a couple of judges who flounder in awkward gowns and wigs, through the ill-paved streets, followed by a few sneering advocates, and preceded by two or three sheriffs, or their substitutes, with white swords, which trip them, and a provost and some bailie-bodies trying to look grand, the whole defended by a poor iron mace, and advancing each with a different step, to the sound of two cracked trumpets, ill-blown by a couple of drunken royal trumpeters, the spectators all laughing, — who fancy that all this ludicrous pretence of greatness and reality of littleness, contributes to the dignity of justice. Judges should never expose themselves unnecessarily — their dignity is on the bench.

We have had some good specimens of the condition of jails. One man was tried at Inverness for jail-breaking, and his defence was that he was ill-fed, and that the prison was so weak that he had sent a message to the jailor that if he did not get more meat he would not stay in another hour, and he was as good as his word. The Sheriff of Elgin was proceeding to hold court to try some people, when he was saved the trouble by being told that they had all walked out. Some of them being caught, a second court was held, since I was at Inverness, to dispose of them; when the proceedings were again stopped from the opposite cause. The jailor had gone to the country taking the key of the prison with him, and the prisoners not being willing to come forth voluntarily, could not be got out. Lord Moncreiff (who joined me at Aberdeen) tells me that when he was Sheriff of Kinross-shire, there was an Alloa culprit who was thought to be too powerful for the jail of that place. So they hired a chaise and sent an officer with him to the jail of Kinross, where he was lodged. But before the horses were fed for their return, he broke out, and wishing to be with his friends a little before finally decamping, he waited till the officers set off, and then returned to Alloa, without their knowing it, on the back of the chaise that had brought him to Kinross, with them in it.

Aberdeen is improving in its buildings and harbour. The old town is striking and interesting, with its venerable college, its detached position, its extensive links, and glorious beach. But the new and larger city is cold, hard, and treeless. The grey granite does well for public works where durability is obviously the principal object, but for common dwelling-houses it is not, to my taste, nearly so attractive as the purity of the white free-stone, or the richness of the cream-coloured. Polishing and fine jointing improve it much, but this is dear, and hence the ugly lines of mortar between the seams of the stones.

We came here by the coast, by far the best way. Except Glamis there is nothing on the inland road. Montrose is one of the most English-looking towns in Scotland, Kelso excepted. I scarcely know a more picturesque street than its main one, with its windings, its gables turned outwards, its painted outsides and general appearance of neatness and comfort. They have built a spire since I was last there, or at least I had forgotten it.

I once more visited the ruins of Arbroath Cathedral. It has been immensely improved by the recent removal of several feet of rubbish, which had been allowed to accumulate within the walls. The removal, besides giving the place an air of protection and decency, has disclosed the bases of many pillars, figures, coffins, and other relics. But the building was made of too soft a stone, and is mouldering rapidly.

I also went this morning and saw the rocks where Scott makes the couple be overtaken by the sea, and saved by Edie Ochiltree. They are noble rocks, and were well chafed by noble waves.

The whole features of this place suit the descriptions of the novel, and now, indeed, they derive their chief interest from their doing so. Arbroath is well painted in the description of Fairport, and as we look at the little harbour, the fishing-boats on the beach, the ruined abbey, and the steep wave-worn rocks on the shore, the whole story, with all its incidents, characters, and names, recur to the memory.

That glorious drive through the Carse of Gowrie was obscured by thick rain.

Edinburgh, 30th April 1838. — We had tough work at Perth, which it took four and a half days to get through. We were only free yesterday about three, and got home in the evening, and a clear, beautiful, though cold evening it was.

Two things deserving of notice occurred in the course of the business.

One was, that we had a bigamist before us. I again threw the case into Moncreiff's hands, in the expectation of hearing the curious sentiment I have already mentioned. But the train failed. He left it out, for the first time I believe in sentencing such a culprit, and made a good rational address.

The other was, that we had an example of that horrid piece of nonsense, invented within these twenty years by the Court of Justiciary, and called by the inventors "The Option." The absurdity cannot possibly last long, and for the edification of posterity it may be as well to tell what it was.

Some people think it cruel, and conducive to perjury, to compel parents or children to give evidence against each other; others — of whom I am one — admit it to be painful, but I think that everything must yield to the necessities of justice, and that nothing is so cruel as that an innocent man should be convicted because a son is indulged in protecting his father by silence, which may happen in many ways. What is thought the humane side prevails at present in our criminal law. But it occurred to some of the judges, about twenty years ago, that, as the indulgence was granted solely from delicacy to these relations, it was competent to them to reject it if they chose. They therefore introduced The Option, by which parents and children might hang each other or not, just as they pleased, unless they happened to be under pupillarity, in which case, being held capable of discretion, they are always rejected.

The practical operation of this folly is this: — A mother is on trial for her life. Her daughter is called as a witness against her. The Court tells her she has The Option. She is a person of right feelings, and declines to testify. The possession of such feelings is a proof that she is worthy of being credited, even in the case of a parent. Nevertheless, truth is defied, and the claims of justice disregarded, for her comfort. But if she had been a monster, to whom hanging her mother was a luxury, that is, if she had been a person who exercised this Option by preferring to give evidence, then she proves herself to be utterly incredible. Yet, just on this account, she is admitted to be sworn. And if the whole family be true to each other, as is commonly (but not always) the case, then all the light depending on parents and children is utterly excluded. A father may cut his wife's throat with complete safety, provided he takes care to perform the operation before nobody but her ten grown-up sons and daughters.

In the case at Perth, a man called Murray was charged with having forged his son's name. But the son, who alone could prove the forgery, took advantage of this notable Option, and refused to answer, on which the witness and the accused walked out of the Court arm in arm.

The thing is particularly absurd in the case of forgery. Because, where the person whose signature is forged is alive and accessible, his testimony, being the best evidence, is indispensable. If the person forged upon were the person injured, The Option would not be allowed. But the Court has decided that the person injured is he who has been defrauded by the uttering. So that all forgeries are safe that are committed by parents or children on each other, and whose respective affection for each other is stronger than their regard for public justice.

This tissue of necessary nonsense is no part of the law of Scotland. The fear of perjury, — a foolish principle, but one that was not unnatural to superstitious barbarians, played on by cunning churchmen, — made our old law reject such testimony altogether and without distinction. But The Option, by which its reception is made to depend on the pleasure or profligacy of each witness, is the production of a few judges, not at all qualified to legislate on such a subject, within these few years.

The true principle is, to disregard relationship, except that of husband and wife, as an objection to the competency of any witness.

Perth is the only place I have ever seen where, in the arrangement of the spectators in a public court, there is an entire separation made between the ladies and the gentlemen. The gallery is divided into a male and female compartment. It looks very odd, but it seems to conduce silence. The eyes flirt more silently than the tongue. I don't understand, however, that this was the object.

When I was at Elgin, I was told that the people there were disturbed by rumours of an intention on the part of the trustees of the late Duke of Gordon to sell the Bishop's House, a large, square, venerable, red free-stone building, almost in contact with the cathedral, and erected at the same time. I instantly wrote to the agent of the Duke of Richmond, who has succeeded the Duke of Gordon, and without whose consent no such proceeding would take place. But on coming home, I find that the disgraceful transaction has been completed, and that since I was there, the Bishop's House, or rather, the Gordon property there, including this house, has actually been sold for about £656. I wish these noble persons, or their representatives, had only let it be known that the saving of such a piece of antiquity depended on their getting £656, for it could easily have been raised in farthings. It is said that the house, which seems to be still entire, is to be taken down, to make way for a villa. _____ them.

I have long been accustomed to watch for my first swallow towards the end of the Spring Circuit, and almost always to find it. This year I looked for it in vain; no swallow has been so foolish as to appear yet.

WEST CIRCUIT

Tarbet, Tuesday, 11th September 1838, 11 p.m. — I left home

last Saturday, the 8th, with Mrs. Cockburn, my daughter Jane, and my son Henry, at eight a.m., and got to Barr by Lochwinnoch about five. We remained there till this morning, two pleasant, lounging, jolly days.

We came away this morning at nine, crossed the Clyde at Renfrew Ferry, and proceeded along the right bank of the water to Dumbarton. The opening of the Clyde there is beautiful and grand. But the tide was out, which greatly impairs it. I have always thought Kilpatrick rather a respectable village, and was glad to see that it still deserved that character.

I have not been on Loch Lomond since (I think) 1824. I am more and more struck with its magnificence and loveliness. I was never so much impressed as to-day with the cultivated comfort and elegance of the lower end of the lake, where every acre of land exhibits the appearance of culture that is old, and of comfort that is improving. Old trees, old hollies, good roads, good houses, good lodges, all well kept, as if by owners who were proud of their places, and knew how much they were looked at by strangers, all, whether they be on the low ground or on the high, kept in connection with their splendid sheet of water. The Church of Luss is, from its charming position, beautiful as ever; but the dirt and squalid wretchedness of the houses and people of that village is a disgrace to the landlords. Such abomination, in such a scene, is one of the unanswerable scandals of Scotland. But the lairds who permit it are the chief brutes. It is perfectly inconceivable, no public infamy is too great for it. And how little it would take, and this little consisting chiefly of kindness, advice, and some authority, to charm the poor people into a higher state of existence, and to make their promontory a paradise. At present, God has planted a garden there, and man a hog-stye.

Mrs. Cockburn searched the churchyard for some lines which many years ago she found, and deciphered, on a very old, hoary, tombstone. She succeeded, but the stone had been renewed, possibly in honour of the lines, which are striking, and to me new —

'Twas when the primrose hailed the infant year,
And all was eye, and all was listening ear,
My sweet rosebud reclined his weary head,
And here he lies among the silent dead.
Uncertain life! How transient is thy show!
How high thy prospects, and thy end how low!
This day in health, a country's pride and boast!
Perhaps to-morrow mingled with the dust!

We were here by three o'clock, and are to remain all night. The day has been good, but not bright, and very calm and balmy. Since I was here the new road up by Glenfalloch, and indeed along the whole loch, has been finished, and it is really a luxury to bowl along upon it. The traveller had the pleasure formerly of mounting over the high point of Firkin, and indeed

14

over all the high points, whereby he no doubt got sundry glorious prospects, but his toil and impatience were not well fitted to make him enjoy them, and it was murderous work for the poor horses. Higher up the loch than this, there was nothing that could be called road at all. The whole edge of water is now lined by a way so level and so smooth, that no dreamer has any pretence for saying that he is jolted out of his contemplations; and I am not sure but the loss of the heights is more than compensated, even in point of scenery, by the increased variety of aspects which are opened up at every turn round the bays and promontories. The daily steamer was grunting and belching, with its long tail of polluting smoke. Nevertheless this too is good; the disturbance is very short, the convenience, even to the solitary pilgrim, immense, and it is impossible not to sympathise with the crowds within whose reach it puts the enjoyment of these recesses.

The evening closed over the loch and the hills in calm, deep darkness, leaving nothing whatever visible, and only one distant little waterfall audible.

This inn is, for a Scotch one, very good, but far too small for the resort in summer, and far too large for the want of resort in winter. I am always ashamed of our country for its inhospitality, in this respect of inns, to the many strangers who now visit it. The inn near the Trossachs could, perhaps, put up a dozen, or at the very most, two dozen of people; but last autumn I saw about one hundred apply for admittance, and after horrid altercations, entreaties, and efforts, about fifty or sixty were compelled to huddle together all night. They were all of the upper rank, travelling mostly in private carriages, and by far the greater number strangers. But the pigs were as comfortably accommodated. I saw three or four English gentlemen spreading their own straw on the earthen floor of an outhouse, with a sparred door, and no fire-place or furniture. And such things occur every day there, though the ground belongs partly to a duke, and partly to an earl, — Montrose and Willoughby. These are the countrymen of Sir Walter Scott. His genius immortalises the region. This attracts strangers, and this is their encouragement. Is there any part of the Continent where this could happen?

Inverary, Wednesday, 12th September 1838, 10 p.m. — A tedius, dull, hot, rainy day, without a breath of wind to move a leaf or a cloud, or a moment's hope that the heavy uniformity was to break up or change. Accordingly it has been true to its promise, and the warm, misty plash has not ceased one moment from seven in the morning till now. Of course we have seen nothing, — nothing at least except the half forms of things, just enough to suggest what would be seen if it were clear, and to revive through the gloom the remembrance of many past expeditions. I trust that Loch Fyne and Loch Long will have brighter faces when I return, and Glencroe a purer verdure, clearer summits, and more sparkling burns.

Tarbet, Monday, 17th September 1838, 9 p.m. — Thursday the 13th continued as humid as its immediate elder brother. But as I was in Court till twelve at night, it was all one in so far as I was concerned. Nothing particular in Court except the account which a worthy sempstress of Campbeltown, a witness, gave of her habits. For about twenty-five years she has scarcely ever been in bed after five. The first thing she does after dressing is, to go to a rock about a mile off, and to take a large draught of sea water. She then proceeds about another mile, in a different direction, where she washes the taste of this out by a large draught of fresh water, after which she proceeds home, and about half past six puts on the tea-kettle and breakfasts. This is a healthy and romantic seeming morning. And therefore I regret to add that it was proved that three or four times a week the rest of the day is given to whisky, as a result of early rising which will delight Jeffrey, to whom morning, except before going to bed, is horrid.

Friday the 14th was a beautiful day. The business was done by two. John Murray, the Lord Advocate, who is living at Strachur Park, came over to us in the cutter maintained by the Herring Board, a very nice vessel, with a master and fifteen men. He and Mrs. Murray, and Mrs. Cockburn, and Cosmo Innes, the Advocate-Depute, and others, went up to a pool in the River Ary, about two miles above the castle, where the annual ploy was held of drawing the water the day before the close of the salmon fishing. It seems to have been a gay and picturesque sight. Mr. Lloyd, who married Mrs. Murray's sister, told me that he had never seen and never expected to see anything like it. To be sure, he is not only an Englishman, but lives near Manchester. But the true Scotchmen all concur in describing the scenery, the people, and the activity of the fishers, as very striking. I was not there, because I determined not to cross to Strachur in the cutter, which was the business of one hour, but to drive round with Jane, twenty-one miles, by Cairndow, which was the business of three.

I can regret nothing that gave me that drive. I can never see a more beautiful evening. All below Cairndow was new to me. The hills were fresh after the rain, the air balmy, and perfectly serene; the sky not flaring with unbroken brightness, but softened by many clouds; the water streaked by long smooth rays, and large spots of it dazzling with trembling brilliancy. Upon the whole, it was a lovely, pensive scene. No day could die away more sweetly. It was near seven when we reached Strachur, and it was not easy to say farewell to the lingering light, and to take one's last look of the still visible outlines of the distant hills.

Our party consisted of the Advocate, and Mrs. Murray, her

sister Mrs. Lloyd, and her husband, the Advocate's brother William, Robert Graham of Lyndoch, Captain Pringle of the Engineers, and ourselves. About eleven at night, Graham and Pringle went on board the cutter, lay down till four, rose and went out in the boat and saw the herring-fishing, came back and lay down again about six till eight, when Pringle went off to Oban to take charge of Babbage the Mathematician, and Graham went to Glasgow to secure a good place for a cow at the approaching cattle show.

Saturday the 15th was still a better day than the one before — brighter, and warmer, and calmer. We passed the whole day, from twelve to half-past six, in the cutter. What a day! What scenery! Our bark lay sleeping on the mirror, so that its motion, whenever we were attracted by a green bit of lawn, a dark grove, or an enviably-placed house, was scarcely perceptible, and it was all that all the airs of Loch Fyne could do to breathe us down towards that most picturesque place, Minard, the hills behind which, seen from a distance up the loch are not unworthy of being compared, in their outline, even with the peaks of Arran. I was much struck with little Pennymore, nestled behind its rock, amidst its soft green copse. It became so perfectly calm in the evening that we were obliged to take to the boats, and to row ashore the last two miles.

About eleven o'clock this night intimation came that Mr. Lloyd's sister, her son, and her grandson, had been drowned a few days before, on their passage to Dundee in the Forfarshire steamer which had gone down after striking on one of the Fern Islands near the mouth of the Firth of Forth. This saddened us all. But there were circumstances in the sister's situation which deadened the blow.

Sunday the 16th was, if possible, still more beautiful. Being a Scotch Sunday we had no boating, and indeed whatever day it had been, sympathy with the Lloyds would have kept us all quiet. So we just sauntered by the shore, — and talked, and gathered shells, and skiffed flat stones on the surface of the sea, and sat on rocks and lay on the turf, and played with the clear water, and gazed, unceasingly gazed, on the hills, and watched the shadows of the clouds, and observed how the prospects varied with our positions, and with the progress of the sun, and in short had a long luxurious day of repose and enjoyment. There was no church, because the minister had gone to the horse fair at Balloch. The day was so calm, that as I was standing on the beach before breakfast, I distinctly heard the barking of a dog on the opposite side of the water.

Tarbet, 9 p.m. — We left Strachur this morning (Monday, 17th September 1838) at ten o'clock, and came here by Cairndow. The weather has continued most delightful. I again came through the grounds of Ardkinglas. It is an excellent place, which however would not be the worse of a little draining, or of a thorough revision of the trees. There is some noble wood, particularly some magnificent (but dying) silver firs.

I turned aside from Loch Fyne with great regret. I had never seen so much of it before, and like everything new that I see, it has greatly raised even my admiration of Scotland. The whole of these Argyleshire sea lochs are glorious. The boldness and beauty of their scenery, their strange, savage history, their wild language, and (till lately) their delightful inaccessibility, all give them a character of picturesque romance which nothing else in this country resembles. But independently of past associations, what an interest is there in the mere present and external features of Loch Fyne! The picturesque hills, the bright water, the occasional masses and constant fringing of wood, the jutting and overlapping of the headlands, the apparent closing in of the loch, and its streaming away again into scenes of distant beauty; the fishing hamlets, with their boats slumbering in quiet bays and little rude harbours; the long poles loaded with brown nets resting horizontally on the branches of two trees springing from the very beach; then sailing under tanned canvas, on a calm peaceful evening to set these nets, the boats sometimes lighted at night by hundreds and sparkling like a moving city, and all moored again by the morning; the intercourse between families and villages by boats, which the narrowness of the loch seems to invite; the bright patches of grain amidst the darkness of the wood, or contrasted by the expanse of the brown hillside; the breeze-varied appearances of the surface of the water, and the shining and roaring of the mountain streams, — these things give it an endless and irresistible charm. All this, to be sure, is the fascination of fine weather. But if other places also are to be judged of in bad weather, these lochs have nothing to fear. The worst thing is the contrast between the quiet little Indian Wigwam-looking hamlets, when seen at a distance, and their utter abomination when approached. It is horrid that human life should be passed in these disgusting holes. It is true that fishing especially when combined with curing, cannot be conducted without filth, but there are many proofs that its slobbery nastiness may be concealed, and kept apart from the fishers' dwellings, and that a fishing village may be a beautiful thing. But until the lairds be civilised and cease to be all regularly and systematically bankrupt, it is in vain to expect decency or comfort in the domestic habits of their people.

The day was perfect for that glorious stage from Cairndow to Tarbet. Few things are more magnificent than the rise from Cairndown to Rest-and-be-Thankful. The top of it, where the rocky mountain rises above the little solitary Loch Restal, and all the adjoining peaks are brought into view, is singularly fine. As I stood at the height of the road and gazed down on its strange course both ways, I could not help rejoicing that there was at least one place where railways, and canals, and steam-

ers, and all these devices for sinking hills, and raising valleys, and introducing man and levels, and destroying solitude and nature, would for ever be set at defiance.

Loch Lomond has been beautiful. The summits of Ben Lomond and all the neighbouring hills have been bright, and it has been one universal blaze of brilliant calmness. It is a difficult competition between the upper and the lower end of the loch; but upon the whole, I rather decide for the upper. The islands scattered over the broad part of it are delightful, and for constant residence, there must be an advantage in the openness of the expanse. But the narrow end is far more Swiss-like. The stern, flinty mountains, with their sharp, high-reared ridges, the deep, clear water, the visibleness of the objects on both sides; the storm-defying, precipitous rocks, that repress the little waves; the soft green promontories that jut out into the loch; the copse tossed about the bases of the hills; the water-falls, and the long, fringed hollows that contain their streams; the solitude, the wildness, and apparent absence of appropriation; — these are the things that would make me prefer a comfortable small house, well placed on a bit of level oasis, two or three miles above this inn, at least for an occasional summer, or during a fit of temporary romance.

Barr, Wednesday, 19th September 1838, 11 o'clock, a.m. — We left Tarbet yesterday morning at ten, and returned here by Luss and Renfrew at six in the evening. I half wish that, for the sake of variety, we had gone down Loch Long, and reached Dumbarton by Ardencaple. But this may be next time, and no one can see Loch Lomond too often. The day was good, and if we had not been spoiled by the super-excellence of the four that preceded it, we would have thought it better than we did. This coming down decides the question in favour of the upper end. The lower one is beautiful, but the Highland character and feelings are gone the moment that the rocky, ridgy mountains become rounded into low, common grazing hills, and agriculture and dressed places appear, instead of bothies, precipices, unchangeable natural features, adventure, and heather.

I go today to Glasgow in order to begin business there to-morrow.

Bonaly, Friday 28th September 1838. — On Wednesday the 19th, I went to Glasgow, and dined with Alison, the sheriff (and the historian), at Possil House; a sort of official dinner. I met one distinguished man there — Serjeant Talfourd, whom I had never seen before. He has the good sense to spend his vacation in Scotland frequently, and has been at Glenarbuck, near Dumbarton, all this autumn. He was very agreeable, though he suffered in the estimation of some people by giving Mrs. Alison very nearly an hour of English Circuit cases in rather a high-keyed voice. There was an old Irish colonel there, brilliant in scarlet and lace, who put me down in grand style, because I ventured to doubt the accuracy of his recollection when he said that it was in 1824 that George the Fourth was in Edinburgh, and I insinuated that it was 1822.

Next day we paraded to Court in great splendour. Talfourd was in my carriage, and I found him so pleasant that I was sorry when the procession reached the courthouse. We talked of the English Courts, Tom Campbell, Brougham, and Richmond the Spy, all of whom he hates. He sat on the bench with us a short while. My colleague was Meadowbank.

We had our public dinner that day. About fifty attended, including Meadowbank's wife, and her sister and daughter. Excellent turtle and venison. Contrary to rule, Meadowbank drank Talfourd's health, and, contrary to a still more necessary rule, his Lordship told him that if he chose, he might reply, on which the learned serjeant made a regular speech. His topics were the excellence of the Scotch scenery he had been living in, and of the Scotch Judges before him. There was another Englishman there whom I ought to have mentioned that I had met, and introduced myself to, at Cairndow. This was Lushington, the new Professor of Greek in Glasgow, in the room of Sandford. He is a very amiable young man, and a great Grecian. His powers as a teacher remain to be seen. I fear he is too soft.

We had eighty-one cases to try, and this took six entire days. There was a Sunday in the middle of them, which was spent by Meadowbank at Garscube, and by me at Barr.

The great majority of the cases were thefts, and, including the whole, I don't think I ever saw so many cases so devoid of interest. A coarse-looking fellow was not only accused of theft, which greatly shocked his friends, he being a laird with a landed rental of £200, but convicted of it. When he was first detected, he was thrown into great agitation, which he accounted for by saying he was in love.

My colleague and I being of the same opinion on the absurdity of the practice, there was no sermonising to prisoners. It is clear to me that the idea of a judge doing good, either to the public or villains, or to prisoners individually, by expounding the moral and Christian law to them, appeals to their consciences, and representations of the consequences of their rejecting, or availing themselves of, the blood of the Redeemer (which has become almost a technical phrase) in each case, is utterly fallacious. The attempt is not merely useless, it is hurtful. There are cases fit for the discourse, and which require it, and the true thing is, to select these well. But practising it in every case only deadens its impressiveness, and applied, as I have seen it, to a dozen of petty thefts successively, it becomes ludicrous. To be sure it is new to each first-convicted prisoner, who gets it fresh in so far as he is concerned, in his turn. But when the judge's address is so habitually repeated that it becomes a form, there can be no freshness in it. The very prisoners know it by hearsay, or probably, from having often listened to it in the gallery, while they were watching the fate of their comrades who had got to the bar before them; and there are very few of the public who do not expect it as they do the proclamations by the clerk, or who care for it more. A pious and benevolent judge who thinks that he can generally move the heart of a culprit, and that he ought not to lose the opportunity, ought to have private interviews with prisoners, or take any other course rather than let what, well used, may be impressive and therefore important, degenerate into a hackneyed ceremony, dull and heartless by mere frequency of repetition.

NORTH CIRCUIT
1839

Bridge of Tilt Inn, by Blair, Wednesday Night, 10th April 1839. — This Circuit promises to be nearly a facsimile of my North one of last spring, so I have nothing to say.

I left home yesterday morning at ten, with Jane and Eliza Maitland, and was at Perth all night.

We left Perth to-day about eleven, and got here by six, though the distance be only about thirty-five miles. But we went about six miles off the road to call at Snaigow, and had to mend the carriage at Dunkeld.

I could not pass Blair-Adam without remembering the excellent old chief. The place shall know him no more.

The Snaigow! Mrs. Keay, the widow, was from home; so I got half an hour of the silent rooms and untrodden walks to myself, a painful, yet irresistible enjoyment. The place is one of the best examples of the triumph of taste within a short period over poor natural features, long aggravated into worse badness by detestable management. Fifteen years ago, it seemed absolutely irreclaimable, and its ugliness was in the worst style of dull, nasty, meaningless inconvenience. It is now a comfortable, respectable, sensible place, with all the old abominations of stone fences, single rows of wind-bent trees, and wet grass fields removed, and a beautiful house, surrounded by well laid-out and well-kept ornamental ground, thriving evergreens, good lawn, and the former wood broken into natural and useful shapes and positions, substituted in their stead. But in all this satisfactory creation, the mind of James Keay predominated, one of the most sensible of men.

These two days have been beautiful — cold, but bright. There has not been a shower for many weeks, which, at this season, gives the earth an appearance that I like. I have always had a taste for mere well-dressed ground, though there be no vegetable life visible on it. It looks clean, and shows care, and suggests the coming crop. During our whole way from Perth to this, we have been looking down upon the valleys of the Tay and other rivers, where rich fields have been spread out, on which human skill has been not only exerting, but exhibiting all its resources, and the dryness of the mould seemed to have made agriculture a pastime, and to have allured the whole population of the straths out to the plough, and the sowing, and the harrows; while the sun, undisturbed by even a zephyr, touched the low grounds with some heat, and the larks and mavises exulted over the scene, as each field was done, and the comfortable horses rattling with their gear, were led into new fields, leaving the finished one to delight the eye, with the dry lines, above all the drains, and all the cleaned ridges, and all the combing and harrowing it had got, with not even a weed to interfere with its purity. It was beautiful. The bare trees looked on in silence, but it was not difficult for fancy to clothe them, and to anticipate summer, and its universal glory.

It is very satisfactory to see the improvement that is taking place in the dwellings along this glorious drive. They used to be worse than even the pig-styes of Luss. But a great number of comfortable stone houses are made every year, and the old mud huts promise soon to be forgotten.

I observed several old women spinning in the sun at their doors, and a great many children playing upon knolls, but lambs only twice, and not a single primrose. It is curious, by the way, how primroses get into districts. Why is Glencroe full of them, and none on the hills or glens between Perth and Inverness? (But query — is this last a fact?)

I am sorry to see so many of Burn, the Architect's, repetitions of himself throughout this picturesque district. There is one of his gimcrack cottage houses at Fascally, two, if not three about Urrard, and one at Lude, all the same, and none of them in keeping with a rough climate and situations of romantic wildness. I lament the destruction of the old house at Fascally; which, though in violation of all the rules of taste, and probably of the more important rules of internal convenience, had become, and very much from its solemn oddity, a striking object in the Pass. If it had been built now, it would have been taken for a cotton-mill. But its age and situation excluded all such notions. It had a very long line of front, very little depth, and was very high, with not one particle of ornament or one inch of projection, its plain windows all in long rows, and was covered with the whitest rough-cast. It was like a compartment of Blair Castle that had walked down the water. I should suppose that it must have had about fifteen windows in front and been five or six stories high, and not thirty feet deep, — a regular, thin, oblong. Ugly enough, no doubt, and not to be made. But standing, staring, in that deep, wild valley — white, strong, and plain, — long built, and unlike every modern-built thing in that quarter, it referred us to the days of Killiecrankie and the 'Forty-Five, and had become by association as peculiar and natural a feature in that scene as either the rocks or the river. But it is all gone, and we have a new polished freestone cottage in its place, with porches, and pinnacles, and oriel windows, and all the rest of it. Half the money would have made the old edifice a good house, and removed its external defect of sameness, without destroying its peculiar and half-feudal character.

Aviemore, Thursday Night, 11th April 1839. — A calm, dry, cloudy, heavy day. All the hills, the whole way from Kinross, have had snow on their summits, and the high ones more than half-way down. By Drumochter it was lying thick, in some places, on the very road. Loch Garry was frozen entirely over, and his surface, instead of blue water, was a sheet of unbroken snow. The massiveness of the grey, motionless clouds rather improved the effect of the magnificent mountains by which the whole valley from Blair to this is enclosed. The silence was impressive. Between Dunkeld and this we have only seen two gigs, one mail-coach, and not a dozen of carts. There is little labour in the fields after leaving Blair, being mostly in natural pasture. The population is far thinner. Except Kingussie, and its neighbour Newtonmore, there is no village, and nowhere any attempt at any manufacture, beyond what can be accomplished by a bad axe or saw, or a little rustic wheel. There is no road so long and so good, from the whole course of which there is such an absence of all that produces artificial sound. And even of the natural sounds I heard none in my walk, except the bleating of a sheep or two, the singing of a few blackbirds, and the roaring of one hill cataract, all of which were heard from a great distance. All this gave the day and the scene a mysterious and somewhat fearful character.

There are only two things wanted to make Aviemore one of the grandest inland places in Scotland. These are wood, and a house. Yes, if it had only wood and a house, it would do. The house must be a noble old castle, strong and large, but commodious for modern habitation, standing on the left bank of the Spey, somewhere opposite the Doune (or Dune) of Rothie-murchus, but on the table-land above the river, not on the low ground, and with its accompaniments of terraces, evergreens, gardens, and above all, a history. As to the wood, we must begin by clearing the country of at least nineteen parts out of every twenty of that abominable larch with which it pleased the late Rothiemurchus, as it still pleases many Highland lairds, to stiffen and blacken the land. Then my wood must be almost all forest trees, chiefly sweet chesnut and oak, the average age of the younger ones being about 100 years, so extensive, that, if collected, it would cover at least 3000 or 4000 acres, but must be scattered over, and dealt out among, the whole tableland and low hills round my castle. There are few places of which it can be said that only these two improvements, which are both in man's power, would be sufficient. But the natural elements here admit of no good change. My river, and my rocks, and my mountains, and my lakes, and my glens, and my plains, are all perfect. Since I am at it, I should like to give the district a little more of a southern climate. But as I am speaking of Scotland, these two may do.

There has been more burning of heather, all along, than I remember to have seen before. The fires on the distant hills were striking at night, but not so much so as the long trailing streaks, and the high curling of the smoke during the day. It was endless watching its forms and directions. Neither in the valleys nor on the mountains was it interfered with by the slightest wind, but took its own way with its own lightness.

Inverness, Monday, 15th April 1839, 11 o'clock, a.m. — I came here on Friday the 12th at three o'clock; was in Court on Saturday till midnight, finishing all the business; processed to church yesterday forenoon; gave a dinner to about thirty people, and mean to be off in a little to Nairn.

The weather has continued beautiful, and few places are more worthy of fine weather than the neighbourhood of Inverness. It is a glorious district, and the spire, the bridge, the river, and the magnificently placed new court-house, give an air of picturesque respectability even to the otherwise mean town. I wish that Playfair had had the planning of the court-house, and not Burn.

There were only eight or nine cases, all insignificant, except to the culprits. I sent a fellow six months to Cromarty jail for his third assault, and predicted publicly that he would one day commit murder. He is a cunning, violent beast; writes and reads very well, but is deaf, though not dumb, and takes advantage of his deafness to make some people believe him an idiot, upon the faith of which he thinks he may give way to his fury with impunity, and keeps the whole country-side in terror. I have little doubt of his being convicted of murder, but he will get his sentence commuted on the score of his mental weakness, which is now the ground always taken up by the pious and benevolent, and it is far too often successful.

Our sermon was by a worthy fanatic called Dr. C———. There are few things more curious than the decorous appearance of patience with which sensible people can sit and hear a man, with an unnattractive manner, roar out two and a quarter hours of sheer absolute nonsense. Yet nothing so common. This is the clergyman whose Circuit prayer Hermand interrupted a few years ago. The reverend gentleman was standing, as usual, beside his Lordship on the Bench, praying away, loud and long, as if there had been nothing else to do than to hear him perform, when Hermand gave him jog with his elbow, and whispered, with his ordinary birr: "We've a great deal of business, sir."

The Sunday costume of the lower orders here on a fine Sunday is peculiar, and rather striking. They go to church with shawls over their shoulders, commonly tartan, and bare heads, their hair tethered in various ways by ribbons, combs, and large brooch-headed pins, but no caps, or any covering for the head. They look like humble people dressed in a room. It suggests the agreeable idea that they think the day good, and that they are enjoying it. They are almost all coarse and uncomely, mostly yellow skinned, with large freckles.

Huntly, Tuesday 16th April 1839, Night. — We left Inverness yesterday about two, and stayed all night at Nairn, where we were joined by Graham Speirs the Sheriff, pious, grave, honest, sound-headed, and very calm; fit, from firmness, sense, and devotion, united to a black, gaunt, thoughtful countenance, to have been one of Cromwell's majors. Nairn, bleak and exposed, and seemingly dead, but Speirs says full of internal bitterness, being fiercely divided into Whigs and Radicals. It produces excellent little fishes, and has a glorious beach. But I have no desire to pass the evening of my days under the brown shade of Nairn.

Forres would do far better. A very nice, clean, thriving little place, with its old gables still to the street, and its magnificent prospects of the ridgy outlines of the blue hills of Ross-shire, Cromarty and Sutherland.

And Elgin would do better still. I am not sure that, except Perth, there is a nicer provincial town in Scotland. Placed in a delightful country, with a climate not exceeded in mildness, and a soil not equalled in dryness, by any that we have, it is dignified by the survivance of many of the old ecclesiastical dwellings, of which numerous obvious vestiges are to be seen in the streets; and the affection of its successful sons is attested by munificent bequests, which their beautiful public buildings show that the existing inhabitants have intelligence to use rightly, while over all there presides the spirit that yet hovers over the ruins of their glorious Cathedral. Old Henry Mackenzie, who married a Grant, and had much intercourse with Morayshire, described Elgin in its old state, before its modern improvements began, as "a melancholy and gentlemanlike place." So it was, being respectable, ancient, and silent. It has now far more new life, graced by due antiquity. The scenery of Perth is better, but it has weavers. Montrose, in its main street at least, is grander, but it has ships. Stirling has every interest, a history, picturesque streets, ruins, prospect and its castle, but the town is squalid and cursed by charity. Kelso, Melrose, and Jedburgh, have each its rivers and its ruin, but they are all paltry, sinking, insignificant places. I cannot recollect such another union of ancient venerableness with modern respectability, and provincial seclusion as in Elgin.

I wasted an hour on Gordon Castle, which I despised so much

when I first saw it, above forty years ago, that I have never taken the trouble to look at it since, often as I have passed it. I find it as contemptible as ever.

From Fochabers to this is Aberdeenshire, and so will from this to Aberdeen be to-morrow, and no more can be said.

Beautiful day.

Perth, Monday Night, 22nd April 1839. — On Wednesday the 17th we went to Aberdeen, and stayed there till yesterday forenoon.

I am more and more astonished at the industry and skill of the Aberdeenshire people in smoothing and drying the horrible surface of their soil. It is the greatest triumph of man over nature, of obstinacy over moss and stones. Talk not of deserts, or swamps, or forests to these people.

Moncreiff and his son James's wife joined us at Aberdeen, and our previous mirth was not diminished.

We were in Court all Thursday, Friday, and Saturday, with more serious cases than usually occur at Circuits, but no capital conviction.

We had a most diverting party at the Provost's on Saturday evening; a quadrille party and a solid supper. His name is Milne, an excellent octogenarian Whig, with a queer, out of the way, capacious, old-fashioned house, and a still more queer and old-fashioned wife, but nice, kind, respectable, natural, happy bodies, with all manner of substantial comforts, and the accent and dialect of the place in great purity. We had the officers of the 74th regiment, remarkably agreeable, gentlemanly men, who had the sense to enjoy the frolic without turning up their noses. On asking the hostess how she got them so soon invited, as it was the idea of a few hours only, "troth," said she, "I just sent up the lass to the barracks an' bade them a' come doon." The venerable spouse's wig, an old brown one, much the worse of the wear, got awry, as she thought, on which she put it right, her own head being too glorious with ribbons and muslin to be seen. "Madam," said he, with great solemnity, "I'll thank you to let my wig alone, I never meddle with yours." Much kindness and much laughter we had.

We went to church next forenoon, and heard one of the very best ordinary sermons by Mr. Davidson, one of the town ministers, I have almost ever heard in Scotland.

They boast much of their new Marischal College. But confined amidst paltry buildings, its position is bad, it has no architecture, and its erection implies the destruction of the old building, which sets all they will do utterly at defiance. They should be all quashed, and only King's College kept up. We, Moncreiff and his party included, left Aberdeen yesterday at half-past one, and got to Arbroath at seven. A delightful day — mild, calm, and clear, with the sea singularly blue. How peacefully Stonehaven lay in its little quiet bay! I scarcely ever saw so many people out, lounging about their doors, and walking and lying on the grass. It was our first truly spring Sunday, and every village was enjoying it in a truly Christian way. It was delightful to see so happy and respectable a population. It was scarcely like a Scotch Sunday, for though everything was peaceful and grave, there was no sourness or gloom. Their hearts were basking in the sun.

I strolled down to the harbour of Arbroath at near twelve at night. The moon was bright, the water trembling in light, and the town impressively still. I walked through all the main streets without encountering a living creature, except one peripatetic cat.

This morning we (Moncreiffs too) revisited the rocks and the ruins, and then came here, amidst the balm of an almost summer day. The Carse was magnificent. I was on the look-out for my swallow, but did not catch him. The whole drive was a crash of blackbirds, mavises, and larks, with bursting hedges and larches, and field after field left, in beautiful cultivation, to the elements, man's power being exhausted.

Bonaly, Saturday, 27th April 1839. — We were in Court at Perth all Tuesday, Wednesday, and Thursday last, the 23rd, 24th, and 25th, from morning to night. There were forty-eight insignificant cases, thirty-five of them being ordinary thefts. My due feet never failed to visit some of the scenery of that beautiful place before breakfast, and about midnight, particularly the North Inch, where the fishermen dropping and drawing in their nets by moonlight is always striking. I purchased two dozen of curious roses (the roots, I mean) but could not get a yellow carnation.

I heard here that my friend Rutherfurd was made Lord Advocate, and Ivory, Solicitor. Rutherfurd's elevation is an occurrence of the deepest importance to Scotland. I have some misgiving about the validity of our proceedings here, because the commission to the Depute-Advocate fell by the fact that the previous Lord Advocate (John A. Murray) had ceased to hold that office, and that no new commission was produced to us. A new commission did exist, because it was executed at Edinburgh just as we began business. But it was not produced in Court, nor was Cosmo Innes, who acted, sworn in under it, nor were we applied to appoint any one. Innes held himself to be safe without the Court's interference, and nothing was said by anybody. But I don't clearly see how a person can act legally under a deputation said to exist, but not exhibited, and not sworn to.

We came home yesterday forenoon. This has been a merry and delightful Circuit. The weather has been, and continues, ethereal. We have only had one shower since we left Edinburgh, — at Aberdeen, — and it did not last above two hours.

I am more and more charmed with Moncreiff, whom it is

impossible not to love and reverence. There never was such a union of the sternness of duty with the softness of affection, of force of intellect, in so far as legal reasoning is concerned, with simplicity in all other matters.

Murray, it seems, has insisted on finishing off by being made a Knight!!! It was he who once praised a sea-captain to me, because when he was told that the Admiralty meant to knight him for some gallant action, he said: "By the Lord! they shall try me by a Court-martial first!" It is incomprehensible.

SOUTH CIRCUIT

Kirklands, by Jedburgh, Wednesday 11th September 1839. — I left Edinburgh for this South Circuit, on Saturday last, the 7th, with Mrs. Cockburn, my two daughters, Jane and Elizabeth, and my youngest son Frank.

We left Edinburgh at eight in a wet morning, and breakfasted with the Tods, at their villa at Kirkhill, on the Esk, a little above Dalhousie, a very nice spot. Mr. Webster, distinguished in this country as the American orator, with several of his family, went just before us all this first, on their way to England, by Abbotsford, I had dined with him the day before at Jeffrey's, — an agreeable and sensible man.

Departing from Kirkhill about twelve, we proceeded over Middleton Moor and down the Gala; a valley associated with my earliest recollections, and which, in a sunny day, still appears to me to be singularly pleasing. The old ale-house at Heriot was the first inn I ever entered. My father, who, I think, was Convener of the County, went out to attend some meeting of Road Trustees, and he took a parcel of us with him. He rode, and we had a chaise to ourselves, — happiness enough for boys. But more was in store for us. For he remained at the mansion-house of Middleton with his friend Mr. Hepburn, and we went on about four miles further to Heriot House, where we break-fasted and passed the day, fishing, bathing, and rioting. It was my first inn, and the first inn of most of the party! What delight! A house to ourselves, — on a moor, — a burn, — nobody to interfere with us, — the power of ringing the bell as we chose, — a lass most willing to answer and obey, — the ordering of our own dinner, blowing the peat fire, laughing as often and as loud as we chose. What a day! We rang the hand-bell for the pure pleasure of ringing, and enjoyed our independence by always going out and in by the window. This dear little inn does not now exist; but its place is marked by a square of ash trees.

We returned to the inn of Middleton, on our way home, about seven in the evening; and there saw another scene which I have never forgotten. People sometimes say that there is no probability in Scott's making the party in *Waverley* retire from the

Castle to the Howf, but these people were not with me at the inn at Middleton, about fifty years ago. The Duke of Buccleuch was living at Dalkeith; Henry Dundas, then Home Secretary, at Melville; Robert Dundas, the Lord Advocate, at Arniston; Hepburn of Clerkington, at Middleton, and several of the rest of the aristocracy of Midlothian within a few miles off, all with their families and luxurious houses. Yet had they all, to the number of twelve or sixteen, or so, congregated in this wretched inn for a day of freedom and jollity. We found them roaring, and singing, and laughing, in a low-roofed room scarcely large enough to hold them, with wooden chairs and a sanded floor. When their own lacqueys, who were carrying on high life in the kitchen, did not choose to attend, the masters were served by two women. There was plenty of wine, particularly claret, in rapid circulation, on the table; but my eye was chiefly attracted by a huge bowl of hot whisky punch, the steam of which was almost dropping from the roof, while the odour was enough to perfume the whole parish. We were called in, and made to partake, and were very kindly used, particularly by my uncle Harry Dundas. How they did joke and laugh! with songs and toasts! and disputation! and no want of practical fun! I don't remember anything they said, and probably did not understand it. But the noise, and the heat, and the uproarious mirth, I think I hear and feel yet. My father was in the chair, and having gone out for a little, one of us boys (I forget who) was voted and put into his place, and the boy's health was drunk, with all the honours, as "The young Convener," hurrah! hurrah! "may he be a better man than his father!" hurrah! Hurrah! very good! hurrah! etc. I need not mention that they were all in a state of elevation, though there was nothing like absolute intoxication, so far as I could judge. They were all happy and glorious, enjoying their unchecked boose. Yet they were within a mile or two of the best and freest houses in the country, all their own, but voluntarily preferred the licence of that little nasty ale-house.

My next acquaintance with the Gala was about two years after this, when my brother Robert and I were sent to pass our six weeks' vacation at Burnhouse, then belonging to the same family (Thomson) that has it yet. The Thomson who had it then was a bachelor, who had to attend to his farm; and so, except when he, who was a first-rate fisher, could go with us to the water, which was not very often, we were left entirely to the freedom of our own wills, and each of us had not only a rod, but a rod with a reel, and a basket, and a superfluity of lines and hooks; nay more, — a pony. Glorious six weeks! The trouts, the open hills, the greyhounds, the ponies, the idleness!

Ever since, I have loved the Gala. But I think I should have loved its pastoral valley without this early attachment. It is bleak and wet, no doubt, but so is most of the pastoral scenery of Scotland, the whole of which requires the attraction of a

30

bright day. But with such a day, the sparkling stream of the Gala, the range of its wild, unenclosed hills, and its impressive solitude, to say nothing of its coming in for a share of the historical interest which belongs to the whole of our southern border, give it charms which I always feel powerful. When I knew it first, Galashiels was a rural hamlet; the house of Torwoodlee stood bare and staring, and the high-road ran on the west side of the valley. The old laird of Torwoodlee survives to enjoy the reward of his having planted judiciously, in seeing his now beautiful place nearly buried in foliage. Galashiels has become the Glasgow of Selkirkshire.

The day brightened up about two, and we saw the rich and interesting district from about Galashiels to Kirklands, by Melrose, in all its beauty. Abbotsford, Melrose Abbey, Dryburgh, the Tweed, and the distant border summits, — these give its interest to this range.

We remained here (Kirklands) all Sunday the 8th, and on Monday the 9th we went to Borthwickbrae, where we stayed till to-day. We went along the right bank of the Teviot, both going and coming. The weather not good; a struggle between the sun and the rain; a battle in which, when it is fought in Scotland, Sol has seldom much chance with Aquarius. But the air was mild, the woods fresh, the fields green, and the drive beautiful.

If any change of our atmosphere should ever render height advantageous, or immaterial, Borthwickbrae may be an agreeable place. But at present seven or eight hundred feet of elevation above the sea is inconsistent with Scotch comfort. A sloppy clay soil, trees imbedded in thick, wet, green fog, — fields of grass which look bright at a distance, but in which, when gone upon, it is seen that every hoof makes a well, and every well is filled with moss water, slimy out-houses, a general chill, a heavy smell, these are the natural curses of such a height. My niece, however, and all her family were very kind, and the party agreeable.

I went to Branxholm, which I had not seen for a long time. It was never much; but a highway between it and the Teviot, and its conversion into a modern house, have now made it nothing.

I also, for the first time, made a pilgrimage to Alemoor Loch, — a small and bleak piece of insignificant water, but interesting as the source of the Ale, which rushes copiously out of it. My juridical eye rested (I hope) with due respect on the high and sterile district which has the honour of having given his title to my predecessor, Lord Alemoor, whom I have always been accustomed to reverence, though I don't know on what grounds, as a respectable judge, classical and pompous, stupid and well-bred.

Kirklands, Tuesday, 17th September 1839. — Still here. The weather since the 11th has been very rainy. Sunday last was flood. Nevertheless thick soles and thick skin make water a smaller evil than it is often thought. And there are always gleams, the more prized from the contrast.

The Court was held and finished yesterday. Only about half a dozen of insignificant cases.

I never see Jedburgh without pleasure. Its position, its history, and its abbey, impress it with that peculiar feeling of softness and of sacredness which pervades all our border scenery, but especially those parts of it which are dignified by fragments of architectural antiquity.

It is a long time since I was there professionally, and this was my first visit as a judge. I was much pleased to see that the Crailing Guard had escaped being anyhow modernised. A delightful institution. The dotage of the feudal system.

The shades of Eskgrove, and of Brougham, of Craig, and of Scott, rose before me. Brougham's only professional occupation for about two years after he joined the Faculty of Advocates (in 1800), consisted in torturing Eskgrove, the Justice-Clerk, a great lawyer, and a testy, avaricious, ludicrous, and contemptible old man. His Lordship once stopped the business, according to the prevailing custom then, to dine, and after teasing his very soul at table, the Evil (Brougham's nickname) disappeared the instant that his Lordship drank good afternoon, in order to process back to Court. It was soon seen why the Evil had taken himself off; for the procession had not advanced half-way when a military-looking gentleman (being the learned counsel), and a respectful servant, with a cockade in his hat, dashed from the slope above the town, through the middle of it, scattering the warriors of Crailing — advocates, jurymen, trumpeters, and clerk, and then before the splashed and dinner-shaken walkers could recover from their agitation, or get well placed in Court, the person, who a minute before had performed the part of a captain in a hurry, was on the floor, gowned and wigged, objecting to everything. The poor Justice was glad to let the devil alone. His step had not been the steadier, nor his temper the calmer, nor his fright the less, from his refreshment, but glad to find his bones all safe, he evaporated in his usual fierce, but insignificant wrath, at "that most malapert young man, Maister Broom or Broug-ham."

Craig was several years after this. The decorous blockhead was deserted on his first Circuit day by everybody else; but as he insisted on drawling on at Jedburgh for three entire days, Scott as a Sheriff, Campbell of Craigie as a counsel, and I as the Advocate-Depute, were compelled to drawl on with him. But for Scott's vivacity, these days must have proved fatal. His Lordship, still in terror of the French Revolution, insisted on himself and us three standing up gravely every day, while he toasted the king, and the trumpeters played God save him. One night when his heart was softened, and his eyes moistened by reminiscence and hot brandy and water, he fell into the days of his "Mirror" and "Lounger", and told us how he was once driven from the paradise of Barskimming where he had retreated for nature and romance, by looking out on a dewy morning and seeing the brute (as he called him) of a butcher killing a calf on the lawn. "Would not you have fled too, Mr. Sheriff Scott?" "No, my Lord, I would have consoled myself by thinking of a good veal cutlet."

We leave this tomorrow for Beatock by Selkirk and St. Mary's Loch. Murphy assures us it is to be a good day, which that scenery well deserves.

Beatock, Thursday Morning, 18th September 1839. — But Murphy was wrong. — We left Kirklands yesterday at half-past eight A.M., and reached this at six in the evening. It was an average day for that country, that is, very rainy, which, however, seems to be universal this season, in the plains as well as on the hills. But its truces let me walk up many ascents, and there were even a few gleams of sunshine.

The first thing that attracted my notice was the statue of Sir Walter Scott in Selkirk, which I never saw before. A sad piece of sculpture, not very honourable to the gentry of Selkirkshire. There are two things good about it, however, — the inscription, which quotes, very happily, his own lines on his favourite Yarrow and Ettrick, and the pride which the people of the town feel in the man, and his effigy. "Have ye seen our (oor) Sir Walter, mem?" said a poor shop-keeper to Mrs. Cockburn, with a strong appropriating emphasis on the pronoun. All the natives seemed gratified whenever a stranger stopped to look at it.

The whole thirty-seven miles, from Selkirk to Beatock, is beautiful, at least to a Scotch and pastoral eye. I had been at the head of St. Mary's loch once before, a few years ago, when I passed a day and a night at a farmhouse of Henderland's, with Richardson and Sir Charles Bell, and their ladies. The rest of the way, from St. Mary's to this was quite new to me.

The woodland part of the scenery, by Bowhill, Newark, and Hangingshaw, is the part that pleases the majority of spectators. But though very beautiful, yet composed, as it is, of wood, river, and hill, not arranged with any singularity, it is not more beautiful than thousands of similar Scotch scenes. By far the best part of it owes its charm to the old tower of Newark.

It is when the trees begin to fail, when the hard-wood keeps back, and lets the fir go on, and when, after ascending the Yarrow a little more, the very fir gives up to the grass, and we are left to the solitude of the hills, that the real peculiarity and interest of the range begins. It is as purely pastoral a district as I have seen in Scotland, with very green grass, unbroken by a single rock, few houses, and no village, except little secluded Yarrow, the clear river, the silent turf-edged loch, the old stories and ballads, and the genius of Scott lingering in every valley, and embellishing every feature and every tale. The bareness, openness, and sameness of the valley might seem to preclude its being interesting, but these are the very things that aid the old associations, and impart that feeling of pleasing melancholy which belongs to the region. There is inspiration in the words Newark, Yarrow, and Dryhope.

There being, as yet, fortunately, no inn to pollute the strath, the Selkirk horses took us to Meggat Bridge, eighteen miles, and there a fresh pair met us from Beatock and brought us here.

The lower part of the descent, near this, is not remarkable. But the first drive down from the Loch of the Lowes till Moffat Water begins to run with some profession of horizontality, is glorious. It is as fine a ravine as we have, of mere turf. In spite of the rain, Lizzie, Frank, and I went up and saw the tail of the Grey Mare, which was fully powdered and frizzled.

Cosmo Innes, our Advocate-Depute, stayed all Tuesday night, in almost a bothy, at St. Mary's Loch, for the sake of fishing. His hostess has two sons, and some other kinspeople, who emigrated a few years ago to Canada, where she says they are all prospering in a Selkirkshire and Dumfriesshire of their own naming. In describing their felicity she mentioned a circumstance which, to be sure, must strike a St. Mary's Loch woman. "An', what d'ye think! in Yarrow kirk ye sometimes canna hear ae word the minister says for the folk coughing. But ye may gang to their kirk the hail year round without either hearing a clocher or a hoast."

Richardson, the most experienced of Scotch London solicitors, tells me that this inn (Beatock) was built on a public view by a tax, being almost the only job of the kind that parliament has ever been cajoled to sanction. They have their reward. The public was assessed about £5000 to pay for buildings, and the establishment is abominable. But Sawney is not an inn-keeping animal. Civility, tidiness, and activity without bustle, are not parts of his nature. The landlord here is a living dunghill.

I have gone this morning to the top of a hill. A few months dry weather every summer over the low ground, leaving the hills to have their verdure brightened by the showers, would make Moffat a very agreeable place; as it is, it is all splash, splash.

Thornhill, Sunday Forenoon, 21st September 1839. — We left Beatock on Thursday forenoon, amidst a torrent of rain, which only stopped for a few minutes, out of respect to the law, as we entered Dumfries in procession. We were joined there in the evening by Meadowbank, with two daughters and a son-in-law. The Court was held next day, and the business was over by four; after which, the usual banquet closed the judicial labours of Dumfries.

I had not been there for several years, and found two or three changes.

The old windmill has been converted into what they call an Observatory; which means a windmill-looking tower, with a bit

of shrubbery round it, ginger-beer in the ground floor, a good telescope in the second story, and a camera obscura in the third. So the astronomical dignity of the establishment is not great, but still it is an agreeable and civilised institution. The views of the neighbouring country are beautiful, and there are few better positions for a camera.

I never entered mad-houses, but the new Lunatic Asylum is very striking outside, and stands on a fine site. While asking a little boy on the road some questions about it, he used a word, which it is to be hoped does not truly indicate the character of the internal treatment. He pointed out a man who was walking in a gallery, as "the Breaker". "What do you call the Breaker?" "The man that breaks the daft folk." A lad beside us also used the term as one familiar.

An ill conceived and worse executed granite monument has been erected to the memory of the Covenanting martyrs, in the churchyard. In order that it might stand on the very spot where some of them were buried, their original tombstones have been lifted, and instead of being replaced properly, are allowed to lie about anyhow, in scarcely legible positions. Some of their inscriptions are very good, breathing devotion and defiance. Those who, like the Committee on Scott's monument at Edinburgh, think that white marble may withstand the climate of Scotland, should look at Turnerelli's horrid statue of Burns in this churchyard. It has only been erected about twenty-three years, and is covered in on the roof and on three sides, yet is completely spoiled. But this does no injustice to the sculptor.

I have always liked Dumfries. It stands high in the rank of our Scottish provincial towns, and owes much to its river, but more, in my opinion, to its churchyard, which contains several most interesting tombs, and the ashes of many families famous in our Southern history.

And my decision is, that its windows are the cleanest in Scotland.

We are going to pay some visits in Galloway; but we can't be received till to-morrow. So, being unwilling to live two days in a wretched Dumfries inn, we left "The Commercial Hotel" there, yesterday after breakfast, and came here, to while two days away.

As soon as we arrived, we set off for Drumlanrig, which I had passed before, but had never gone up to, and loitered some hours in and about the house and the grounds. It would be unjust to condemn any place utterly, which is in such a pitiable state of disrepair. But I doubt if anything, even the restoration of the old wood, which has been so barbarously destroyed within my own time, in order that its produce might be wasted on foolish profligacy in London, would make it a fine place. The incurable defect is the paltriness of the natural features. No lake, no sea, no rock, no mountains except some lumpish ones too far off to belong to this place particularly, and not even a

36

river, for the Nith is so hidden and so distant that practically it forms no part of the home scenery, at present scarcely any good wood, and no ruin. The house, architecturally, is excellent, as might be expected from Inigo Jones, who, I believe, designed it, and the terraces below are on a greater scale than anything else of the kind in Scotland. But they are not good, because, like everything else about the place, they are obviously incomplete and ill kept. To be right, they ought to have balustrades, statues, and fountains, whereas at present they have not even decent gravel. The inside of the house seems to be in a mean taste, and it is said that the whole fabric is dangerously frail. If this be the case, the best thing that could be done would be to leave it as a ruin, to get a noble design for a new castle from Playfair, to build it more in visible connection with the river, to renew the terraces in better style, to plant largely and judiciously, and to do everything in anticipation of how the whole is to look after these woods shall have sucked the nourishment of a hundred summers.

I walked home, and saw the valley of the Nith lighted up by a sweet and splendid autumn sunset. The day was beautiful, and so is this day. I like the character of the strath, lined by respectable (though not picturesque) hills, the low grounds, and even some of the high, brightened by agricultural cultivation, and darkened by masses of straggling wood, and a beautiful stream playing itself through the whole. The smoke of the village fires yesterday — a Saturday evening — gave it the last charm of which any scene admits.

I have been much pleased with the floral taste of the people, whose gardens and windows abound with good flowering shrubs. There are more fuchsias and geraniums at the doors and in the windows of that beautifully placed Penpont, which I have just strolled through, than in all the hamlets in Midlothian.

And this inn, which, though I should not suppose it contained above half a dozen of rooms, is ludicrously called "The Buccleuch and Queensberry Hotel," is the very best little country inn it has ever yet been my good fortune to fall in with in Scotland. In kindness, purity, quiet, comfort and good cheer, it would be a formidable rival to any of its English sisters. Like most other perfectly well-conducted small inns, it is managed entirely by women, Mrs. Glendinning, a tidy and sensible matron, with a lively eye and soft voice, being the Lady Abbess, who bustles about actively, but very gently, amidst her nice hedge alehouse nuns.

We mean to return to Dumfries to-night.

Cumpstone, near Kirkcudbright, Thursday, 26th September 1839. — We went to Dumfries last Sunday evening, under the influence of a mild and bright moon, and left it next day about eleven, and went round the coast by Southwick to Dalbeattie, and from thence to Gelston Castle, where we remained until Wednesday forenoon, the whole distance being only about thirty-two miles. The early part of the day was foggy, but after twelve it was calm, warm, and sunny.

We stopped and did homage to New Abbey, which I had not seen for above thirty years. It is a beautiful and venerable fragment. It would be difficult to find any building where the stone and the ivy combine more harmoniously. But though as yet time has only blended them beautifully into one position, and breathed an unbroken reverence over both, the further insinuation and clustering of vegetable life ought to be repressed; as it is, it has covered quite enough. The chief value, however, of this abbey, consists in its standing as a monument of the brutality of Scotland in these matters. It is only about twenty-five years ago that the whole pile was not only sold, but was bought actually for the purpose of being taken down and made into stone dykes! And this purpose was partly carried into effect. No proprietor could have made such a transaction in any country of right feeling, nor in such a country could any person have dared to have avowed such a design. The liberality (combined, I hope, with the indignation) of six or eight gentlemen saved the residue of the ruin by repurchasing it. It is theirs still, but I grieve to say that another specimen of our unworthiness to possess such relics is to be found in the disgraceful state in which it is kept. It is a byre. Beasts!

"The unlettered muse" seems never to have entered the churchyard. There is not even an attempt at an inscription in it, beyond names and dates. The name and the years are there, but no holy text around is strewed. They have even removed (at least, I could not find it), the stone which, when I was last there, contained the posthumous defamation of first stating that a young lady was an affectionate sister, and a dutiful daughter, etc., and then adding "and a chaste virgin."

I had been told (but only by Galwegians) to expect something uncommonly fine along this part of the shores of the Solway, and from this highway. I was disappointed. It is the stupidest of all our Firths. Few rocks, no islands, and especially no edging of picturesque mountains. For to point, as the natives always do, to the dim ghosts of some distant hills, of which only the outlines are visible, and to explain, with an air of triumph, these are the English mountains, is mere stuff. They are too far off to be felt as parts of the real picture. They may serve the part of remote distance, but not of foreground.

Southwick is too far from the sea, at least for a place so near it; but still it has all the appearance of being excellent.

We stayed at Gelston — ugliness itself — till yesterday forenoon, that is, from the forenoon of Monday the 23rd, till the forenoon of Wednesday the 25th, when we came here (to Cumpston) eight miles further.

Cumpston, Friday, 27th September 1839, Night. — Went up the Tarf yesterday, seeing and visiting. On the way home, I went with Edward Maitland over the eminence called Tongue-land Hill, from which there is a good view of the Royal Burgh of Kirkcudbright and its waters, and down to the Dee, at present a noble stream, with its bridge, one of the largest though certainly not one of the handsomest, arches in Scotland. A bad day.

To-day we went and saw the Abbey of Dundrennan. Though greatly abridged, it is still a beautiful and interesting mass. But every other feeling is superseded by one's horror and indignation at the state in which it is kept. If it had been an odious and offensive building, which the Crown and the adjoining landowners were trying to obliterate as fast as possible, and to render disgusting and inaccessible in the meantime, what else could they do? Five pounds worth of draining, £20 worth of clearing and levelling, and £200 of masonry, would preserve it, in decency, for centuries. But (though a little has been done, and ill done) it is left a victim to every element, man included, by which architecture can be effaced. Not a trace of it will be discoverable in fifty years. Arches and windows might be rescued by the labour of one man for a single day; but it is dealt with as if spite hated it. No execration can do justice to the careless or selfish insensibility that can obstinately persevere in the daily perpetration of such atrocity. My excellent and esteemed host, in whose house I now am, and on whose ground this abbey stands, is the chief delinquent. And the value of the case is that he is a most liberal and right-minded gentleman, because this shows that the mischief proceeds from no positively improper object, but from that absence of right feeling which, on such subjects, seems to be nearly universal among Scotch proprietors. They gaze on the glorious ruins of noble buildings, over which time and history delight to linger, and which give their estates all the dignity they possess, with exactly the same emotion that the cattle do, to which these impressive edifices are generally consigned. It is a humiliating national scandal.

A rainy, rainy day. Where's the old rainbow?

Cumpston, Saturday, 28th September 1839, Night. — The first half of this day had a famine-like appearance. Heavy stock-rotting rain. About twelve it cleared up, and we had a rather splendid day for Cally. We passed some hours there. I had seen it before, but not since the new front has been added to the house, and the marble lobby made, and the furniture put in. The place, with its wood, its well-kept home ground, its varied surface, its distant, bounding hills, and its obvious extensive idea of a great and beautiful domain, is one of the finest in Scotland. As to the house — granite and marble though it be — and though its portico be designed by Papworth and admired by Playfair, I was disappointed. Solid, grave, and in good proportion, it ought to please, and I fancy I am wrong in not being sufficiently pleased. But for such a place, and such a house, it is all too small. And accordingly the chief defence of it, particularly of the portico, is that it is of granite, a strong stone, and that there are no larger granite columns in this country. Well, neither are there larger gold or larger ginger-bread pillars, but if, whatever their substance be, they be not sufficiently large to satiate the architectural appetite, the peculiarity or difficulty of their material is nothing. Granite is admirable for fortifications, bridges, or other works of eternity, where durability is the only beauty. But for houses it is too cold (I speak only of the grey), and its seams don't admit of being well joined; and though great reverence be due to hardness, and to any size, however small, that for the material, is un-usually large, it won't do to give us a mansion of great pretension, though perhaps the pretension were of modesty, and then, when we object to its want of greatness, to say, it is built of very hard and rare stone.

The marble lobby is new in Scotland, and beautiful. But for a thing of the kind, it is too little and far too fine for a mere common lobby. I advise whoever means to lay out enough of money, to cover a lobby with pure white marble, and adorn it with beautiful busts, to put it well into the inside of the edifice, and to use it for sculpture, or music, or anything dignified, rather than as a passage.

The factor told me that the whole marble of this lobby was cut, and polished, and put up by a common workman from Whitehaven.

I wish I had the two busts of Napoleon and Washington.

Cumpston, Sunday Night, 29th September 1839. — A beautiful day. I passed it in the temple not made with hands. But I have nothing to record. The Dee after the late rains, was glorious; not so much however from fulness, as from rugged, foaming whiteness. The prospect from Tongueland Hill is beautiful and peculiar. Kirkcudbright stands like a little Venice, in the midst of its surrounding waters.

Thornhill, Monday Night, 30th September 1839. — We left Cumpston to-day about half-past ten, and got here, by New Galloway, about half-past five.

The whole of these thirty-five or forty miles were new to me and we had a perfect day for enjoying them.

The space is all partly agricultural, and partly pastoral; that is, better than either separately; though with a great preponder-ance of the pastoral. With moor and mountain enough to preserve the feeling of wildness, the prevailing character of the range is that of advancing cultivation, interrupted by many a tumbling stream, and broken by innumerable hillocks, and streaks and masses of wood, by which the whole surface of this half Highland country is diversified.

A shepherd, with whom I had a crack, was much offended at

the slight put upon his river by my asking him if it was the "Tarf?" "Tarf! deil a drap o' Tarf's in't. That's the black water o' Dee! the auncientest water in Scotland."

By far the most striking thing I've seen of late was the Loch and Castle of Kenmure. It is a very curious scene. Whenever we hear of lakes in Scotland, we are apt to think of Highland ones, and to be disappointed if we do not find rocky promontories, and the water set in a deep frame of mountains, and all the other circumstances of Celtic scenery. There is nothing of this in Kenmure, nor in almost any of our southern lochs. Its bank is flat on the one side, and not picturesque on the other, though there be a hill, which however, with the exception of the single peak (of Dennans), is lumpish, and from the surface not lofty. But the cultivation on the low ground gave the loch an air of civilisation, and the water lay shining throughout its whole extent, under a bright, soft sun; and everything was calm and silent, while at the upper end the dark rebel tower frowned from its high mound, over all this peaceful loveliness, as if still retaining the scornful spirit which drove its owner to the ruin of his house in 1715. We stopped and made a slight, unobtrusive inspection of the restored Peer's eyrie. Everything denotes poverty. Money laid out chiefly on repairs and on planting, would make it a proud feudal keep, with a worthy subjected domain. One of the best, because one of the most barbarous, prospects of what is called the castle, is from the bridge, about half a mile after leaving New Galloway. There is only a streak of the loch visible and very little wood, but the high, solitary, old building is seen, backed by a bare mountain, and its vassal village cowering at its feet, exactly as it was in the days of the Stewarts. The Peer, now in his 90th year, I understand, is as much of the old school as his tower is.

Next to Kenmure, we were delighted with what a geologist would call the Basin of Minnyhive.

It's a wretched, half-dead village, which should either be regenerated into a clean, nice, thriving country town, or be altogether superseded by a great mansion. Because its position, at the confluence of several pastoral valleys, is extremely beautiful, and the district is distinguished by everything pleasing in the half-natural, and half-cultivated scenery of the Scottish strath. All the low grounds and much of the hills, were gleaming with bright corn and grass; a great deal of wood is tossed richly everywhere, the surface is full of knolls, some of them very regular, and plainly shaped by water; comfortable, embowered houses are perched on heights; the river sweeps in a full flow of liquid crystal; and there is a prevailing air of industry. I walked, or rather lingered, here for above an hour, and was never more charmed. To be sure, I saw it all under the magic of the sweetest sunshine that ever blessed the close of a calm autumnal day. But, with its elements, that scene can never be but beautiful. We lost the glow of the Happy Valley, as we got into the narrow defile, but the wood and the stream joined us again about two miles from Penpoint, and as I looked back from the bridge over the Nith, close by Thornhill, I saw a day incapable of being made better, ended by a magnificent, gorgeous sunset, and did not bid the last day of September adieu till "the gradual, dusky veil" had fallen over all nature.

Bonaly, Tuesday Night, 1st October 1839. — We left Thornhill to-day about nine, and were here before seven.

But how was the fine gold of yesterday dimmed! We were persecuted by a rainy fog, which destroyed the magnificent Pass of Dalveen, and after following us here, is now pattering, as if in spite, on the poor drenched Pentlands. We saw nothing, fairly, and our enjoyment consisted in the prospect of getting under the cover of our own tower.

My printed companions (but I have been very idle), have been Goodman's History of his own times, too grave for a chaise; Grattan's Life of his father, the very worst book that has ever yet been penned by man; *The Fair Maid of Perth,* read for the twentieth time and always with fresh pleasure, and some frivolities in the department of the ladies.

Meadowbank took Ayr himself. In arranging the Circuit, Moncreiff and I shed mutual tears at the necessity of our being divorced, and vowed our reunion next spring.

WEST CIRCUIT
1840

Bonaly, 11th May 1840. — But our reunion did not take place, Moncreiff was married to the Justice (Boyle), and I to Meadowbank.

I went to Stirling and Meadowbank to Inverary, and both of us to Glasgow.

It was not worth while taking any note of so short and common journeys, and I only put down the dates and places after returning home, in order to keep up the Log-book.

I went with my daughter Jane and Rosa Macbean to Stirling, visiting Linlithgow Palace by the way, on Monday the 27th of April. Before dinner that day, I went and visited Lord Abercromby at Airthrie. He had been very ill, but was then better, and his place was in the perfection of young vernal beauty. It has been the finest spring ever vouchsafed to Scotland. There are few Julys like this April. And the verdure of Abercromby's grass, the bright, fresh, tenderness of his foliage, the clearness of his lake, the mirth of his lambs and water-fowl, and the softened richness of his rocks and hills were all blended into a scene of singular loveliness.

I was in Court the whole of the three next days, the 28th, 29th, and 30th. There was nothing particular in any of the cases, except that in one of them we had an excellent specimen

42

of that beautiful option. Four people were under trial for theft, and two for reset. A villain, who would have cut the throats of all his relations for a shilling, was called as a witness by the prosecutor. It was objected that, being the son of one of the thieves, he was not bound to give evidence. The prosecutor (Cosmo Innes) endeavoured to make the objection inapplicable by saying that he only called him against the two resetters. But the reply, that still his parent was one of the accused, and that he was in the same position with a wife called to testify in a case where her husband was one of the accused, is at present deemed sound by the Court. So I was obliged to disgrace the law by explaining to him the respect paid to his sensibilities, and that in order to spare his filial piety, he had the option of defeating justice by telling the truth or not, just as he chose. No censure of this modern piece of judge-made legal nonsense could be severer than the grotesque and villainous leer with which he said: "Odd! a' like that hoption, ma Lord!" on which he retired amidst the laughter of the prisoners, and the amazement of the jury, and saved the two resetters.

The Lord Advocate (Rutherford) and I made out a Bill lately, which has just passed the Commons, for preventing the repetition of such disgraceful scenes by abolishing the objection of relationship. But its passage through the Peers is by no means certain; for a majority of the Faculty of Advocates is actually opposing it. They call such a blackguard's declining to speak, "the voice of nature", and profess to be moved by the *metus perjurii*. The opponents always take the case in which nothing worse can happen than that a guilty man escapes. But under this rule an innocent one may be convicted. Take this case. A is on trial along with B for a murder, which B alone committed. He calls B's son, who saw his father alone do it. In this case the life of the innocent person is sacrificed to what, at the very best, is the filial injustice of the guilty one's relation.

When at Stirling, I heard of the death of Mrs. Cockburn's brother, William Macdowell of Barr, an event not anticipated, and which clouded all the rest of the Circuit, and will long cloud the recollections of all who knew him. We came to Edinburgh during the night of the 30th of April, as I had to attend an Estate Bill, and then to go to Barr next day. We reached Edinburgh at four in the morning, through a dull, but most refreshing, fog, left it at two next forenoon, and reached Barr that night about ten. The funeral was next day. I remained there with Mrs. Cockburn and Mrs. Maitland till the morning of Tuesday the 5th of May, when I went to Glasgow, which I reached in time for a public breakfast, and was in Court by ten that day.

We had five days of work, from nine in the morning till six or seven in the evening, having been liberated, however, on Saturday the 9th in time to reach home that night.

There was nothing particular in the cases, the great mass of them being aggravated thefts, followed by seven years' transportation, *ad nauseam*. There was one capital conviction for murder. But even this was commonplace; the common Scotch case of a brute, excited by his own liquor, and pretending to be provoked by that of his wife, and finding himself alone in his own house with his helpless victim, proceeding to beat her to death. This man seemed to think it a sort of defence that it was a Saturday night, when "he was always worst, it being his pay-day". His wife was perfectly sober, and though "she could take a dram", was not of dissipated habits generally, and was never known to show any violence towards her husband. Yet though the proof could not have been clearer if the jury had seen him murder her, they unanimously recommended him to mercy on the ground of provocation, of which there was not a tittle, either in evidence or in truth. Such is the modern aversion to capital punishment. His name was Thomas Templeton.

There was also a shocking case of a poor child, scarcely eight years old, a climbing boy, who was compelled by threats to go up, or down, thirty-eight new chimneys successively, and without any interval for rest or food, though he was quite exhausted, cold, wet, and excoriated, and imploring that he might not be sent down the thirty-eighth vent, in which he died. The labour and danger were greatly increased by the vents being new, and the object being to clear them, by a chisel, of the lime and rubbish that adhered to their sides, a task requiring time and strength, and the rubbish greatly obstructing the passage at every turn. It was only charged as a culpable homicide, and the master had rather an affection for the boy, and worked him to death from no anger or selfishness, but merely from the general brutality of his craft. We longed to transport him, and will be abused by the benevolent for not doing so; but, in the circumstances, we could not go beyond imprisonment.

Our public breakfast was a substitute for the public dinner, and has been tried twice at Glasgow with success. It does not supersede one or two small, rational, dinners, of eight or twelve friends, or respectable connections of the Court, but only the abominable gathering of all the monsters who, as a matter of right, have long been permitted to scandalise Scotch Circuits. Though often sorely grudged, the old judges deemed these festivals indispensable to the dignity of the law. They were deemed essential for the preservation of Church and State. But, for some years past, much business, the want of the judges, picking the jurors, the cessation of the attendance of the gentry, and the weakness of the modern stomach, have introduced a distaste among most of us for these judicial and stately feasts. There are only two of us who now don't loathe them; Moncreiff, who enjoys the refreshment of meat and drink, and the Justice (Boyle) who, besides the conviviality, still deludes himself with the notion that the Circuit dinner exhibits him and the law in an imposing attitude. These two delight to sit down at two in the

44

morning to salmon and roast-beef, though they have to return to Court at nine, and to do Provosts the honour of taking bumpers of claret or mulled port with them; every shut eyelid in the house starting open at the sound of the glorious trumpets, as they drink the royal health. When these two shall be gone, there will not be a judge of such bad taste as to endure these horrid and mirthless meetings. But how Hermand would have despised this. With him the jollity of the Circuit was the only thing respectable about it. Nothing made it contemptible, even judicially, except sobriety. I once heard the servant of his serene colleague, Pitmilly, who had a strong taste for decorum and law, and none whatever for laughter or liquor, tell the chambermaid at Perth to bring his master a large kettle of warm water. Hermand, who was passing to his dinner at midnight, said, "God bless me, sir, is he going to make a whole kettle of punch, — and before supper too!" "No, no, my Lord, he's going to his bed, but he wants to bathe his feet first!" "Feet, sir?" exclaimed Hermand, "what ails his feet? Tell him to put some rum among it, and to give it all to his stomach!"

My book on this Circuit was Romilly's Memoirs of his own life, just published. The first part, being the account of his youth, is excellent. The Parliamentary Diary recalls many interesting discussions, and discloses many valuable views, particularly those of Romilly himself, but on the whole, it is not so striking as I thought that a record of the parliamentary life of such a man would have been. It is difficult to understand how he could record his impressions and proceedings at the time, yet keep so entirely clear of the characters, conduct, manners, or curious doings or sayings, of his associates or opponents. The charm of the whole book consists in its development of the character of the author, whose high, severe purity is softened, in these pages, into greater amiableness than appeared in the original in real life. There never was a better man. He had a capital head, and a capital heart, for criminal justice. His proposal that the Court should be entitled to award costs to the unjustly accused against the prosecutor is wise and humane, and perhaps original among moderate and practical reformers. Why should the public be permitted to charge an innocent man with a crime, and though he be acquitted, to ruin him by costs, when it is not allowed to bring a civil action against him unjustly, with the same consequence? Such a law would soon introduce public prosecutors into England, by the necessity it would create of greater caution of prosecution and preparation. In Scotland it would probably not burden the public with £50 a year.

WEST CIRCUIT

Dalmally, Saturday Night, 29th August 1840. — I am here on

this Western Circuit, Meadowbank going to Stirling, and I to Inverary, and both to Glasgow.

I left Edinburgh on the morning of the 26th, with Mrs. Cockburn, Jane, Elizabeth, and Frank, and went that day by Stirling and Ardoch, to my nephew's, Sir David Dundas, at Dunira, four miles west of Comrie. We stayed there all the 27th and 28th, and left it this morning and got here about seven in the evening.

As yet we have had delicious weather, and have enjoyed it. Nothing except what good weather reveals, in the finer scenery of Scotland, has occurred worthy of being mentioned, though our two days at Dunira were merry and kind.

Strathearn, meaning the strath of about twenty miles from Crieff to Lochearn Head, though by no means the grandest, is, I suspect, perhaps the most picturesquely beautiful district in Scotland. The rapid and steep descent upon it from Ardoch, especially when it is lighted up by the glow of a summer evening, is very striking, not nearly so Swisslike as the descent on the opposite side of the valley, from Amulree, but still surprising and beautiful. We snuffed the Comrie peat, and hailed the singularly lucid water of Earn, and soon found lowly Dunira sleeping calmly, as usual, in its magnificent cradle of crags and woods. The two next days were entirely given to explore that delightful strath, which though I had formerly been in it for days together, never appeared so fresh and clean. I exclude Drummond Castle, for it is on the flat, but what have we in this country more perfect, in mixed cultivation and rocky wildness, than Ochtertyre, Lawers, Dunira, and Strowan? though its preponderance of mere agriculture, perhaps, would justify the exclusion of the last from the society of such glorious places. And then how their interstices are filled up by the tufts of Clathick, Comrie House, Dalchonzie, and Aberuchill! The eye and the mind wander incessantly from the rich, low, flat, gravelly, alluvial holms, bright with verdure and grain, though perpetually darkened with knolls of wood and rock, to the lofty sierras of black and grey crags, their bases all covered profusely with good wood, till the solid masses are broken and dissipated as they get higher, till at last they die away as the height still increases, into streaks up the sheltered ravines, till vegetation ceases, save where one or two successful adventurers may be seen far beyond all companionship, defying the storm, braving it, like the strong men of the world, and calling on their timorous associates to come up to them. I never tire of getting on the summit of one of the Strathearn crags, and sitting and surveying the scene below, obviously once a lake, and still the best preparation for a new lake in the world.

The whole drive from Dunira, to this was glorious. The day calm, balmy, and bright, and everything, from the rich placidity of Lochearn, to the alpine grandeur of Dalmally, seen in the most favourable circumstances. It is about thirty-one years since I was in these regions. What a district it is! Lying along the bases of Ben Voirlich, Ben More, and in the company of Ben Cruachan and Ben Lawers, four of the greatest mountains in Scotland. Their summits were all played with by the sun and the clouds all day. How the shadows swept over them! Amidst the milkiness of such an air, and the gorgeousness of such lights, nothing is wanted to entitle Scotland to stand up whenever even Switzerland is named. The approach to Dalmally, where the valley opens out, as if to give fair play to the amphitheatre of mountains, and the solitary church marks the presence of men, forms one of the noblest prospects I have almost ever seen. And the hills! They have driven Aviemore out of my head.

Oban, Sunday, 30th August 1840. — We left Dalmally this morning before eleven. The day still incapable of improvement. The superiority of the Cairngorms is in their ridginess. The Dalmally mountains are more earthly and lumpish. But what lumps! And how well placed! Oh for old oaks, a huge old castle, and a feudal history, about the centre of that amphitheatre.

The country from Dalmally to this was new to me, and it is now gratifying to an aged gentleman to have the omissions of his youth rewarded by being able to say that so is the journey from this to Lochgilphead, and from Lochgilphead to Inverary.

The upper, that is the Dalmally, end of the Loch Awe, dignified by the ruins of Kilchurn Castle, and bounded by the steep and stony Ben Cruachan, with its wooded base and the magnificent corries that flank its northern bank, is all very fine; the southern hills, near the lake, are low, but this implies shallowness of water, which gives islands, with which accordingly this part of the loch is more richly supplied than most of our Highland waters.

No river has a more striking outlet than the Awe, with its sides roaring with cataracts, and so steep that, though sheep were browsing on their oases of verdure, it defied us to find out how they had got there, or were ever to get away. The river makes short but violent rush to Loch Etive, amidst a profusion of mountain, wood, and many well-placed cliffs, till Muckairn Kirk, from which the surface recedes on both sides, tells us we have gained the summit, and must now descend to the sea.

Lest Ben Cruachan, whose summit was glittering to-day as well as all the other sublimities of the district, should not be sufficient for the honour of Muckairn, the heritors or somebody have erected a thing in the churchyard, about the size of a large broomstick, and not more attractive in its form. I asked the driver what it was. "It's a moniment to a gentleman." "What gentleman?" "Ou, a dinna mind his name. He dee'd a while ago. Ou ay. A mind noo. It's to Lord Ne-e-elson."

The descent from this summit to Loch Etive is all very fine.

The very rapid ebbing of the water towards low tide as we saw it, suggests the notion of an American river; the dun hills remind one who has never been among them, and knows them only from opinion, of something more poetical; and the appearance of little, comfortable Oban, with the feudal fragment of Dunolly, makes the traveller, even of two days, feel as if he had reached a haven of repose after a long and perilous voyage.

This is the gem of sea villages. A small bay blocked in by hills; five little vessels sleeping on the quiet water; a crescent of white houses almost touching the sea, backed by a corresponding curve of cliff; the old tower of Dunolly at the end of the one horn, and high knolls at the end of the other; no manufactures, no trade, and scarcely any bustle, several strangers attracted by mere beauty and tranquility; all this completes one's idea, or rather one's feeling, of a peaceful summer sea retreat. How gloriously the sun set behind the hills of Mull! and with what deep and ineffable peacefulness has the night gradually, and as if reluctantly, closed over the silver waters.

I half tremble to think that to-morrow is destined for the Sound of Mull in a steamer, in order to see Iona and Staffa, by me for the first time. Hitherto my stomach has only been for the solid earth, and I am shabby enough to half wish for the apology of a storm.

Lochgilphead, Tuesday Night, 1st September 1840. — Well! I have actually had my piety warmed by musing over the ruins of Iona, and my faith in Ossian excited by being in Fingal's Cave.

Francis, Elizabeth, and I left Oban yesterday morning in the Brenda, a rumbling steamer, at six o'clock, and were relanded there, after a prosperous voyage round the Island of Mull, at eight in the evening, going by the south end and returning by the Sound. Consequently we not only saw Iona and Staffa, but about 120 miles of islands, and nature never produced a better day.

I saw little after the tenth or twelfth mile till I reached Iona, for my very unmaritime stomach was rebellious, and for about four hours I lay abusing my folly, and vowing that this should be my last voyage. In this state I was landed on that island, but my infirmity instantly ceased, and, getting into water like glass, it never came over me again during the day.

The ruins greatly surpassed my expectation. I thought that all I was to see was the mere stools of buildings, whereas I found as many legible old inscriptions, carved tombstones, and standing walls, as in most very ancient, fallen edifices. Being walked round by the Captain, and only an hour allowed, and a whole cargo of travellers to be satiated, it was not a visit that could do more than leave a general idea of the appearance of the place, and enable one to know hereafter what people are speaking about when they speak of Iona. Were it not absurd, after all that has been said and written, it would be irresistible for any one of ordinary sense or feeling to indulge in the visions which this remote and deserted little island is so well fitted to inspire. They came across me, and the recollection of the scene will now for ever suggest them more easily and vividly.

I must confess that my contemplations of the past were greatly marred by the reality of the present. A more wretched set of creatures than those that crawled around us I doubt if even Ireland could exhibit. Certainly no other part of the world that I have ever read of could exceed it. It might have been accounted for by supposing that Argyleshire had sent its most humiliating destitution to affect the visitors of Iona, had it not been for the sad truth, that the naked and diseased dirt which greets and follows the tourists there, will meet and follow him in many other islands of the Hebrides. My sensibility has perhaps been too little blunted by the past reality of such spectacles, for I doubt if I was ever on one of the western islands before, but it is dreadful to think that these poor creatures are not only human, but countrymen. Yet they have an infants' school, which I saw in action, and a church where the Sacrament was dispensed the day before. So easy is it to combine the forms of religion and education with the degradation of human habits, if not the prostration of the human character. They are the better of the church and the school, but still are about as brutish in the economy of life as their very nasty cows and swine are.

But what can be expected, though they had all the churches and schools in Christendom, of people who live in the constant view of these still more brutally kept monuments and temples. What a disgrace to their owners! who I understand are the Argyles. All the waters of Loch Fyne will not cleanse them from the shame of these neglected solemn ruins. They are the most interesting relics in the British Empire, and might, by mere attention, and with very little expenditure, have been protected for centuries; the flat, carved tombstones might have had their venerable letters saved from being worn out by regardless feet; and the grass might have been kept as smooth and pure as the turf at any of the Oxford colleges; but no foul beast ever trod a pearl in the dirt so unconsciously as these titled men have, for many ages, but particularly during the last hundred years, deliberately allowed fragments, that have been the wonder of thinking men, to be reduced to a worse condition than most pig-styes. If proprietors who behave so had all the apology of bankruptcy, this might be a consolation, for a well-disposed mind could not fail to consider this as God's punishment for their crime. But every one of them wastes yearly, on contempt-ible importance, what would be quite sufficient to transmit these sacred gifts of a former age to succeeding ones, and in such a condition that they might be admired, as they descend, without having the veneration they inspire marred by unnecess-ary disgust. Even the Argyle is diminished in my sight.

We landed easily on Staffa, and I was one of four who went to the very innermost recess of the cave. It is one of the very few much-spoken-of wonders to which my fancy had not come up. And I cannot say that my expectation had been lowered by the opinion of Serjeant Talfourd, who told me, two years ago, that he thought Staffa "contemptible", a crotchet to be ascribed, no doubt, to the poet's stomach not having come to its senses so soon as mine had. It is one of nature's great geological feats. No thunder is more awful than the roar of the wave as it breaks along the sides, and on the inner end of the cavern. And then there is nothing human about it. It is all pure nature. Not a single ass has even painted its name upon it. The solitude and storminess of its position greatly enhance its interest.

On the whole, I have rarely been more gratified than by at last beholding these two sights, one of the wonder of nature, the other of man. I had been anxious to see them almost all my life, and the recollection will now be more exciting than the fancy of them was.

The rest of the sail was delightful. We moved over a sea nearly of glass, past places, but particularly past islands and points, and other things called castles, the names of which were familiar, and where the mere surprise of seeing what one had so often heard of was a pleasure. In their present state there is very little beauty in any one place along that coast, and not a single old building of any architectural interest. The great want is of wood, even of larch, which, however, for scenery, is rarely wood. Nor is it true that wood would not grow on these tempest-beaten and foam-washed spots. A thousand small and exposed, but still oak-clad islands, and promontories, and bays, and knolls, and ravines, but especially islands which are most in the way of the spray and the wind, attest that, even though not planted in great masses, the whole of the Hebrides might be adorned and warmed by trees. It is sheep and poverty, not the ocean or the storm, that keep them hard and uniform. What an Archipelago it would be had it only due summer!

As it is, the charm of the region consists in the picturesque grouping of the features of the scenery, particularly of the hills, in the barbarous history, and above all, in the desolation that seems to prevail over everything. We did not see two dozen of vessels, including boats, throughout the whole day, no town, or even village, except Tobermory, very few, and very insignificant houses, and no people; we heard no sounds except the oars of the few boats that came alongside for passengers; everything was silent, hard, and still, under the impressiveness of which one sails along, amidst scenes which time had been incapable of changing, and which seem as if they had been preserved merely that they might be the localities of old stories.

The two finest prospects are, a little after leaving Aros, when the whole of Ben Cruachan, and a little after leaving Ardtornish, when the Appin mountains stand before us, both as we saw them, blazing with the setting sun, and contrasted with the shaded, and almost black groups behind us.

I suspect that had I seen Tobermory first, I should have said of it all I have said of Oban, which it is very like. Tobermory has the advantages of a steeper immediate background, fringed with scattered wood; of a high and low town, the one on the summit of the cliff seeming to stand on the top of the houses on the beach; and of a church with a sort of a spire peering out from among the trees amidst the upper buildings. Our twenty-five passengers, or so, were mostly English, and all of them were struck with its resemblance to Torquay in its primitive condition.

The number of foreign, but chiefly of English, travellers is extraordinary. They fill every conveyance, and every inn, attracted by scenery, curiosity, superfluous time and wealth, and the fascination of Scott, while, attracted by grouse, the mansion-houses of half of our poor devils of Highland lairds are occupied by rich and titled Southrons. Even the students of Oxford and Cambridge come to the remote villages of Scotland in autumn to study! I found ten of them three years ago, with two tutors, in lodgings at Callander; and a party, also with the tutor and the Greek books, at Inverary last time I was there; and I found both English and Irish youths established now at Oban. The quantity of Greek imbibed, even by the dominie, I can only conjecture, but they can do nothing better for their minds or bodies than breathe such air, in such scenes.

Yesterday morning I went and saw Dunstaffnage. It would be difficult to fancy a more glorious position for a great castle, old or new. Indignation is never satiated with abusing the unworthy owners of such shamefully neglected ruins, nor imagination with arranging and improving the material of the scenery, recalling the former condition of such places, or reviewing them for modern life. I was very anxious to steal a curious round thin flat stone, of about a foot in diameter, with a hole in its centre (part of a quern, probably), and ventured to ask a sort of a fool of a lad, who was attending me, if I might take it, but he completely disarmed me by fidgeting, and clawing, and drawling out, with a look of pain, "Ou ay — I dinna ken — but it's been a lang while here," putting a most appealing emphasis on the lang, which he spun out to five times its ordinary length. "It's been here a la-a-a-ng time," plainly implying the question — "And wad she tak it awa?" So there it lies for me. There is a tender epitaph in the burying-ground by a swain over the remains of "my modest love, snatched from me by death." But it turns out that in spite of all her modesty, the lamentation proceeds from her spouse and numerous offspring.

We left Oban to-day at eleven, and got here at eight. Another perfect day.

There is little to be seen between Kilmartin and this, — eight miles — but all the rest of the road, from Oban to Kilmartin, about thirty-two miles, is most admirable — most admirable indeed. A great deal of it quite inland, consisting of deep valleys, profusely enriched by wood (real wood, not filthy mercantile larch) and water; but then we met, every few miles, with our friends the arms of the sea again, and as our way lay mostly across the upper bays of their most inland touchings of the country, and was consequently far from the storm, the whole of these delightful little seas were surrounded by wood, and sprinkled by knolly islands. Loch Melfort is beautiful, and has the advantage of having sometimes defied engineering to make a road along its precipitous approaches.

I found a lad carving a monument from a design of his own, in Kilmartin churchyard, whom I mention because I should not wonder if he should hereafter be distinguished as an artist. He told me his name was Mossman. His conversation, and that design, a blasted tree, standing over a broken column, gave me the impression of his being an able young man.

There are a great many old, and curiously carved, flat tombstones in this churchyard, generally without inscriptions, but probably identified to the families by the carved devices. There is also the remains of a cross, which had been in the form of a human figure, on a cross, with outstretched arms. Though it be nearly covered with dirt and nettles, and the arms be broken off above each elbow, enough remains to evince considerable taste and skill in the artist. It was Mossman who pointed it out to me. There is also a very respectable and hoary monument, built into a wall, to the memory of the last Catholic minister of the parish.

Strachur, Sunday, 6th September 1840. — We left Lochgilp-head, and went to Minard, on the forenoon of last Wednesday the 2nd, under a deluge of rain which was thought great even in Argyleshire, and endured the whole day.

We remained at Minard till Friday morning. The place had struck me so forcibly two years ago that I visited it now chiefly that I might be better acquainted with its beauties, especially as I had seen it advertised for sale "as the most beautiful Highland residence in Scotland". I was disappointed, chiefly — (which applies to nearly the whole western side of Loch Fyne), — because the opposite side is so heavy and uninteresting. The eastern is clearly the side to look from. The hills too, which had seemed, and still seem, so picturesque from where I now am, were lost at Minard itself. That place, however, projects so far into the sea that it is distinguished by the rare peculiarity of having no road between it and the water. I saw many proofs there, as I have elsewhere, of the favourableness of these regions for vegetation. Besides gorgeous fuchsias and very considerable passion-flowers, a myrtle has sustained itself healthily for many years, though uncovered and on an unheated wall. But much of Argyleshire is south of Edinburgh, on a gravelly soil, and on the level of the sea.

I made acquaintance, for the first time, with Castle Lachlan, opposite Minard, with nothing castellated in its modern style, but a remarkably sensible small house, standing in a sheltered valley, with a beautiful prospect of the sea, which turns the waves of its little inland bay at its feet, excellent interspersed turf and shrubbery, and altogether a comfortable place, in judicious taste, and without any of the nearly universal symptoms of the idiot of a laird having built or improved, or idled himself out of his estate.

After an agreeable visit to a kind and cheerful family of ladies, we left Minard early on Friday, and held the Court that day at Inverary. A very wet day.

The business (three cases) was over by six in the evening. Having palmed off a public breakfast upon the people, I gave them no public dinner. The only peculiarity in Court was, it was the first time I had been on the bench since the recent passing of the bill which I mentioned that Rutherfurd and I had prepared last spring for quashing the objection of relationship, with its consequent Option, the initial examination, and the necessity of having every witness out of Court. All this tedious and unjust nonsense is now extinguished. It is a satisfaction to recollect that in my own practice, and unless when compelled by a weak brother, I had never put the initial interrogations.

We crossed to St. Catherine's and came here yesterday, where we found Maitland (Solicitor-General), and Archibald Davidson (Advocate-Depute), Lord and Lady and William Murray, Mrs. Rigby, and Mrs. Wildman. An agreeable evening. But this is another bad day.

In crossing from Minard to Castle Lachlan we all — ladies too — tried the line-fishing with no success. But it reminded me of the day I think in 1808, when I had tried Loch Fyne in the same way with Lord Hermand. He was the judge here, with his wife, and his two nieces — one since married to me, and one to Maitland, — and I was the Advocate-Depute. Robert Bell, now Procurator to the Church, was at Inverary, with Lord Cullen. It was a bright, calm day, and we paddled about the whole forenoon. I rowed. His Lordship brought up some great fishes, but not without many a drive, and many a loud direction, and not a total absence of abuse, from the fisherman, who was all deference to my Lord so long as no fish was on the hook, but no sooner saw that one was in danger of being lost by his Lordship's awkwardness, than his whole respect was forgotten, and he bawled, and shook his fist, and directed and scolded most energetically, to the learned judge's vast entertainment. The night before, the two judges, who were of opposite politics, and no friends, had met (at supper) for the first time for several years. They were cold to each other at first, but at last liquor soldered them, and by two in the morning (John Richardson, Bell, and I, alone being present) they were embracing and vowing eternal friendship, and toasting each other's wives, and giving us young ones imitations of the old lawyers. I scarcely ever saw such a scene. But it was not unjudicial in those days. Cullen was in bed all next day, and never saw his own Circuit Court, but the immortal head of Hermand was clear and cool next morning by six, and after a few hours of business and a long sail, he returned to the charge at dinner with a picturesque and cordial exuberance of spirits which the concentrated kindness and gaiety of all Argyleshire could not have equalled.

Hermand, Friday, 11th September 1840. — On Monday last, the 7th, we left Strachur for Kilmun, a beautiful day, and a delightful stage of sixteen miles. And we had ample time to enjoy the melancholy beauty of Loch Eck, for our steeds did not choose to hasten through the scene faster than three and a half miles in the hour, and one of them at last stood still, and had it not been for the vicinity of a Samarittin cottar, who lent us a substitute, we might possibly have been obliged to survey that narrow strip of water by moonlight, and under the morning dawn. It was comfortable to see that our proper beast was not much fatigued, for no sooner was he liberated than he at once proceeded to a most active graze. We were in time, after all, for the steamer, which soon swept us out into the busy and glorious Clyde, the most varied, magnificent, and enjoyable of inland seas. The sun was hastening home and threw his parting light on almost the whole circle of bright and striking towns and villages, by which its edges are specked; on Kilmun, Dunoon, Gourock, Greenock, Helensburgh, and on many hamlets, besides kindling the summits of the finest collection of noble and picturesque mountain peaks in the world. After a shamefully awkward debarkation of the carriage at Greenock, we proceeded to my daughter's at Erskine Manse, where we stayed that night.

Next morning (Tuesday the 8th) I went to Glasgow, but was compelled by a mistake about horses, to go, with the vulgar, by a steamer! a degradation of the judicial dignity whereat the Justice-Clerk will be greatly shocked. Our 54 or 55 cases were got through yesterday by four o'clock, that is, in three short days. They were mostly trashy thefts, and we literally had not two hours' speaking from the bar, taking it all together, and neither Meadowbank nor I think it our duty to preach regularly to every prisoner.

As soon as we got off I came here.

I forgot to mention before, that twenty youths from Oxford and Cambridge, with two tutors, have been living for about two and a half months at Inverary, and eight at Oban.

I heard some lamentation at Inverary, when I was extolling the woods of Glenfeochan and Loch Melfort, about the probable consequences of their all having been sold to the Bunaw Iron Company for charcoal. Such sales are hurtful, or the reverse, according to circumstances. However injurious to any particular spot a senseless massacre of wood may be, nothing can be more favourable to the general cultivation of trees than a market for them. Accordingly, I see that this groundless foreboding about the Bunaw Company was made above seventy years ago, and the country, though not timbered, is foliaged still. "At Bunaw, near the north end, is a large salmon fishery, also a considerable iron-foundry, which I fear will soon devour the beautiful woods of the country." So predicted Pennant in the year 1769.

I had so much to see that the only book I could get read was the *Pathfinder*, which I was told was Cooper's best novel. It is his worst. The occurrences that marked the period when the French, the English, and the original natives fought for the soil of North America, supplied some excellent materials both for true and for fictitious narrative. But they were too few and too simple for much of it. They are devoid of the variety and interest which history and society alone furnish. Accordingly, Cooper, in these stories, is always copying himself. It is all one what the title of any of his Indian tales may be, for they all produce exactly the same impression, through substantially the same scenes and characters. It is always the wily Indian with his rifle that never misses; the brave, honourable, and obstinate English officer; the gentle and heroic woman, braving bullets, tomahawks, long marches, and the fiery sieges of the wooden fortress; the noble savage, with all the gallantry of chivalry, and all the magnanimity of Christianity; the trail through the forest; the canoe and the rapids; eyes glaring through bushes; red skins and pale skins; hostile tribes, with their skilful leaders and odd names, etc. This does well once, but not often. Cooper is never original, or in his element, except in a ship. His home is on the deep.

GLASGOW CIRCUIT
1841

Edinburgh, 11th January 1841. — I returned yesterday from holding the Glasgow Winter Circuit.

On Monday the 4th, my daughter Elizabeth, Miss Rosa Macbean, and I, went, amidst heavy snow and bitter cold, to my daughter Mrs. Stewart's at the Manse of Erskine. I stayed there all night, and went next morning to breakfast at Moore Park, near Govan, where my colleague Lord Medwyn was, at his nephew's, Charles Forbes, banker. We went from that, in procession, to Court.

There were 68 cases, of which 65 were tried, the other three being put off from absence of witnesses or of culprits. There were two cases which occupied a whole day from nine in the morning till four next morning, yet, except one immaterial case which Medwyn remained to try to-day, (Monday), the whole business was leisurely and patiently gone through on Saturday night, and I came home (still through snow and frost) yesterday.

Medwyn, though more of a monk in matters of religion or politics, than any man I know, is an excellent, judicious, humane, practical judge, with great industry, and a deep sense of official duty. Though pious and acquainted, by long administration of the affairs both of the innocent and the guilty poor, with the feelings of the lower orders when in distress, he agrees with me in the uselessness, if not the hurtfullness, of the judge preaching to every prisoner who is undergoing sentence.

We had three capital cases, a murder, a rape, and a robbery. But though each was as clearly proved as if the commission of the fact had been actually seen, and each was a very aggravated case of its kind, such is the prevailing aversion to capital punishment, that no verdict inferring such a punishment could be obtained, and these horrid culprits were only transported. It can't be helped as yet, perhaps, but this want of sympathy between law and the public is very unseemly. The public is wrong.

We had also a bad case of bigamy, for which, according to our usage, we could only send the heartless, perfidious villain for one year to jail. This, till lately, was the English punishment also, but within these two years they have got a statute extending it to seven years transportation. I have already renewed my recommendation to the Lord Advocate (A. Rutherfurd) to try to pass such an Act for Scotland.

SOUTH CIRCUIT

Langholm, Saturday Night, 10th April 1841. — I left Edinburgh, on this South Spring Circuit, on the morning of Wednesday last, the 7th instant, with Mrs. Cockburn and my niece Graham Maitland. Meadowbank is to go to Ayr; I have been at Jedburgh and am proceeding to Dumfries.

After being dragged up, with our backs to the glories of Edinburgh, to Middleton Moor, we swept down, amid the silent peacefulness of Gala, to Melrose. It was about thirty years since I had gone into the Abbey, and I was very glad that the necessity of showing it to Graham compelled me to see it again. It is greatly improved in keeping, being really, at last, decently clean and respectable. But they have allowed a brewery to get up within, I should suppose, 100 yards of the principal window. John Bowers too, who has shown it for about forty years, and who even makes drawings of it thought worthy of being engraved, though, I dare say, a worthy man, has two faults, — one that somebody has told him to eschew plain Scotch, and so he called the ruin "a grand Rowen," and gave it as his opinion that if the great window were to be destroyed it would "create a vast vacuum;" the other that, although for anything I know he may

56

be qualified for the Presidency of the strictest Temperance Society, he has a very whiskyfied visage. Shall we never see these Scotch fragments, waited upon by attendants worthy of them? By the respectful, well dressed, reverential old man, the nice, tidy, decent, kindly woman, or the gentle and intelligent girl.

We stopped at Kirklands (Richardson's, near Ancrum) for about an hour and a half. Beautiful, but there is always sadness in the emptiness and silence of a friend's house.

I processed into Jedburgh that day at four, and next day (the 8th) disposed of the criminal business, and of a dull public dinner. I went back to Court for two hours next day, to hear two appeals, and this ended the Jethart Justice of this spring. The Court was crowded on the second day to hear the discussion of an appeal, which, divested of all surplusage, came to this point, whether the burial, by an owner, in his own ground, of a dead horse implied such dereliction that the abstraction of it was not theft? The Sheriff-Substitute had decided no theft, which I reversed.

I went, duly, morning and evening, to linger over that massive and curious ruin, to which, far more than even to its sweet and secluded position, Jedburgh owes its principal interest. A glorious pile, nobly placed; but disgracefully, most disgracefully, abused. What extenuation can even charity suggest for the atrocity of converting one-half of the building into the parish church, a proceeding by which, for the sake of saving the heritors from the expense of a new church, one-half of the old cathedral windows have been nearly built up, and the antiquity of the place has been interfered with. Letting a Rutherford of Edgerston get a bright new gimcrack, and richly ornamented tomb put over his bones, within the old building, and a whole aisle of it locked up for his special comfort, is a piece of taste of the same kind. The Barons of Exchequer had great merit in clearing Arbroath Abbey unsparingly of the whole of this "rubbish", as it was called, to the immense indignation of the descendants of the intruding defuncts. The apology for the Edgerston abomination is, that his titles gave him a right to it, which, being interpreted, means that as usual, some of his cunning ancestors chose to put this right into his private parchments. Then the manse, and a private school, and a dyer's work, and many hovels, all permitted to jostle and elbow the unprotected majesty of the sacred, mouldering edifice. One hundred thousand pounds, or certainly two, would clear and purify all the old historical buildings in Scotland, and would keep them permanently right, and I don't know how the money could be laid better out. But I believe the whole four abbeys of Roxburghshire are private property.

Yet in spite of all its surrounding bad taste and selfish disregardedness, how beautiful was this one! With its clear stream, its hanging gardens, and its young foliage. This is a

very early spring, and many of the planes, and more of the poplars, stood out amidst primroses, and a whole world of bursting buds, rich, bright, fresh, verdure, exhibiting one of the best pictures of the decay of the works of art, in combination with the eternal youth of the works of nature, and of the holy softness that is breathed over the latter by the pathetic interest of the former.

We left Jedburgh about one yesterday, and came up the Teviot to Hawick, and from that to Borthwickbrae, where we stayed till this forenoon, when we came here by Moss Paul.

The weather had been beautiful, the perfection, indeed, of a Scotch spring — bright, calm, and very dry, and with no foolish prematurity of heat, but on the contrary, with a sensible, prospective sharpness, which, though it may make us sometimes envy the opening of a more southern climate, gives us the comfortable assurance that every leaf that is born will live. The whole country has been beautiful, the hedges nearly green, every bank sweet with primroses and wood anemone; the larches clothed in their early, short-lived freshness; all the village gardens gay with yellow daffodils and green gooseberry bushes; larks revelling in the sky, and mavises in every wood; the fields in that delightful state of weedless cleanliness, that shows the exact nature of every agricultural operation, and makes one think it would be pleasant to play upon them. And then these quiet pastoral hills! The descent, through them, from Moss Paul to this tranquil place, was delightful. Langholm was lying in its valley, at the junction of its waters, under an evening so sunny and so sweet, that one can scarcely avoid believing that every poor man would be happy if he could only get all his Saturdays to close so softly. And what a fact to be able to record of any town, that though comfortable and well ordered, it is so simple that there is not a single lamp in any part of any street within it. It was all pitch dark to-night at nine. Except from the shop of "Anderson, Baker and Grocer," there was not so much as one candle shining from one window. Yet the people were not all asleep. On the contrary they were walking about in considerable numbers, only as no one could see his, or her neighbour, they seemed to feel the necessity of hailing, for I never heard so much whistling.

We explored Langholm Lodge. Nothing. And ill kept. But Buccleuch is a many-placed Duke.

Lochmaben, Sunday Night, 11th April 1841. — I saw this morning that there was a gaswork at Langholm, and gas burners in the streets. But the work seemed cold, and the burners were without glasses, and rusty.

We meant to have come directly from Langholm to this, but, attracted by the beauty of the drive, which I knew, and by the hope of English muffins, we went round by Longtown, where we breakfasted to-day.

It is indeed a beautiful drive, one of the most beautiful in the Scotch Lowlands. But we were too early in the season for it, for it depends much upon its forest trees being in leaf, not merely from the charm of the foliage, but because this valley is the better of having the poverty of its hills — if they deserve the name — hid. But still the river, the pines, the evergreens round almost every house, the comfortable villages and farms, and above all, the general appearance of care, culture, and of an interest in the beauty of the district, make that a delightful stage at any period of the year. It is the most gentlemanlike stage in Scotland.

And the muffins were excellent. Dinner is the English meal, breakfast the Scotch. An Englishman's certainty of getting a good dinner, seems to make him indifferent about his breakfast, while the substantiality of a Scotchman's breakfast impairs, or at least might impair, his interest in his dinner. However, the vicinity of Scotland has instructed the people of Longtown, and the whole morning set-out was capital. But the peculiar glory belonged to the muffins; things which Scotland never succeeds in imitating.

We went from Longtown to Ecclefechan, where we stayed an hour to let the horses rest. I tried to reach Hoddam Castle during this pause, but could not. It seemed the only thing worth seeing on that road, except a place which had the appearance of being a very nice modern house, with its bank, river, and old castle.

We got here from Ecclefechan about half-past three, 24 miles from Longtown, — the whole way respectable in point of agriculture, so far as one who is no farmer could judge, and there its merits end.

Contrary to our expectation, we have found a decent hostelry in this wretched carcass of a royal burgh. Yet they have their provost and their town house with a spire, and their cross, which last reminds me to mention that the people of Melrose have lately repaired the pedestal of theirs, and well. Hermand used to say that he always detected a royal burgh by its stink.

I went and saw the castle. It must have been a strong place once, but is truly a ruin now. I don't see how any fragment of it can survive above ground fifty years longer. It has plainly been skinned. The ashlar work has been removed both outside and in, for the sake of the materials, and nothing left but the interstice, a rude conglomeration of mortar and of water-worn stones, in their round, natural state. The walls stand by the mere tenacity of the lime, without any solidity from the weight or position of the stones. It should be all given up to ivy. In its best days it must have been the least interesting of all our great castles. Nothing can exceed the paltriness of its situation, with its flat, bare, rockless, islandless loch, its own few wretched trees, and the poor beggarly idiot of a burgh that stares at it.

We go to Dumfries to-morrow morning, and I fancy my next

note will be at Thornhill, on our way home on Tuesday.

Thornhill, Tuesday Night, 13th April 1841. — We left Loch-maben yesterday morning about half-past seven, and went to Dumfries. This ended the new part of my road, which was from Longtown to Dumfries. There is nothing to be recorded concerning this last stage, except the prospect of Dumfries and its vicinity from a hill about half a mile before reaching Torthor-wald kirk. It was extensive and splendid, the bright sun glitter-ing on the roofs of the Dumfries houses, and on the sides of countless farms and country mansions, all of which had their white sides exposed to the clear morning light.

I was in Court yesterday till six in the evening, with very common cases, after which we had a grand dinner. The draft ale excellent. To-day I was in Court till four, when we came here.

We includes James Craufurd, the Advocate-Depute, who has been with us since Jedburgh, but leaves us to-morrow for Ayr — an honourable, able youth, with more of an Irishman in his manner than any Scotsman of my present acquaintance.

I saw nothing whatever of Dumfries this time. Mrs. Cockburn brought me the following epitaph from a Covenanter's tomb in the churchyard:-

> Stop, passenger, read! Here interred doth lie
> A witness 'gainst poor Scotland's perjury;
> Whose head, once fixt up on the Bridgeport stood,
> Proclaiming vengeance for her guiltless blood.
> Wm. Pentland, 1667.

I was told a singularly pleasing fact about their Lunatic Asylum. A box is occasionally taken in the theatre for the patients, who go respectably in coaches and sit happily and enjoy the play. A very curious and delightful fact.

Mr. Montgomery Bell and Mr. Young, both advocates, who are going to Ayr to-morrow with Craufurd, dined with us here. Very pleasant. Except myself, the house is all snoring, and I proceed to snore too. Dalveen to-morrow!

Wednesday Morning, 14th April 1841, Thornhill. — Just leaving Mrs. Glendinning and her hotel, which are both as worthy as I found them in 1839 of the traveller's attention. The day is not what I would have it, being showery, but we may possibly have a gleam for the Pass. His Grace has built a new and respectable-looking church here since I was last at this place, for which, of course, he has the curses of the Dissenters, who greatly prefer the decline of the Church to the rise of knowledge. I have heard it said that there is an extent of wretchedness in Thornhill beyond what is usual even in High-land villages. But I don't believe it, because it is inconsistent with the prevalent air of decided comfort that appears, the cleanness of the streets, the substantiality of the houses, and, above all, the wholeness and cleanness of all the windows.

Troloss Toll-Bar, half-past 10 a.m., 14th April 1841. — I have stopped here for an hour in mercy to the beasts, for whom this twenty mile stage from Thornhill to Crawford is far too long.

I adhere to my former feeling about Drumlanrig, chiefly that the hills round it, in so far as they can be considered as connected with the house, are stupidly lumpish. But in reference to farms, keeping, and attention to the people, the whole country exhibits those constant proofs of judicious munificence which mark the family of Buccleuch. But for the repetition by Burn of himself in every building, the farmhouses are beautifully placed, planned, and kept, and a great land-owner's history cannot be more honourably read than in the comfort and obvious improvingness of the whole district.

The day is bright, and I have had a walk through the Pass, the finest, certainly, in any pastoral region of Scotland. I should like to see it by moonlight. The smoothness of the velvet hills, which indeed forms the principal charm of the scene, is very strange, considering their steepness and the wateryness of the climate. I should have expected the rills to have broken the surface into a hundred gullies thousands of years ago.

But the horses say they are ready for another pull, and I am not sorry to get quit of William Anderson's squalling bairns. But no wonder they squall, because as soon as we came in they were dragged to a pail and got their faces washed, and then Mrs. Cockburn gave them oranges, the cutting, and skinning, and eating of which, with all the consequent competition, and battling for the knife, and interference of the mother, only increased the confusion.

I ought to have mentioned Durisdeer, which, there is no reason to doubt, is as shabby inside as most Scotch villages, but outside, and seen from a distance, has always struck me with its remoteness and solitude. I first saw it when I was walking along from Closeburn school — where I had been commissioned by my father to go and place my brother Montague — to Edinburgh, in my nineteenth or twentieth year, and have never lost the impression made upon me, early in the morning, by the loneliness of that still, smokeless, and silent village. It is like a town one would expect to meet with in the wilds of Arabia.

Bonaly, Thursday Evening, 15th April 1841. — We got to Edinburgh last night about seven, after a cloudless day. Under such a sky, desolate though it be, the whole region from Thornhill to Edinburgh is excellent. To me, its desolation is its charm. The wide open hills and moors, unbroken by wood, the solitude rather deepened than interfered with, by an occasional hut or farm-house; the appearances of life and of human care, in the

62

white clothes laid out on the patch of bright grass beside the sparkling burn, in the little bit of garden, and in the dirty children chasing the mutinous pig; the admirable fields that are reclaimed, wherever they are reclaimable, by skill and patient labour, the sound of the mail-coach horn surprising the ear in these wastes, and then dying away with the rattle of the carriage, and leaving the wilds again to their natural, thoughtful stillness; making acquaintance with Clyde in his infancy, and when he has scarcely collected himself into a visible river; the gradual descent from the higher district till we get down into Lothian, and are absorbed in the metropolis; what is wanted to make this course delightful, except a just impression of the interest imparted to it by what is called the dreariness of the upland districts?

My books were the treatises on *Political Philosophy* written by Brougham and published by the Society for the Diffusion of Useful Knowledge, but not in his name, and *Master Humphrey's Clock*. His Lordship's expositions are able and vigorous, and have the great advantage of containing the views and feelings of a practical statesman. But on the other hand he ventures, and with great confidence, as might be expected from the man, into subjects such as China and the Antiquities of the Feudal System, of which he apparently knows less than ordinary writers, and, on the whole, I thought him dull. But who could be anything else than dull, when reading him implied not reading Dickens! This man seems likely to do, in novel writing, for England, what Scott has done for Scotland. He has opened a new era in the art. All his works are excellent, but Nell has set this one above them all. What a beautiful conception, and how beautifully executed! I doubt if there be anything in nature to justify such a strange monster as Quilp, a London Caliban. The *Clock* and the *Club* seems an awkward apparatus for the author to trouble himself with. Scott excepted (who I think as yet far Dickens's superior), no man but Shakespeare has fancied and wrought out so many original characters. But even this is not his chief praise, which is due to the warmth and sincerity with which he uniformly encourages right principles and good affections, not by vague or grandiloquent declamation, but by adhering to truth and nature. I saw a letter from Jeffrey to-day, from London, in which he says that Dickens tells him that the sale of these weekly numbers of the *Clock* amounts at present to 45,000, and is on the rise. Very honourable to him, and very good for the public, but it is bad for a man of genius to be fettered, though by chains of gold, till he perform any weekly task.

But there is nothing, even in all Dickens, so agreeable as the lunatics at the play.

Tyndrum, Monday Night, 30th August 1841. — I left Edinburgh for this North Circuit on Saturday last, the 28th instant, with Mrs. Cockburn, my daughter Jane, my son Frank, and my niece Graham Maitland, in and about an open carriage.

Our first day's journey was by Stirling to Dunira, where we stayed all yesterday. And to-day we came on, by Lochearn Head and Luib, here.

Up to this point I have nothing to say beyond what I said last autumn. But I think it is exactly thirty-two years since I last put up at this unchanged inn. I ran past it last September on my way to Dalmally, merely getting fresh horses, and did not come out of the carriage. I have sauntered about to-day, both in the forenoon and evening, and renewed my acquaintance with the numerous and glorious peaks which distinguish the district. It is a magnificent region, most picturesque in the forms of its mountains, and sublime in its solitude. It was a fair and rather mild, but a calm, cloudy, melancholy day; the sides of the hills moved over by films of vapour, like Ossian's ghosts, and the thin clouds through which his heroes behold the stars. There was but one moment of sunshine all day, just at the day's close, when a whole world of light haze, which had clustered round the summits of the mountains, was enflamed into red, and then faded again into the dead grey in which it wrapped them for the night.

Some variety is given to this Highland scene by its mining, — wretched mining in reference to science, and, I suspect, in reference to profit, for the poor human emmets have been scratching the same ravine, and apparently only on its surface, for above sixty years. But the high placed apparatus, the peculiarity of the operation, and the detached, colonial, appearance of the workmen, give it all a picturesque air.

The dwellings of the people in Tyndrum proper, that is, the holes in which they burrow, are disgraceful, and nearly inconceivable, even in Scotland.

To-morrow for Glencoe!

Ballachulish, 31st August 1841, Night. — And when will there ever be a more glorious Glencoe? A mild, calm, brilliant day, the sky garnished by gorgeous, huge, white clouds, sailing above their shadows, over the mountains, and not a drop of rain, though in a very rainy season, not even the fear of a drop, till a short, fairy shower imparted the only other desirable charm to the upper part of Glencoe.

We left Tyndrum about nine, and got here above five.

The whole thirty-six miles are a range of unbroken, and in so far as Britain or Ireland are concerned, I suspect, of unrivalled mountain magnificence. The great peculiarities are the detached position, and the peaked form, of the hills. Each is magnificent, both by itself, and as one of a collection. The first five miles, including the retrospect, after leaving Tyndrum, — the six or seven after leaving Inveroran, — and the whole sixteen from King's House to this, not only defy my powers of description, but of fancying improvement. Last year Dalmally superseded Aviemore, this year Tyndrum has superseded Dalmally, and I only hope that the Cuillin Hills, towards which I am veering, may supersede Tyndrum.

What I have been in the society of all this day have been mere mountains. There have been no arms of the sea, no lakes (for Tulla is but a pool), no buildings, modern or in ruins, no woods, no islands, no distant prospects (except of summits), nothing to interfere with the claims of the solitary majestic heights on our thought, and I can scarcely conceive the mind that can be insensible to their sublimity.

Yet, with what rapture is a day of admiration, or rather of awe, succeeded by the mingling of beauty with grandeur, when we emerge from the stern gully of Glencoe, to the more open brightness of this delicious Loch Leven. Never but twice, once at the very place, when I last saw it in 1819, and once, still further back, when from the coast of Ayrshire, I saw the sun sink behind Arran, have I beheld a more glorious sunset than this evening. What a blaze over the heights behind Ardgour! And when these heights intercepted the luminary, and showed us nothing but darkness on the sides of the hills next us, with what a soft vapoury splendour did he stream down the valleys, till he at last resigned the whole scene to slow-coming, gentle night, and to a moon which did what it could in its way, but though about full, and with a placid, inland, lake-like sea to work upon, could make itself no rival to such a close of such a day.

I cannot hope ever again to see such 36 miles. And I have to remark two facts. One is, another example of mining, or rather of quarrying, being picturesque. The Ballachulish slate quarries are singularly so. The other is, that though the faces of the people, and particularly of the women and children, would certainly thole a little water, they positively seem to be much cleaner than they used to be. I mean the whole way from Dunira to this. But the people are tolerably educated, and every way well behaved; and if their habits could be raised, and the climate would sometimes make it possible for their clothes or skins to be a week dry, their comfort in dirt would soon cease. So long, however, as they are worse housed than their swine, nothing above the habits of swine can be expected.

I see that Anderson in his generally very sensible *Guide to the Highlands and Islands,* gives it as his opinion that "the stage of 18 miles to King's House (from Tyndrum) is bleak and sterile". What the devil would he be at? Does he want wheat-fields, and larch weeds. His sole praise is to Loch Tulla, the only paltry part of the scenery which he calls "picturesque". And the road over the Black Mount, which exhibits the most glorious mountain prospects, and which nature plainly compelled the road to be taken over in order that these might be seen, is described as crossing "a tedious, high, and tiresome hill", called the Black Mount". But he probably saw it all on a bad day, when his knapsack was fretting his back, and his shoe his toe, and his inward man longing for the King's House whisky.

We have found this inn on the south side of the water decently comfortable, better, so far as I could judge from merely calling, than the one at the north side.

But the north one was still kept by Angus Cameron, who had it when I passed three days under his roof in 1819, the most perfectly beautiful days my memory can recall. Even this evening it has been chiefly through the eyes of those days that I have been able to see this paradise of Scotch sea scenes.

Angus was the best piper in his day, and, when only eighteen, gained the competition prize at Edinburgh. But he had the misfortune to marry what was called "a leddy", — a very good wife, I hope, but who thought the pipes below her dignity, and so fiercely discouraged them, that at last she has compelled her spouse totally to abandon the source of all his glory. On one occasion, when he was delighting a crowd of admirers, and would not take a gentle hint, she stepped forward with a knife and stabbed the bag.

Though giving great praise to old rivals, and to young aspirants, he bemoaned the general decline of the art, for he said that there was not now one single "real piper — a man who made the pipe his business", in the whole of Appin. I suggested that it was probably owing to the want of county militia regiments, for the Highland colonels used to take their pipers with them. But he eschewed this, saying that we had plenty pipers long before the militia was heard of. I then suggested the want of training. "Ay! there's a deal in that, for it does tak edication! a deal o' edication". But then, why were they "no edicated"? So he hit it on the very head, by saying it was the decline of chieftains, and their castles and gatherings. "Yes", said I, "few of them live at home now." "At hame! ou, they're a' deed! an' they're a' puir! an' they're a' English!"

His complimentary reasons for our sitting down in his house were very Highland. "There's a chyre for you, mem, for ye're heavy, an' no' able to stan' like ither folk." "An' here's a chyre for you, mem, for ye're young an' tender!" "An' here's a chyre for ye, ma Lord, for your Lordship and me's gettin' doon the hill noo." We thought there was neither weight, nor weakness, nor age among us.

Invermoriston Inn, 1st September 1841. — We came here from Ballachulish, by Fort William, yesterday, through a torrent of uninterrupted rain. It was dull — dull and horrible; made worse, I have no doubt, from the way not being new to me. But we were very merry, and had a sumptuous repast of oatcakes, eggs, and whisky, at Letterfinlay, the worst shelter for poor travellers I have ever been in. But I slept soundly in it in 1819.

There is not much (for Scotland) in the space between Linnhe Loch and Loch Ness. But all of these are beautiful, and the rain and the mist just disclosed enough of them to let us know what we were losing.

I was surprised by seeing that brutal obelisk still standing near Invergarry Castle, which the late Glengarry erected about 1812 to commemorate what his inscription styles "the swift course of feudal justice", which means the murder by one of his ancestors of seven men. It was defaced for many years by passengers and the people, and when I saw it, with Thomas Telford, engineer, very soon after its erection, he could scarcely keep his hand off it. But it was protected by a lodge.

The great Highland estate of Glengarry, consisting of a magnificent country, was sold last year to Lord Ward, by the son of him of the obelisk, to pay his father's debts; and this son, the existing Glengarry, a respectable young man, I am told, is trying what he can do in Australia. His father was famous in his day, and by flattery and the affectation of Highland usages, had the good fortune to get Sir Walter Scott to immortalise him in several of his works, as a fine specimen of the chieftain. But none knew better than Scott that he was a paltry and odious fellow, with all the vices of the bad chieftain and none of the virtues of the good one; with the selfishness, cruelty, fraud, arrogant pretension and base meanness of the one, without the fidelity to superiors, and the generosity to vassals, the hospitality, or the courage of the other.

Scott used to account for his enduring these sort of people, by saying that they were "savage and picturesque, both of which is in my way".

The only fearlessness he ever displayed was in an act of madness which Telford (the engineer) and I saw, and to which, as to his duel, he was driven by insolent fury. A boat, in which he wished to cross Loch Oich, or Loch Lochy, left the shore without him, and a laugh showed that it had done so on purpose to avoid him, on which he plunged with the pony he was on, into the water, to swim after it. The people pretended not to see, and rowed as hard as they decently could. Telford and others were in ecstasy with the hope that they were at last to be relieved of him. And certainly he ought to have been drowned. But after being carried very nearly across (a mile I should suppose), by the vigour of a creature more meritorious than its rider, he got on board, and was praised for what it had done.

A rainy day brings out the full measure of the wretchedness of ill-housed poverty. We saw mud hovels to-day, and beings with the outward forms of humanity within them, which I suspect the Esquimaux would shudder at. And this, as usual, close beside the great man's gate. We shall see what the

English purses, and the English comfort, of the southern supplanters of our banished, beggarly, but proud, lairds will do.

Shiel House, 2nd September, 1841, Night. — We left Invermoriston this morning, and got here in the evening. The stages are Torgyle 8 miles, Cluany 16, Shiel House 12. As we have been told that there are no post-horses kept along our intended route, we ordered a pair from Inverness to Invermoriston, and we keep these till we reach Inverness. There are none kept indeed after leaving Fort William. And there is not even an inn at Fort Augustus. The steamer carries all the world past. Nor, so far, is there a habitable inn between Fort William and this. Letterfinlay I have mentioned. The one at Invermoriston ought to be good. If kept by an Englishman, Mrs. Glendinning, its position at the outlet of Glenmoriston, and within 28 miles of Inverness, would secure its success, even without the aid of its charming scenery. As it is, it is shameful. But it is not a bad specimen of what is called a good Scotch country inn, because, though they knew of our coming, and had seen it pouring all day, they had neither fire nor food prepared, a tea tray was receiving the rain from the skylight of what was given to me to dress in; and the landlord, though married only last week, was drunk. Torgyle, Cluany, and Shiel House are mere drovers' quarters, — and bad quarters for the poorest drovers; but very civil — with good oatcakes, some tolerable Glasgow "loaf bread", as they call it, excellent eggs, cool water, and passable whisky; bad wet peats, but good moss timber, and some English coal. Animal food they seem scarcely to know; and when they catch a lord — even a poor paper lord — they charge him (most properly) higher than he would be charged in the Clarendon Hotel. But these hostels have only whetted our mirth, which is excessive.

The whole way from Invermoriston till we shall reach Inverness, has been, and will be, entirely new to me.

And so far it is admirable. I have been told to go and see Glenmoriston almost all my life, and now that I have seen it, I am satisfied that I have never got this advice too strongly. And I say so, though I grieve to add, that in point of weather this day was worse than yesterday. But I sat out the whole of both days, and, thanks to caoutchouc, so perfectly dry that I did not require to shift an article on getting housed for the night.

For our first hour the rain checked itself in order to let us see the lower part of the glen in peace. I cannot pay these four wooded miles, — where the softness of the birch contrasts so naturally with the savage rocky stream — a higher compliment than by saying that they reminded me of some parts of the unrivalled Findhorn, by far the finest of British torrents. All the rivers here are swollen at present, and Moriston was in his fiercest strength.

As the valley opened and rose, its masses of wood disappeared, though it was long adhered to by sprinklings of fine birch

68

and of noble old, branchy Scotch fir; till at last it was a composition of mountain and of water alone. And it would not be easy to find better specimens of either. The character of valley is never lost, and indeed throughout it is a glen so narrow, that everything within it — even to near the tops of the countless and almost perpendicular cascades that tear up and whiten the sides of the hills, — is very distinctly visible. There is no cultivation, singularly few inhabitants, not one single seat, scarcely above two farm-houses, and these both towards the lower end, not a village, nothing but mountain and water. And I saw enough to satisfy me that the mountains had everything that rock, precipitousness, and peaked summits could give them. Seen in a fine day it must be a noble range. I have been particularly struck with the great profusion of peaked knolls and hills. That blockhead Anderson (whom I notice only because he is in fashion as a guide) first says that they are "like so many sugar loaves," and then explains that "the slope is like the side of a tent," these two things being quite dissimilar. The truth is, that they are not so much peaked as mammalated. It is at this end at least, a very pappy glen. Loch Cluany, though not to be named among even our fifth-rate lakes, is beautiful, chiefly from its steep sides. Yet this is the very thing that Anderson objects to. "The mountain on the south side rises rather abruptly from the water," — ass! Except as to miles I'm done with him.

The sky is now clear, and the moon beautiful, as the bright surface of Loch Duich and the dark sides of the hills opposite this caravansera attest. I go to bed praying, but trembling, for the day to-morrow. I wish I had the price of all the superfluous water I have seen to-day, if it were properly distributed and sold in New South Wales.

Shiel House, 3d September 1841, Morning. — The day does not promise to be decidedly bad. Blue sky visible, and all the hill-tops. A delightful place this; touching Loch Duich, all along ridged with precipitous hills, over which the rainbows seem to take a pleasure in smiling. That dog Anderson has excited my wrath again this morning, by saying, which I had not observed before, that "from the east end of Loch Cluany to about four miles beyond the inn, the glen is pretty level, and barren without grandeur." There is not half a mile level in the whole 36 miles; and except that there are no grapes or even wheat, there is not an inch of barrenness in them. Is there any barrenness of torrent or rock; and for what else did God toss the earth about so?

In the garden of the only other house here (which was formerly the inn) I see about sixteen sweet chestnuts and walnuts, the former about thirty years old and very healthy, and some more chestnuts at the opposite side of the house. It is a pity that the sensible man, whoever he was, who planted these once not uncommon trees, in this sea-beach place, had not set them in larger masses. They would have kept possession of all the ravines, and all the meadows they had got.

Kyle Rhea, Skye, same day, i.e. 3d September 1841, 2 P.M. — Here we are in Skye, as proud as Columbus when he first landed in America.

The Laird of Ratichan, who lives within a mile of our last night's quarters, sent us a pair of horses to help us up his hill, which is as long a steep pull as I have seen, except perhaps on Corryarick, I should suppose, but it is a mere conjecture, that it must rise from the level of Loch Duich (the sea) at least as high as Arthur Seat, in three miles. But the Laird's beasts, not understanding why they should be set to pull up a Saxon coach, had the skill to keep their rope traces almost always slack, a propensity which the whip of the Saxon driver behind them only increased.

There is a good view of Loch Duich and its hills (which rise "rather abruptly") from the top. It is the scene of this region; but, though very good, it is surpassed by hundreds of other Scotch firths. The road throughout the rest of the twelve miles to the ferry on what we now call the mainland opposite this, insinuates itself very skilfully through the same succession of hills that distinguished yesterday; but they get gradually lower and more open, till near the ferry they spread themselves out in good open south country pasture.

This ferry, though boasted as the best in Skye, is detestable, at least for carriages, and as ill-conducted as possible. But what can a ferry be for carriages, where ours is only the third that has passed this year, and the object of the landlord of the ferry-house on each side is to detain instead of advancing the passenger, and where, when at last it is seen that they can carry it on no longer, the only machinery for putting the vehicle on board consists of dozens of lazy and very awkward Highlanders, all scolding in Erse, who almost lift it and throw it into the groaning boat.

Broadford, Skye, 3d September 1841, Night. — The first six or so of the twelve miles to this are a continuance of the same striking mountain scenery. There is a still worse ascent immediately after leaving this side of the ferry. It is a worse road, rises as high, or nearly so, and is in one place steeper, altogether more formidable. We hired two leaders for it, and without them, our making it out would have been very doubtful. So far as we have gone, these two hills and the ascent up Glencoe (which however we came down) are the only three places where there can be any pretence for putting more than two horses to a light chariot with six people, besides the driver, and all their indispensible luggage.

The last six miles next this, open and descend into a

commonplace pastoral country. But (observe this but) there is from that descent a good view of the landlocked sea ending with this Bay of Broadford, and bounded on all sides, except round its upper end, with good stern hills. This (the upper) end or head of the bay, is flat and mean. But all below is beautiful. Perfectly treeless, hard looking, and bare, but still capable of all beauty that a bright sun can bestow on calm water, and on silent massive hills. The day has proved excellent.

I thought Broadford had been a town, — not a toon, but a real town or respectable village. But I find that it consists of three houses, the inn, the school, and "the shop", near which there are a dozen or two of hovels, not standing together, however, so as to form even a toon, but scattered at distances, and all so like the black moss they stand on that till we came up to the holes which are termed the doors, and saw the ragged human rabbits looking out of the warren, we did not take them to be houses.

As soon as we arrived, I called on Mr. Mackinnon of (or on) Corry, who lives half a mile from the inn, and with whom I had been in correspondence about getting to Coruisk, etc. He had expected the whole party to have gone and taken up their quarters at his house, but the word "you" used in his letters, and "I" by me in mind, produced a misunderstanding which gave him only me individually, and this only to dinner. However, the badness of this inn, which is only not just so bad as Shiel House, and therefore might have had so much the less fun, joined to Corry hospitality, have made us resolve to be his guests from and after tomorrow morning.

Meanwhile I go to be at the inn, anxious about to-morrow, and much moved for a poor cat, which has been mewing incessantly in some undiscoverable recess of the parlour here, but which we have satisfied the people has been lately built up under the floor. If so, they say it must have been there two days. I have vowed to have it out tomorrow.

Corry, near Broadford, Sunday, 5th September 1841, Night. — Well! I have seen the Spar Cave, part of the Cuillin Hills, and Coruisk, the two last objects of all this travel.

But let me proceed regularly. The cat gave up mewing as soon as we gave up talking or moving, and was as silent as we were all night. But no sooner did I begin to stir yesterday at six in the morning than it renewed its supplications, though in a much weaker voice. I broke up the skirting of the floor, but this would not do, and the carpenter who was repairing the house had not arrived. So I was obliged to leave it a little longer in durance, but left proper injunctions. On coming home in the evening I learned that the carpenter had never come, and that the mason was averse to touch wood. The general opinion of the household was, that though no doubt it was the best cat in the house, it should be left to die, because why did it go in? and could they be expected to lift the carpet which had been just

71

nailed down. The cook alone was tender-hearted, and talked of the "puir crater", and "how would we like to want our own meals", and "what a smell it would make in the room if it died", and besides they should consider "the feelings of the leddy". The smell was the only thing that seemed to make any impression. But still, had it not been for Mrs. Cockburn and our servant Robert, death by starvation would have been its fate. They got a bit of the precious carpet removed and a board raised, when out jumped pussy, and made the best of its way from that floor, and I find to-day that it is quite well after its three days' abstinence.

Now for Coruisk. And as it, and the way of getting at it, are little known, let me be particular. Corry is the best guide to it in the world, and I did as he directed, for he could not go himself.

Frank and I breakfasted yesterday morning a little after six, and left this in our own carriage at seven, with cloaks and a basket of provisions, and drove about five miles, in a south-westerly direction, past the old kirk of Strath, and till the road stopped at the sea. It is a good road, and, it is impossible for a person who sets off upon it, and goes on, to avoid reaching the sea. It is necessary to have a boat bespoke there, for there is no village, and no proper boat can be got upon chance. The minister, who lives (but not in the manse, for there is none) close by, can always provide one if properly applied to, but a better way is to engage a boat and four men from Broadford, and to cart the boat across the five miles if necessary. Corry did this for me, so I found my bark and my crew waiting for me. I sent back the carriage, with directions to return to the same place at six in the evening.

So we got on board, and set off from that place (I never heard its name), which is at the head of Loch Slapin. It was a strong, clumsy fishing-boat, with no mast, sail, or rudder. The crew consisted of three men and a boy — only one of whom spoke English. The boy rowed as well as any of the men, and they were all civil and merry.

The day was perfect and the sea like glass. They said that the distance to be rowed was 16 miles going and 16 coming; but I should think 14 nearer the truth. The course lay down Loch Slapin and up Loch Scavaig, these two being adjoining lochs, separated by one promontory.

We coasted down along the west side of Slapin, a space of about seven miles, rarely 100 yards, and often not so many feet, from the shore, over water so clear that we often fancied we saw the monsters of the deep. The hills bounding the loch are not striking, either in their height or forms. But the more distant eminences, blended as they were, were beautiful, and would have been so even without the aid of the islands, which, however, very powerfully contributed to the composition of the scene. But in truth it was difficult to withdraw one's eyes from the objects that were close at hand. The whole shore along which we were passing is lined by a perpendicular, though not an absolutely continuous wall of rock, into which the sea has eaten by washing off the soil till it has formed a barrier against its own further encroachments. It was low tide, yet the water was deep enough for the boat to sail close up to the rock, so that there is no beach. Without quarrying and smoothing no bathing-machine could work on all the seven miles along the west side of Slapin, except at one place near the upper end. The line of rock varies in its height, from 20 to apparently 200 feet. The average, I should think, must be about 100 feet. The rock is all laid in horizontal laminae, and is separated vertically into detached pieces at almost every 50 or 100 feet or oftener, so that it is not an unbroken wall, but a long series of detached and horizontally laminated masses, cut into all sorts of forms, from great solid lumps to tall pillars, and worn into all sorts of curious appearances. The fissures between the cliffs are often cleared out entirely so as to leave no roof, but in other places a roof is often preserved, or in other words a cave is formed, and into every crevice the fresh sea entered and laved the pebbly bottom and the clean sides. Even in the interstices and on the tops of the fantastic rock, such is the general severity of the storm or the want of soil, that there is scarcely any vegetation, in so much that the rowers stopped to point out a crack in which a single ash had attempted to root itself, for which it is now bleached nearly white. It is all strangely worn rock, which, though at last the employment becomes idle, it is impossible to give up observing and wondering at.

We passed close by the Spar Cave, which I did not know we were to do, and so yielded to the rowers, who seemed to think it ominous that any stranger should pass their wonder without entering. Not thinking of this as a part of the day's work, we had brought no lights, and had to send for candles to a house not far off, but which I never saw. We wasted an hour on this piece of nonsense. It is not worth describing; even MacCulloch, who saw it when its stalactites were unbroken, thought it insignificant. Now that not one remains, the whole charm, which was in its sparriness, is gone, for in its mere dimensions it is nothing. There is no dirt in it, I mean no mud, but it is very wet, a pool of about thirty feet has to be crossed on a Celt's back, a steep and slippery incline plane of about 40 feet has to be scrambled up on one side and down on another, a feat requiring skill even from the guide; and after all this splashing and straining, and wetting of hands and feet, there is nothing whatever, absolutely nothing, to be seen. The only way to deal with it would be to shut it up for a century or two and let the dropping reconstruct the white figures, which alone can ever give it any interest. At present the only reward for going in consists in the pleasure of getting out. And indeed I suspect that even in its best days, the outer entrance was always the finest part of the show. It consists of a fissure between two

73

rocks, which, were it not open to the sky, would have made a cave worth entering. I paced it as well as I could, and it seemed to me to be about 500 or 600 feet in from the sea, that is, in depth; about 40 wide, and about 150 or 200 high; each side being of solid rock, and either quite perpendicular or leaning inward, and every tide brightens its sea-weed and channelly floor.

But my thoughts were of Coruisk, which is pronounced here Coruishk. So we proceeded and were now near the point which we had to double in order to get into Scavaig.

Ever since we reached Kyle Rhea, we had been excited by glimpses of the summits of Cuchullin, and were so in Slapin this very morning. At last, after rounding that point, at the distance of about seven or eight miles, across a sheet of calm bright water, the Cuillin Hills stood before us! — seen from their bases to their tops — some of their pinnacles veiled in thin vapour, but most of them in the light of a brilliant meridian sun. I gazed in admiration, and could not for a long time withdraw myself from the contemplation of that singular assemblage of mountainous forms.

The Cuillin range extends to eight or ten miles, but the portion before me was not probably above from two to three. But I am told it is the best portion, and may safely be taken for the whole. I had two full hours to observe them during our approach, which lay up and across Scavaig; but indeed, their features and characters may be apprehended in a very few minutes. Black, steep, hard, and splintered, they seem to stand amphitheatrically, and rising from the very level of the sea, their irony and shivered tops stream up to the height, MacCulloch says, of 3000 feet (but I suspect that this is too much), and are fixed in every variety of peak, and precipice, and ridge, and pillar, made more curiously picturesque by forms so fantastic, that were it not for their position and their obvious hardness, it might almost be supposed that they were artificial.

There was a considerable shower as we advanced, and the whole scene was wrapped up. I began to fear, but it cleared away in a quarter of an hour, and confidence returned with the sun.

On looking round, I found new ground for admiration. Loch Scavaig, in the middle of which we were, I saw to be one of the finest sea bays I had ever beheld. The eastern side is bounded by a hill, which till it actually reaches the Cuillin, is low and pastoral, and the grass (such as it is) comes down to the shore, the belt of rock I have spoken of ceasing at the point of Slapin. But on the opposite or western side, the whole shore was lined with the same stern barrier as Slapin, above which the mountains rose high, and hard, and sharp, till they too fell into the Cuillin range. Towards the north end the loch is enclosed by these Cuillin mountains. The southern and far wider end, is locked in by several islands; of which Eigg, Rum, and Soa are the largest, and these, and the projecting promontories of the mainland of Skye, group most beautifully. I was particularly struck with Rum, which I don't recollect having heard praised for its shapes. But it is very striking, both in itself, and as part of the general landscape. It is not equal, or nearly equal, to Arran, either in height or in form; but it is the only island I have yet seen that can justly remind us of that one. The beauty that shone over all these objects was the beauty of mere light and form: for there was little visible vegetation, not one tree, no verdure, no apparent house, no ruin, no sound. But the positions and the forms of the objects were admirable, and a depth of interest was impressed upon the whole circle around me, by its universal hardness and sterility, which no softening could have increased.

So we went on, till, almost palpitating with anxiety, we were landed on a rock at the head of the loch. I found an oar lying in some heather, and on looking round saw a boat seemingly deserted, on the beach, and eight barrels at a little distance. These, I learned, were the still ungathered store of a poor fisherman, who was drowned three days before, in trying to cross the stream which flows out of Coruisk, when it was in flood.

The level of Coruisk is not, I should suppose, more than from 30 to 50 feet above that of the sea; and the fresh loch is not above half a mile from the salt one. The space between them requires scrambling, for it is rocky and boggy. I bade the boatmen remain with the boat, to rest and refresh themselves, and went forward, and in a few minutes stood on the side of Coruisk.

I was foolish enough, considering what I knew, to feel a moment's disappointment at the smallness of the cupful of water. But it was only for a moment. And then I stood entranced by the scene before me. Subsequent examination and reflection were necessary for the details, but its general character was understood and felt at once. The sunless darkness of the water, the precipitousness of the two sides and of the upper end, the hardness of their material, consisting almost entirely of large plates of smooth rock, from which all turf, if there ever was any, has been torn by the torrents; the dark pinnacles, the silence, deepened rather than diminished by the sound of a solitary stream, — above all, the solitude, — inspired a feeling of awe rather than of solemnity. No mind can resist this impression. Every prospect and every object is excluded, except what are held within that short and narrow valley; and within that there is nothing except the little loch, towered over by the high and grisly forms of these storm-defying and man-despising mountains.

On withdrawing one's mind from the passive impression of this singular piece of savage wildness, and looking to particulars, I could not help being certain that the lake was not three miles long, which some state it to be, and I doubt if it reach even to two. MacCulloch's test, of the time he took to walk round it is quite fallacious, because the walkingstrip, extending to about 100 yards in breadth, between the water and the hills, is covered with large rocks and bits of bog, and getting over these (for it is not walking) is difficult and precarious. However, he may be right, for the largeness of the hills makes the water seem smaller. Besides two or three specks — just showing themselves above the water, — there are three islands, seemingly about a quarter of an acre in size, all low and covered with shrubs, heather, or stunted grass. The lake lies from north-west to south-west, which I mention because MacCulloch's description is somewhat confused by his calling its direction from east to west. Each of the hills seems to consist of one stone. They are not rocky mountains, but mountainous rocks. Hence the·sharpness into which they have been cut, and hence the large plates, or rather fields, of smooth stone which the two sides exhibit. I need scarcely say that there is no path, no grazing, no human symptom. When it rains the sides must stream with water. But the surfaces are so steep that it soon runs off, and when I was there, there was not a rill either to be heard or seen; except one, which ran down an open grassy slope on the east side of the lake towards the lower end. The hills enclosing the upper end may, on being examined, be found to be not at all semicircular, or to have any approach to that form, but as seen either from the sea or Coruisk, they seemed to be curved inwards, and part of the seclusion of the place appeared to be owing to their doing so.

Some things are stated which misled me, because they are not correct. It is not the fact that the loch is set in a frame of actually perpendicular rock, like a wall, and that hence it has never been approached by even a shepherd's foot except from the sea. The hills may, in one sense, be called walls, and they are very steep. But they are not perpendicular, and have no wall-like appearance. They are not steeper than the turfy hills forming the left bank of the River Awe, on which I saw sheep browsing very comfortably last September. It is the hardness, not their steepness that makes the access difficult. Yet, hard though they be, I thought I saw places where even I could have found my way out; and Mackinnon assures me that the shepherds find their way in by the hills, whenever it is necessary. At the open and grassy slope a horseman might trot both up and down, at least in so far as steepness is concerned.

Then it is said that there is no vegetable life. Scott won't admit either mosses or heathbells. This may be fair enough in a fancy piece, but it is bad in a portrait. There is abundance both of mosses and of heather. I picked up about a dozen of the ordinary wild-flowers of Scotch hills and valleys. The sweet gale or bog myrtle is in profusion; MacCulloch makes the islands shine "with the brightness of emeralds." This, to be sure, is on the flat, but even on the "solid wall", as MacCulloch calls the steep hills, there are thousands of fissures, and generally where there is a fissure there is accumulated rubbish, and where this is there will be vegetable life, and so there is here. There are also hollows on the islands.

These exaggerations are unnecessary for this place; enough of stern sterility and of calm defiance remains.

After lingering over the solitude for above an hour, it being now three, and other four hours rowing before us, I withdrew from a scene which far less than an hour was sufficient to comprehend, and which once comprehended, there was no danger of forgetting. So turning backwards and descending, a few steps, what had given me Coruisk, deprived me of it — suddenly and utterly, — and we proceeded, homeward bound.

As our bark receded from the shore, the Cuillins stood out again, and the increased brilliancy of the sun cast a thousand lights over Scavaig, and over all its associated islands, and promontories, and bays. The eastern side of everything was dark, while the opposite sides shone more intensely in front of the evening sun. One horn of the curved Cuillins, though quite clear, seemed almost black, while the opposite horn was blazing. The dark side of Rum was towards me, but its outlines, like all the other shaded summits, were made distinct by the glow behind them. And as far as the eye could reach, bright spots, especially light-touched rocks, attracted it; and almost the whole line of wall by which the eastern shores of everything but Scavaig were barriered, was gleaming in the distance. It was a glorious scene.

I should feel it as a sort of sacrilege to prefer, or even to compare anything to the Firth of Clyde. But one great difference between the sources of its beauty and that of Scavaig was forcibly impressed upon me. How much does Clyde owe to human association, to culture, to seats, to villages, to towns, to vessels! The peculiarity of the interest in Scavaig arose from the total absence of all human interference. The scene would have been the same had man not existed.

As we sailed close by the shore of Scavaig and near the point of Slapin, the rowers stopped to point out five huts. It was there, they said, that the drowned fisherman had lived, and where his remains were lying, preparatory to their being interred in a burying-place (not a churchyard) about two miles off, next day. I thought of Steenie, and felt as if I were ashamed of enjoying an evening which was probably closing so bitterly over these poor hovels.

On coasting along Slapin again we found the many herds of nice, clean, free goats we had shouted to in the morning almost all in the same nooks. And I was even more satisfied than before, that if the people would but examine the innumerable openings in that line of rock, instead of one spar cave, they would probably find several.

We landed at half-past six, and found the carriage waiting.

The only error of this day's work, but it was a material one, consisted in mode of returning. I ought to have been directed to go from Coruisk up Glen Sligachan, and to have slept at Sligachan, 9 miles from Coruisk and 16 from Broadford. This could have been done either by walking the 9 miles, or by getting a pony sent to a place occupied by a Mr. Macmillan, near Coruisk, and the carriage should have met me at Sligachan. The walk or ride down the glen would have shown me the whole of the Cuillins. Mackinnon (called Corry here) says he did not advise this, because after what I did see, the rest is immaterial.

Another mistake was in not letting me know this till this forenoon, when it was near church-time, that there was a view from the high, but very accessible hill hard by, of almost all Skye. A "red Lord" as it seems the Skye Erse calls the Justiciary Judges, would not abstain from church in so small and noticing a place, but I was told I could ascend it after it came out; and when it did come out, — being three — I had no time. So I lost my view.

We Saxons went in to the English part of the service, which closed with Gaelic prayer and psalmody. I never saw a more respectable country congregation. There were about 350 present, all except Corry's party in the humblest rank. The men had almost all strong blue fishermen's jackets. The women, with only one exception, so far as I could observe, had all on red tartan cloaks or shawls and clean mutches of snowy whiteness, with borders of many plies. I can't comprehend how such purity can come out of such smoky hovels. There was not one child or very young person. This was perhaps the reason that there was no beauty. The reverse. One old woman, however, reminded me of the late Mrs. Murray of Henderland. Some of them had walked eight miles, and some sailed three.

The cat is well.

Jean Town, Ross-shire, 6th September 1841, Monday Night. — We left our kind entertainer at Corry this morning. He was coming here on business, and Frank went with him in his yawl.

Our route was to Kyle Akin, nine miles, where we crossed again into the mainland of Scotland.

The inn at this Kyle seems excellent, and the Kyle itself is beautiful. I mean its position, placed as it is at the junction of Loch Carron and Loch Alsh, and not far from the opening into Loch Alsh of Loch Duich; made respectable by the old fragment of Castle Muel or Maoil, and gay by fishing-boats. It was intended, it seems, to have been a small metropolis, but like other over grand building plans, has stuck at about a dozen of two-storied houses. The ferry is ill provided with a boat and machinery for carriages, but hands, and the hope of whisky, did the business, though certainly their knocks and jolts, if survived, are the coachmaker's triumph.

We said farewell to Skye from one of the heights on this side.

We had seen little of it, but quite enough to give us an idea of the whole. The sun, if the wind keeps quiet, makes anything pleasing. We have seen this island rose coloured. But its prevailing state is marked by features that cannot be mistaken. The cold, cheerless rocks, the treeless desolation, the perpetual tendency of the clouds to rest, as if it were their home, on the tops of the hills, the great corries into which the weather has hollowed one side of most of the mountains, the utter want of natural verdure, the grey, benty colour of the always drenched pasture, the absence of villages and of all human appearance, — these things mark Skye as the asylum of dreariness. The value of black cattle and sheep has no effect in landscape. The tempest seems to have said to an island of cloud-attracting mountains, standing on the north-west of Scotland, surrounded and everywhere pierced by a fierce sea, Thou art my brother! and everything we behold attests their cordiality. To one who visits it for such purposes as mine it is only redeemed by Cuillin and Coruisk, by the projecting of its promontories, the receding of its bays, and the varying intermixture of its Scalpas, and Rums, and Eiggs, and Cannas; its Loch Eisharts and Loch Snizorts, and Loch Follarts; its Sounds of Raasay and of Rona, and the whole host of things and of forms which go to make up its strange composition.

The stage to Strome Ferry (12 miles) is very hilly, and few of the hills have much to recommend them. But it was a beautiful drive, because much of it lay along Loch Alsh and Loch Carron. Wood returned to us, and the day has been fine.

Strome Ferry is like the rest — picturesque — (and for this the worse conducted the better) and as well managed as mere hands, without proper boats, piers, or any apparatus, can ever manage a ferry. When our ferrymen were loitering on the south side, it was curious to hear them excited to activity by the Mail-horn on the other. I had forgot in these solitudes that there was a post.

The road from Strome to Jean Town (six miles) runs along the shore of Loch Carron, which was glittering under a serene sun.

We had been told that the inn here was very superior. But it is just a good bad inn.

Kinlochewe, upper end of Loch Maree, Tuesday, 7th September 1841, Night. — And I have now got a glimpse of Loch Maree, the last new object I wished particularly to see. But being as yet only a glimpse, I shall say nothing about it.

We came from Jean Town this morning to Craig Inn — 10 miles, — a mere feeding-place, though with one room styled the parlour. But it has been one of the peaceful bright days, in which there is a parlour on the top of every wall, and by every burn-side.

Our next stop was — other 10 miles — to Auchnasheen, bad even for horses, for not choosing to stop at Luib, which being only seven miles from Craig, made a bad division of the way, we had to bring oats from Craig with us.

Here (Auchnasheen) I discovered that all my information about reaching Maree was wrong. As there was no stopping there (at Auchnasheen, I mean), and the opening of the new inn here (Maree or Kinlochewe) was uncertain, I had been advised to go to Auchanault (10 miles) for the night, and to proceed next morning from that place to this, which was said to be only about 10 miles — to see this loch — and to return there at night. Now it was found on inquiry that the new inn here was not open, that the distance from Auchanault to this was about 20 miles, that to sail down even the half of this loch, which as yet is the only way of seeing it, would take four hours, and consequently that doing all this in one day was impossible. I therefore sent the ladies to Auchanault for the night, and finding a return two-horsed phaeton going to Dingwall, Frank and I got into it and came here.

And I am glad that we did not attempt to bring the carriage to this place, for the road down Dochart, though new and hard enough, is more narrow, steep, and dangerous than any new road I have seen, in so much that a carriage could scarcely have been got either up or down. The inn, moreover, as it is called, is the most deplorable I have ever been within, worse by far than either Letterfinlay or Shiel House. No party of ladies could put up here. As to the new inn, which is to be opened next week, besides giving up the best of it on lease to a shooter, it is very small, and has a flat composition roof. A composition roof in the wilds of Ross-shire!

We engaged a boat for to-morrow morning. While our hideous dinner was preparing, I walked to the top of a hill, and had a good sight of the loch.

Garve, 8th September 1841, Wednesday Night. — It has been a beautiful grey day, perfectly still, mild, and with the full measure of the light that is consistent with the absence of positive sunshine, a steady, pensive day.

Frank and I breakfasted at six, took the phaeton to the boat, two miles off, and were on board and the oars in action by seven. We sailed down among and a little past the islands, one of which we ascended; and re-landed after being above four hours on the water. After this, and the two views I had of it yesterday, one from the road and one from the hill, I think I have a good general notion of the loch.

I have heard it called the Loch Lomond of the north, and an intelligent person who unites a knowledge of art to an intimate acquaintance with Maree, told me before I left Edinburgh, that the truest idea he could give me of it was, that it contained about six miles of Trossachs. This is all nonsense.

It is a noble lake, both in its splendid sheet of water, and in the great, black, sentinel mountains that guard it.

Certainly about 16 or 18 miles long, it is said to be not wider at any part than three, but this width its apparent openness about the middle would make me doubt. I think it must be more there.

Except at one part it is lined by a range of lofty hills on both sides, but particularly on the northern margin, which in every respect is far the finer of the two. All these hills are stony and black. Besides those close on the edge of the lake, every opening discloses others at a distance, striking both in form and in dimension. Not one of them is spiculated, in which feature one of the poorest Cuillins would laugh them all to scorn. But there are some conical and some saddlebacked, and indeed all forms: except that they all avoid lumpishness, the greatest opprobrium of hills. The chief are Ben Lair, and Sleugach, both on the northern side. Ben Lair, I believe, is the highest; and MacCulloch, who ascended it, gives a striking description of the prospect with which it rewards him who has the sense to mount it, as what hill ever fails to do? And, had I never been at Tyndrum, I would have agreed with him, that "the effect of Sleugach, seen from its base to its summit, is perhaps more striking than that of any mountain in Scotland." Its top is like what had once been a cone, crushed down into something more solid, and its obvious hardness attests the storms it encounters and defies.

The part where these respectable hills are not, is for about five miles towards the centre of the southern side of the water. This space is low, stupid, and insignificant; being occupied by a long, dull sort of a tongue, lining the loch, and ending in a large flattish peninsular promontory, out of which the water in some geological yesterday has plainly cut the islands, which are sometimes foolishly described as the glory of Maree.

For these islands are the worst things in it. One of them is beautifully wooded, and being the one farthest out into the centre of the loch, is a very prominent object. Its verdure, and that of the very few patches of wood that are to be met with along the water's edge, show what might be done. But except it, all the other islands are bare, or worse than bare, their squalidness marked by a few old stunted Scotch firs, of from 3 to 10 feet high, beneath, or rather beside which, there is tall but scraggy heather, and wet bog. Then the whole twenty-four, or so, of them are set so close, that though it be possible to sail between them, they might as well for the landscape be all joined, or all covered by water. Without height, for not one of them is 50 feet high, or wood, or rock, or ruin, and so huddled together that there is no gleam of water between them, it is the poorest of fresh-water archipelagos. To have seen the Trossachs or Loch Lomond, and to talk of these!

So that the peculiar features of Maree are its long extent of water, and its near and remote ranges of great mountains, the remote ones rather suggested than seen. Except that, I

81

suppose, there are salmon in both, it is absurd to speak of it as resembling any part of Loch Lomond or Loch Katrine. Its want of wooded islands and wooded hillsides settles the matter as to Loch Katrine. It has no narrow gullied part like the upper strip of Loch Lomond; and its broader expanse wants all the delicious foliage which so softens the margins and the islets of that beautiful lake.

What the effect of human familiarity might be, it is not easy to predict. An inn, or even a house, or perhaps even a sheep, would extinguish Coruisk; and a mail-coach horn heard along the side of Maree, or a steamer panting and grunting over its surface, with crowds of happy and giggling ladies and gentlemen, would certainly make an odds on that water. But at present, the belief that it is little known, and the certainty that whether known or not, it is beyond the intercourse of common tourists, gives it that irresistible interest which remoteness and silence can alone confer.

We saw to-day one single house on the north side, inhabited by "an Englishman", which I observe that the Highlanders always think description enough for the whole of these foreigners. It is their Linnaean term for a class. Besides this, we could detect no house, and not six turf hovels. There was no smoke, no sheep's bleat, no colley's bark, no sail. The only sounds we heard were the call of two fishermen returning tired from the east coast, and of two persons something like gentlemen, who seemed to be laired in the heather, who wanted to be taken to the opposite end from that to which we were going. Not above two rills whispered down the precipices. All was stillness and solitude.

And there stood the black mountains looking at the water. The deer possess the land. It is all rock, — not the gigantic flags of unbroken rock that inlay the sides of Coruisk, but the ordinary fragments that refer themselves to the mountain mass they have fallen from. It is woodless, ploughless, and nearly heatherless and grassless, — a region of stone. It seems as if the genius of sterility had sometimes left Skye and sat down upon the top of Ben Lair.

The infrequency of society may, nay, certainly will, cease, and it is possible that hundreds of nooks on this, and on all our lochs may be gay with human habitation and happiness. But the physical aspect of Maree will continue — a long lake — roughened by an unusual number of steep promontories, lined by dark mountains, that will ever command the more admiration the more they are known, presided over, when left to nature, by sublime silence; and to be enriched by its islands, only when these shall follow the example of the solitary emerald into which one of them has been converted.

We found the phaeton waiting for us at the water-side, and left Maree about twelve, and were here by five. The loch is not above nine miles from Auchnasheen.

Two things make these nine miles very remarkable.

Suppose you are going from Auchnasheen to Kinlochewe. Well! You pass a poor idiot of a four-mile loch, called Rosck, or Rosque, with nothing but insipidity in its face or dress. After this the road rises very considerably. All up this ascent, but particularly towards its height, there is a grand view of a range of monsters of hills, which I was told were about the head of Loch Torridon. I know few such mountain prospects. And one peculiarity in them arises from their being made of quartz. They are whitish, not white, but whitish, pepper and salt, with a great preponderance of salt. There is a grand one near Kinlochewe called, I think, Ben Eaye. It is literally powdered with its own dust. Except from snow I never saw a whitish hill before.

The road then descends rapidly into Glendochart. And at a sudden turn, about three miles from Kinlochewe, almost the whole of Maree lies stretched out before you. Neither the hill I mounted, nor my sail, gave me a better view of it than these three miles did. In truth if you only wish to see its general features, either of land or of water, stop at that turn for an hour and go back.

Bog Roy, Alehouse, six miles from Inverness, 9th September 1841, Thursday, 1 P.M. — Disturbed all last night at Garve by a company of jovial, i.e. drunken, fishermen, who chose to sing, and dance, and yell, in spite of all entreaties, remonstrances, and threats to be quiet. Lord! How they kicked the floor and howled!

We were glad to escape that otherwise not uncomfortable inn this morning at seven, and breakfasted at Dingwall. And we are now at this decent little place, giving our steeds their last feed.

We have now crossed the southern end of Ross-shire, from Strome, I may say, to Inverness. It is a drive worth any one's taking. The inns are all comfortable, and as to roads, though there have been about four severe unavoidable ascents, we have not come upon one bad quarter of a mile since we left home; and all the Government roads are uniformly admirable.

The country from Jean Town eastward has some lochs, and rivers, and hills, but they are not sufficient to save the most of it, till we reach Contin, from the character of uninteresting dreariness; except in the eye of a grouse-shooter and fisher, or of one who, like me, thinks there is something bordering on sublimity in mere solitary vastness of surface. There are shooting-boxes all along the road, generally ill-placed. Mackenzie's of Scatwell is by far the best, both well-placed and handsome.

The change from wildness to civilisation is completed in a few miles after leaving Garve. The region of wheat succeeds that of heather instantaneously. And when this region begins, the justice of all that is said in praise of the richness of Easter Ross cannot be denied. It is a half-Highland country, beautifully cultivated, still improving, well wooded, and adorned by many good seats.

We passed, but only passed, Kilmorack and its falls; and my time did not permit of our going out of our way for the Drem.

If Dingwall was in its ordinary state, it must be an excellent place for sleeping a life away in. The whole royal burgh was still as if not awake. Anderson says it has nothing to boast of except the cross and the pillar to the memory of the Cromarties. No boast in either. But has it not to boast of the following epitaph, which I found in the churchyard on "William Potter, Ship-master," who departed this life only in the year 1830?

> Loud Boreas' blasts, on ocean's waves,
> Oft has tost me too and fro;
> But God's decree, you plainly see,
> Has harboured me below.
>
> While here I safe at anchor ride,
> With many of our fleet,
> Untill that day we anchor weigh,
> Our Admiral Christ to meet.

Very meritorious tomb poetry for 1830.

We stopped and disgusted ourselves by going into the ruin of the Priory of Beauly. The poor building has little in itself to recommend it. But it was something. It has old windows, and other obvious marks of an ancient ecclesiastical edifice. But it has a deeper interest in its position and its history. Six hundred years plead for its protection, in which they are powerfully supported by the sacredness of ancient and the tenderness of recent sculpture. Yet a spot more absolutely abandoned to abomination never disgraced a community. Rubbish, nettles, and that filth so dear to Sawney, have their triumph over decency. The very bones of the modern dead, allowed to be exposed, are not spared. Yet the guide-books tell us of the famous Frasers, and Chisholms, and Mackenzies, etc., who repose within these odious precincts. The Lady of Sir Francis Mackenzie of Gairloch was buried in one of the aisles within these few years. I saw the same or even worse brutality at Dingwall. It is owing chiefly to inveterate bad habit and to the want of good example, but partly to the nature of Calvinism, at least of Scotch Calvinism, which holds spirit to be everything and matter nothing. The Scotch despise, if they do not even abhor, ornamented churches; because the devotion of the place is all that they respect, and they waste none of their reverence on stone and timber. They have neither the consecration of religion nor of affection for churchyards. Any field will do. Because provided the soul be safe, why misapply a sigh over the dust it animates no more? Accordingly there are probably not now one hundred modern tombs in all Scotland that are even decent; not fifty that are much above mere decency, and not twenty or even a dozen that are beautiful and beautifully kept; and these almost wholly among the Episcopalians. We are pious and affectionate people, no doubt, but if I were required to produce the tribe of men most regardless of their dead, I would turn to my countrymen.

Forres, 12th September 1841, Sunday Night. — All since we reached Inverness is hackneyed. I shall therefore make the log very short.

We got there on Thursday the 9th. Dined that day with our cousin William Fraser, at Laggors Cottage. Moncreiff had arrived at Inverness with his spouse, a son, a daughter, a manservant, and (horrible) a lady's-maid. It is but justice to record the merit of my wife, daughters, and all my Circuit companions in this respect. They have never afflicted me with the monster called a lady's-maid. She is no joint of my tail. For the which, God be praised!

The criminal business was over in one forenoon.

On the 10th we had our Circuit trumpet-tongued dinner.

On Friday the 11th, Moncreiff began the trial of a civil cause. I sat with him some hours, and then, being useless, went and dined at Ness Castle with Lady Saltoun.

This day we went to church. A metaphysical roaring sermon.

The civil case is not done, and Moncreiff is obliged to stop for it. I have come on here.

A delicious day.

Inverury, Tuesday, 14th September 1841, 2 P.M. — Left Forres yesterday morning and breakfasted at Elgin. Visited the Cathedral. John Shanks is dead.

From Elgin we went to Arndilly, 15 miles, where we stayed two hours. Then to Keith, 12 miles; then to Park, 12 more.

We were very kindly received by our friends the Gordons, with whom we dined and stayed all night.

We left them this morning at eight, and have come here by Huntly (which is 13 miles from Park). And as we were here by one, and four is the hour for meeting the Magistrates, we have had to wait here one hour, and have another to wait; which my companions will keep up for ever against me, as one of the ten thousand proofs of my impatience; but for which they say that they might have slept in peace two hours more at Park. But, say I, where would you have been if you had broken a wheel, or even lost a show? Never shave close with the Bailies.

I ought to have mentioned before that the Tories have come into power since we left home, and that their first fruit appeared at Inverness, in the form of Adam Urquhart as Advocate Depute. He had no commission, and there was no evidence that his principal, Sir William Rae, had been sworn in. But

Moncreiff and I had no difficulty in appointing him *valeat quantum.*

Castleton, Braemar, Friday, 17th September 1841, Night. — I processed into Aberdeen in vast pomp, on the 14th. Moncreiff joined us there in the evening.

Next day (15th) we both processed, under the charge of the 71st Regiment, to Court; where we remained till near six, when we had a grand judicial festival, — the most numerous, it was said, that had ever been seen in that place. On the following morning, after a re-procession and some more very stupid cases, we all dined (ladies and all) at a Mr. Crombie's, a bailie; who, on a few hour's notice, had collected enough to make a party of twenty-one to dinner, and of about thirty-five to dance and sup in the evening. He lives in one of the large, excellent old houses, entering by a close, and containing a more spacious lobby, staircase, dining-room, and drawing-room than any house in the New Town of Edinburgh. We were all very merry, and the worthy host did one of the duties of hospitality with great effect, not merely by precept, but by example.

Aberdeen is improving rapidly in public taste, and King Street, a creation within these five or six years, is really beautiful; and Marischal College, though covered, I have no doubt, with defects, in the eye of correct architecture, is a wonderful production for such a place. Their granite wrought as they now work it, is, when fresh, not much, if at all, inferior to marble; but modern Aberdeen shows that it never can be polished sufficiently for houses to preserve its brightness long. They have a manufactory for polishing and shaping it for slabs, pillars, chimney-pieces, vases, urns, and such things, which produces articles far more beautiful than could be made out of most marbles; but houses can never afford to be polished like these.

I made a remonstrance about the cross, which stands in Castle Street, by far the finest thing of the kind in Scotland, but from which the cheek of the queen, the horn of a unicorn, and half the head of a horse, have been chipped since I was last here. The apology was that the hustings were always erected close beside it, and that it generally suffered at elections. An excellent reason for holding the elections elsewhere. However, I was told that it was to be removed (being its second change of site) to nearer the top of the street, in a few weeks; when it was also to be repaired and cleaned, and to have its arches, which are at present closed, reopened, and windows put into them, so as to convert it into a shop, and then to be all protected by an iron fence. I hope that these intentions may be adhered to, but Town Councils and taste rarely draw together.

We left Aberdeen this morning, breakfasted at Banchory, and were here by six in the evening.

The whole of this district — from Aberdeen to Perth by

Braemar — is new to me. I have wished to go by it a hundred times, but have never made it out till now. And I have got it done in the most favourable possible day; sunny, calm, mild.

We have come about 60 miles, and the whole of this long strath merits all the admiration it generally receives. It is beautiful.

In their forms the hills are defective, scarcely a ravine; except about Invercauld, very little rock; and not one peak or pinnacle — all heavy monotonous masses. Their size and quantity however, make them very respectable, and they fully perform their main duty of enclosing the valley. The whole valley is far less narrow, ridgy, and picturesque than I had supposed. In truth it is only after passing Ballater, about 42 miles up, and getting into the higher region of Invercauld, that the really Highland character of the landscape begins. But nothing can exceed the beauty of all this lower portion of the strath. The lateral country is never once let in, so that the seclusion of the proper strath is always preserved. And while considerable portions of the low ground, and almost all the visible high, are richly furnished with excellent Scotch fir, and with birch which Loch Ness alone can equal, the valley is constantly brightened by finely cultivated haughs, comfortable cottages, seats, and the best of wild culture that forms the true charm of the whole district, the brilliancy of the yellow grain, set off against the dark pine, and interspersed by the comfortable habitations of those who work, as well as of those who own, the soil; while the Dee, after it is once got to, gleams in its long, distant reaches, and sweeps past with great purity and little turbulence, presenting a constant succession of delightful pictures. And after these withdraw and leave the mountains to deal with Invercauld, or rather with Braemar, as they please, the scenery becomes strictly Highland, and the great masses of wood distinguish it from most of our Highland scenes.

The villages of Banchory, Ballater, and Castleton (including both sides of the Cluny) are not surpassed in position, comfort, or rural beauty, by any that I can at present recollect, and they are all remarkable in their openness, the separation of their houses, and the free ground within and around them. I wish I could have got up to see the old Castle of Crathes more nearly. I did go up to Aboyne, saddened by bankruptcy, the windows boarded up, the furniture sold, the axe ringing in every wood, and the whole place desolate. Abergeldie is beautiful, and Balmoral (at least it sounded like this) still more so. They have both preserved the picturesque style of building which so eminently distinguishes Aberdeenshire above any other Scotch county, and their positions are admirable. Indeed I do not recollect where I have seen any place that struck me more than Balmoral. And the strange mass constituting Braemar Castle, closes the upper end of the valley by a striking and solitary edifice.

On the whole, it has been a most agreeable day. There is no such way of passing a day. If any man wants to be happy, I advise him to get a public allowance for travelling, to cast out any devil by which he may be possessed, and then to get into the dickie of an open carriage, with a suitable assortment of books and cloaks; an amiable, affectionate sensible, and very quiet niece beside him, and a wife, daughter, and son, with whom he is on good terms, behind; and to drive 60 miles through a new and beautiful country, in a sweet and bright autumn day.

The sun never did his duty better than he did it today, including his whole career, from his dispersing an alarming-looking fog in the morning, to his sinking in gorgeous splendour behind these Braemar hills in the evening.

Castleton, Saturday Morning, 18th September 1841. — I have been down looking at Braemar Castle. I am not architect or antiquary enough to be able to determine whether it be ancient, or what may be called modern. But if I were its owner, I would remove the wall round it, which is loopholed for musketry, and all other modern symptoms about it, and leave its tall solitary knoll-placed form, with its five odd turrets, to tell its own tale.

This castle, and the two churches, give the village and this upper end of the strath a respectable and striking appearance. One of the churches is the Established parish one, and on its side of the water stand a few stone and slated houses composing Castleton proper. The other is Catholic, twice the size of its rival, and on its side are scattered the more humble and more numerous dwelling-places of what is called Auchendyne. Each church is quite new, each beautifully set up on a platform overlooking the valley, and between them flows the sparkling Cluny. I know no country place in Scotland where the Papist beards the Protestant so ostentatiously. Strange that men can't go to heaven the same way, or let each other take their own road in peace, to the same end. Here are a few poor people of the same tongue, and tribe, and pursuits, living in a remote and mountain-bounded spot, which if they chose, might to them be the Happy Valley. Yet religious differences, not nearly so clear, even to themselves, as the stream that divides them, and small though it be, as easily passable by reason, separates them into two sects, each of which thinks the other travelling to hell, towards which neither would probably be averse to give the other a push.

Another glorious day.

I ought to add before leaving this region, that the inns of Banchory, Aboyne, Ballater, and Castleton, are all most excellent for country inns. Nothing can be better. And each, except Aboyne, keeps horses. Banchory is perfect.

Perth, 20th September 1841, Night, Monday. — We left

Castleton after breakfast, and went to the Spittal of Glenshee, and from that to Kindrogan, where we remained from Saturday forenoon till this morning, when we came here.

There is much to be enjoyed, though little to be described, between Castleton and Kindrogan. Huge clumsy mountains, merely made for the muirfowl grouse, and prairies. But bulk and loneliness suggest awe, and therefore inspire pleasure. Sheep and turf are rapidly encroaching on heather and muirfowl. There is no better pasture on any Highland hills.

The household of Kindrogan was kind and honest. No hospitality could be greater. This is one of the virtues that is very easily capable of being made disagreeable. Nothing saves it except simplicity, consideration of others, and frank sincerity. Let a friendly stranger go to Kindrogan and be reasonable, and he will know what true hospitality is.

The 30 miles from Kindrogan to Perth are that last stage of the descent from the mountains to the plain, and wheat and hedges furnish no subjects for a tourist. But I must notice Craighall, a second Hawthornden. I very reluctantly passed that singular place with no other knowledge of it than what passing it can give. But this was enough to make me doubt its comfortableness as a residence. No flat ground.

Kinross, Friday Night, 24th September 1841. — The Perth business has occupied us four days. Not one case of the slightest interest, except to the culprits. Assaults, which are on the increase, formed very nearly a fourth of the whole. We left that place to-night about six, and after sleeping here, our plan is to go and breakfast tomorrow at the Tower of Tulliebole.

And I cannot part in the meantime with the owner of that tower (as I understand it to be, for I have never seen it), without recording my love of the man, and my admiration of him as a judge. I have had another Circuit's experience of Moncreiff, and have again not only acted with him in public, but been privy to all his private official feelings and views; and I am confirmed in the conclusion forced upon me by forty years' friendship, that there cannot possibly be a better man, or a more pure, honest, anxious, or high-minded judge. With no superiority of talent, and a great inferiority of general knowledge, little taste, and no fancy, a look and manner far from commanding, and a very bad voice; no one ever overcame such defects by so few excellences. But two things, and only two — his force of reasoning and his virtue — make him very powerful, both as an object of affection and of fear. Nothing can withstand the concentrated energy of his logic, and that man must have a very hard, or a very thoughtless heart, who does not reverence his goodness. I differ from his system of addressing prisoners — as a uniform system, — but when he falls in with a proper occasion, his tone and sentiments do honour to the Bench, and bring upon it the grateful esteem of all right-minded hearers. Simple, pious, and

warm-hearted, a superior being, exhorting and encouraging a guilty but still reclaimable creature of this lower world, could scarcely impress the scene with a deeper feeling of reverence and of kindness. With some peculiarities to amuse his friends, who occasionally smile at the very intensity of his honesty, and the seriousness of his zeal, few men have so much solid excellence to secure their respect and esteem.

I am delighted to learn that Perth, like Edinburgh, as appears from the recent census, has increased very little, if at all, in population during the last ten years. Almost all the material additions to the number of the people have been in towns, where it has chiefly been an addition of precariously fed manufacturers, who are constantly making others tremble for the effects of their seditions of the belly. It is comfortable to have a few Goshens, a few spots where taste, and intellect, and peace can enjoy themselves in their old way, undisturbed by steam-engines, mobs, and upstart temporary wealth. I scarcely know a more singular fact, than that the people of Glasgow, who with plenty better things to boast of, are proudest of that very excess of population under which they fret and groan, were very angry that the statute ordered the late census to be taken on a Sunday, because this excluded many of their inhabitants who went regularly out of town that day. The Sheriff, I am told (the Historian of Europe as he is termed), actually issued a sort of official recommendation to the natives, either to stay at home that day, or, though really absent, to return themselves (contrary to the Act) as if present. This Glasgow zeal is not for truth, but for Glasgow. As if the best thing that could happen to them would not be to have a hundred thousand fewer.

Bonaly, Saturday Night, 25th September 1841. — We did not get to Tulliebole. It rained too heavily for us to go seven miles out of our way in an open carriage, merely to sit wet to breakfast. But though it was cruel, I forgive the rain, because it was the only umbrella shower we had since leaving Shiel House upon the morning of the 3d. So we came straight home, after exactly four week's absence this very day.

My book has been Combe's *Notes on America;* that is, *Notes of his recent travels in America,* by George Combe, Writer to the Signet, and now the Apostle of Phrenology, an excellent book by a most excellent man. Deducting his unhappy science (as he calls it), he sees everything clearly and fairly, and in a right spirit. His candour, even on his own subject, never forsakes him, and his benevolence never cools. And a zest is given to every part of his diary, and of his proceedings, by his honest phrenological credulity. He can see nothing except through phrenological spectacles. He is now in Germany, where he means to lecture in the native language; and in a land where thousands have faith in animal magnetism, and where mysticism and craze seem to be indigenous, lecturing on phrenology, he cannot fail. He is well suited for the apostleship of a new absurd sect, zealous, calm, and unobtrusive, benevolent, modest, and as unpretending as as consistent with a firm conviction that, Spurzheim being gone, he himself is the head of the phrenologists, and that all other philosophers are wrong. Independently of his arguments there is a great attraction in his worth and simplicity. The very plainness of his appearance and elocution, which have nothing beyond perfect naturalness to recommend them, takes people in. And no one who knows him can doubt his honesty. What he believes may possible be nonsense, but there can be no question as to the belief being sincere.

And so ends the best Circuit expedition that was ever performed!

NORTH CIRCUIT
1842

Cupar Angus, Monday Night, 11th April 1842. — North again. And with Moncreiff.

Jane and I, and Helen Maitland, left Edinburgh this morning at eight, and got here by Perth at about four. It has been a beautiful dry transparent day. But I have nothing to say of a route so common to me.

My object in coming this way has been to see Glamis, which I have tried to see all my life in vain, and I doubt if I shall be more successful now; because I must meet the Magistrates of Aberdeen to-morrow about four at the Bridge of Dee, nearly seventy miles from this, which admits of little delay for castle seeing. However, we shall start early and try. Had it not been for two confounded factors, I should have passed this evening at the village of Glamis. But my friend John Dundas, who acts for the Strathmore trustees, wrote to them to be sure to pay me every attention, the consequence of which was that if I had gone there to-day, instead of being let alone, and left to loiter over the castle as I chose, I should have had to dine with these two brothers, — excellent men both — one said to make up for being only 22 years of age by being 25 stones in weight, — with probably some of the gentry "to meet me"; and copious bowls of hot whisky punch, I am told, is the habit of the house, even in July evenings. This hospitality I have had the barbarity to avoid, even at the risk of not seeing the finest castle in Scotland.

Was not there some flaw in the marriage of Helen Fell, who put the following statement on the tombstone of the person she calls her husband, and which I found in the churchyard here? —

"Erected by Helen Fell, in memory of Donald Stewart, her husband, who, after having lived with her in a married life, departed this life the 10th June 1779." It must only have been a marriage of cohabitation. At least it has a left-handed appearance.

Aberdeen, 12th April 1842. — As I expected we did not see Glamis; we got to its outside at eight A.M., which, early though it was, left us by no fair calculation above half an hour to spare for the inside, which is the real thing to see. This half-hour was wasted in vain efforts, by bells and knocking, to rouse any one to open the door and show the castle. So we were obliged to move off, but had the pleasure of seeing a woman standing to admit us when we looked back from the first park gate. The closed shutters showed that the factors were still asleep.

I don't think I shall ever see Glamis more; for the Strathmore approach to Aberdeen is so incomparably the worst, that my present resolution is never to repeat it. Except to an agricultural and fox-hunting eye, the whole seventy miles or thereby, from Perth to Stonehaven, are utterly uninteresting. The Castle of Glamis is the solitary thing worth stopping to see; though perhaps the abbey, or whatever it is called, of Brechin, is not undeserving of a look.

The day has again been splendid.

Moncreiff joined me at Stonehaven, and we processed into Aberdeen grandly.

Fochabers, Saturday Night, 16th April 1842. — We were in Court in Aberdeen all Wednesday, Thursday, Friday, the 13th, 14th, and 15th, and I was there to-day till eleven, when I came away in order to get to Inverness with as little of what is now called "Sabbath desecration", which chiefly means travelling on Sunday, as possible. I left Moncreiff yoked to a long case of fire-raising, by a black-looking fellow called Rosenberg, a Prussian Jew, and his wife, at one time an actress in London; and got here about six.

The only unusual bar scene at Aberdeen was in the lifting of a prisoner, the only one I ever saw so introduced to be tried. She was an otherwise respectable woman, who if she had not directly murdered her infant, had caused its death by wilful neglect at bringing it into the world. And remorse, as was said, had deprived her of the use of her limbs, and prevented her from being capable of being tried till her crime was three years old, and she had become a truly pious woman. As it was necessary to get quit of her case one way or other, she, though not small, was lifted like a big child into Court, in the arms of an herculean porter, who, after she had pleaded guilty, and had been sentenced to a short imprisonment for the neglect, put his left arm under her as a nurse does to a child, and (she steadying herself by placing her right arm over his neck) carried her away.

The only person I ever saw absolutely and entirely lifted into Court, was one Smith, who, because he chose to work for less wages than they thought proper, was shot by these scoundrels the cotton-spinners on the street, in Glasgow, in open day. The ball shattered his spine, and paralysed him all over, but left his mind unimpaired. He was brought in as a witness, lying in bed, the bed (without any posts or curtains) being laid on a flat wooden frame, and placed on the table of the Court. He was pale and emaciated, with a fallen chin and feeble voice, but with a clear eye, though obviously dying. I scarcely ever felt more than when he lay before us, and raising his thin hand, swore, in answer to the absurd initiatory question, of which we have only last year got quit, that he had no malice or ill-will at the prisoner, to whom he owed the painful and lingering death which closed his sufferings in a few days. My client would have been hanged if the law had allowed it, but unfortunately, the statute which makes shooting, though not fatally, capital, had not then been extended to Scotland. This miscreant had the merit of getting it done.

We had a premature sort of a villain at Aberdeen, an advocate's clerk aged only nineteen, but who was old enough to conceive and execute the sending of three threatening letters, in order to extort money. They were well-written and well-contrived letters for his purpose, for each of them held out to a different person the certainty of utter ruin, by having crimes imputed to them, if they did not comply with his demands, which demands were always made very slender, but if once yielded to, would of course have risen. We cordially transported the heartless dog for ten years.

We went to an evening party at Aberdeen. If their usual society be, as I am told it is, in the same style with any I have ever seen, they are a kindly, hospitable, unceremonious, happy people.

Their cross has been removed further up the street, a much better site, and has been cleaned, repaired, and set all right; the original stones have all been preserved where they were broken, the broken ones have been replaced, the carving has been dealt with in the same way, and in short it is the old cross, only in a better place. Very well done.

The great present defect of the town is the want of a tolerable access to the pier. They should take down the houses which now close in Castle Street at its upper end, and make a street from that down to it. It would be well worth doing, were it only for the sake of letting people get an easier walk to the pier, which carries them further out into a blue and stormy sea than any pier in Scotland.

Marischal College is finished. If they do not succeed in getting the front of it cleared, they have been wasting their money. And even though they do, the building will be poor, and the attempt to maintain two Universities in such a place absurd. "For you must know, Mr. Speaker," as somebody said a few years ago in the House of Commons, "that England has two Universities, and so has Aberdeen." They should have given up the one in the town and made the old, venerable, well-placed, academic-looking King's College, the single seat of their science. It is in vain to speak of anything so reasonable to either of these two parties, each of whom would rather see its favourite establishment, and science besides, extinguished than yield to the other. But their folly ought to have been disregarded.

It is the fashion to abuse Aberdeenshire, but our drive here to-day, through its large, reclaimed, well-cultivated, and well-walled fields, was very pleasing. It is the beauty of utility, the rejoicing of the desert. There is more of the blossoming of the rose in Strathmore, but there they have a far better soil and climate, and have had more time. Theirs is the rose of nature. In Aberdeenshire it is the rose of art. And it is art laid out purely in subduing the appalling obstacles to their conquest over the soil. No towns, few villages, no stack of any manufactory, nothing but agriculture, which, besides its own proper triumph, has produced regions of surface, of which the purity and order, especially in this weedless season, when the clean line of every harrow is visible and the only herbage yet green is that of the cultivated seeds, delights the eye of taste.

The inn here is excellent. And if the village had been less regular, and less obviously withdrawn in its structure from the will of the people, it would have been better. But the truth is that during the lives of the two last dukes, — a period probably of sixty years — it was neither meant nor used as a village for villagers, but as a kennel for the retired lacqueys and ladies'-maids of the castle, and for the natural children and pensioned mistresses of the noble family, with a due proportion of factors, game-keepers, and all the other adherents of such establishments as their two Graces and their household rejoiced in.

Inverness, Monday Morning, 18th April 1842. — We came here last night, having had some difficulty in steering through the various parishes, so as to escape the people going into or coming out of church. But, on the whole, though I have no doubt that a judge travelling on Sunday, even though it was absolutely necessary, will be publicly denounced by some reverend zealots, we contrived to make it as little offensive as possible. Moncreiff, however, is in a worse plight, for his case of Rosenberg, which began on Saturday morning at nine, was not over till yesterday afternoon at twelve. He could not adjourn till Monday, because as the Circuit Court was to be held here to-day, and can only be held in one place at once, it would have been illegal. It is diverting that this desecration should have fallen to the lot of Moncreiff, a deeply religious man, a known anti-desecrator, a strict observer of Sunday, and an acting elder in Candlish's church. If it had been me or any other ordinarily pious man, we would have been excommunicated to a certainty. And probably they would perform this operation even on Moncreiff, if they were to detect that after getting out of Court, breakfasting, taking a walk and a nap, he dined out, and only got home about twelve at night. His fire-raisers were convicted.

Our drive here to-day was delightful, for the sky was still blue, and the air milky. And old Lithgow is right in calling this eastern district of Morayshire "the pleasant planure of the north." The road frequently winds through wood, where it did not require much fancy to make us suppose that we actually saw the larches greening themselves as we passed them, and it was difficult to say whether the glorious edging of the bright burnished whin, apparently exulting in having its roots cherished by the warm sand, gave more delight to us or to the bees. The coast of Ross-shire, seen across the serene blue sea, appeared as if it were beside us, with its rocks, and crevices, and sutors; Fort George glittered on the point of its promontory; as we advanced up the Moray Firth, new objects attracted the eye and the heart, for all the people were enjoying the scene in the evening of their day of well-clad rest. Ben Wyvis presiding over all, the long level ridge of his summit sparkling in the purest snow, the idle boats lay on the shore, two vessels vainly courted air enough to move them towards Inverness, which, backed by its singular group of picturesque eminences, reposed peacefully at the head of the Firth.

Of course I took Helen to the Cathedral of Elgin. The Bishop's House is still standing, and they say it is to be allowed to remain. I was sorry to find one grave marked by an insignificant flat stone containing only the four words "John Shanks, Shoemaker, Elgin." So patient and successful an Old Mortality deserved a fuller epitaph, and I said something to induce the Elginites to give him one. He, as well as Wren, may tell the stranger who asks where his monument is, to look around. But not far from John's dust we found the following excellent specimen of sycophancy, over the ashes of Mr. Hoy, a decent man, the best part of whose life was spent in performing the part of Macwheeble to the family of Gordon.

Here Lieth
The Body of
JAMES HOY
More than 46 years
Secretary at Gordon Castle
During which time
He enjoyed the confidence and friendship
of two Noble Dukes and two Dutchesses
Of the illustrious House of Gordon
He departed this life on the 19th Decr.,
In the year of our Lord 1827, aged 80 years.

Departed in that constant hope of trust
To rest eternally among the just;
To live and die well was his whole endeavour;

And in assurance died to live for ever.

He was — but words are wanting to say what,
Say what a Christian should be, — he was that.

Few men lived better certainly, for he dined at Gordon Castle
every day. And it is pleasing to think that the friendship of
noble dukes and duchesses can give such consolation in death,
and such glory after it.

We stopped to look at the Forres pillar, and after walking
through that nice old country town, which was so silent that I
was afraid my solitary step might disturb the people in church, I
played with the Findhorn at its beautiful suspension bridge,
from which the view of the town is very striking.

We went to the Frasers, at Laggan, four miles beyond Inverness, without stopping, and, having dispensed with the
procession, crept into town, quietly at ten at night. Yet I have
been told that my friend Dr. Clark has been composing abuse
against the two judges for desecration. It is a pity that I shall be
out of the place before he can get an opportunity of letting it off.

Bridge of Tilt, Wednesday Night, 20th April 1842. — I was in
Court two days at Inverness. There were two cases of fire raising, in which each of the culprits was a boy considerably under
twenty; not an ordinary juvenile offence. One was acquitted.
The other was convicted and transported for seven years. He
was about nineteen, and went into a barn, one end of which was
used as a dwelling-house by two fishergirls. He attempted to
use liberties with them, on which they turned him out. Stung
with what he called the "insult", he swore that he would not
sleep till he had burned the house over their heads. He was as
good as his word, for, returning that night about twelve, he
stove in the door, and took peats from the fire with which he
kindled a mass of straw that was in the opposite end of the
place, and made dust and ashes of the whole concern in a few
minutes. This, I presume, was his first adventure in love.

The weather was perfect during these two days, and my due
feet did not fail, as they never do, to go morning and evening
about half a mile up the left bank of the river — one of the most
beautiful of walks, more so, perhaps, than even the North Inch
of Perth. However these two places may settle it between
themselves, there can be no such competition between them
and any other towns in Britain.

Though we left Inverness this morning at six, we did not
reach this till half-past seven in the evening, a long while for
about eighty miles. But we stopped to breakfast at Aviemore,
and there is a good deal of hill on the road. And I wish it had
taken us double the time. For what a tract! And what a day!
Calm, bright, warm, silent. The snow of last winter still
whitened the corries of the mountains, while all their exposed

sides and heads were free; the little patches of hamlet farms in the valley, having been spared their usual rain for about a month, were clean and in good order, and the waters sparkled in their purest blue. But it is the solitude of this magnificent strath that awes and delights, — the deep and long solitude. I do not know any other so long tract, fairly within the reach and the daily use of civilised man in this island, which is so utterly unobtruded upon by the appearances of the sounds of art or population.

The firs that I mentioned four years ago have done the job. They have very greatly obstructed the western prospect from the high part of the road, for some miles after leaving Inverness.

This is an excellent inn, a very excellent one, small, nice, and well placed. It is to be hoped that its vicinity to its brother at Blair will be a check upon each; but it is somewhat absurd to have two hostels, on a lonely road, within three hundred yards of each other. This is one of the effects of the ridiculous rivalship that used to subsist between the houses of Athole and Lude. Each laird built his inn and his village; and Lude consoled itself for Athole's getting the church by Lude getting the poor bit of an Episcopal chapel, which stands in the field below the mansion-house.

The Place of Blair used to be open to everybody. And no wonder. For its only pleasure-ground is mountains, and there is no town to make intrusion formidable. It was not easy indeed to be found by the late duke on his domain, without getting not only welcome, but dinner. Under his second son Lord Glenlyon, however, who, during the insanity of his elder brother, is the acting duke, strangers are warned off by threatening placards at every corner. This is thoroughly Scotch. There are very few of the owners of our great places who have sense or humanity to make the enjoyment of their places a source of enjoyment to themselves. They seem to think that they get it best when they get it all, and frown at every stranger as an enemy who does not do them due homage if he walks in, not because the owner permits him, but merely because the beauty of the spot invites him. The proprietor of a place like Blair, which is composed of solitary mountains, should be thankful for all human intercourse. Glenlyon's placards should have announced that every properly-behaved person who would enliven the place by walking in it, should be rewarded by oatcake and whisky. I am aware of what is said about the mischievousness of the Scotch. But nothing provokes this vice, or rather habit, so much as our practice of stern exclusion from everything beyond the line of the highway.

Perth, Thursday Night, 21st April 1842. We left the Bridge of Tilt at ten, and were here at half-past four.

The strath between Blair and Dunkeld could not have been

98

seen to greater advantage; it was in the perfection of its vernal beauty. The day has been delicious, — June-like. The earth, the air, and the trees, were full of happy animal life, lambs, insects, birds. Labour had withdrawn from the flat, warm haughs, and had finally resigned its seeds to the undisturbed nurture of the elements. How softly the blue stream flowed through the valley. The larches were everywhere covered with that delicate and short-lived verdure, which makes that tree one of the best emblems of the Scottish spring. The planes, the first forest trees that display their confidence in the departure of winter, were bright with their rich gummy foliage. And what a world of brown bursting buds were the limes, the elms, and especially the birches, silently turning out into leaves. The whole scene was worthy of Charles the Fifth's praise of Florence, — that it was too beautiful to be looked upon except on a holy-day.

But the most pleasing circumstance is the obvious improvement of the human beings who inhabit what was lately not the Happy Valley. I remember it one of the most squalid regions in Scotland, with the duke's two houses at its opposite ends, and mud hovels and beggary between. It was an established Athole custom for the children to run like savages for miles alongside of every carriage, calling out for charity. The change that is taking place is striking and satisfactory. The mud tenements are disappearing every year; respectable stone houses, with their little gardens, are rising; busy, civilised villages are multiplying; the schoolmaster with the basin and the towel. So that we could scarcely detect a very dirty face on any child throughout our whole drive, nor were we assailed by a single beggar, youth or old.

Of these reformed villages, Pitlochry and Blair (including the Bridge of Tilt) are the most important. They exhibit too many symptoms of the determination of some single owner to have his capital picturesque, in which respect, though finer, they are less natural than Kingussie, which is plainly done by the people themselves. But time will correct this, by taking off the newness of the more pretentious cities. By the way, I was struck with a village somewhere near Elgin, called Lhanbryde, I think, which I don't remember observing before. It is in the transition state towards a better condition, and if its master, whoever he may be, shall adhere to the preservation of the trees, and the scattering of the houses, I predict favourably of Lhanbryde.

I called at Urrard, a most beautiful spot, and wished I had only £1000 and two years time to dress it up.

Helen and I also went into the grounds of Dunkeld — always odious; because there is nothing to be seen beyond what can be seen out of them, and because a walk there is subjected to restraints which destroy the pleasure. I had to get the landlord to send somewhere to ask leave for me. This leave came in the form of a printed permission, which was to be kept in the hand till a person took it. The person took it at the gate. Then our names had to be signed in a book at the lodge. And after all this preparation, the heels of a guide, impatient for the strangers' contribution to his wages, had to be followed step by step, with a check and an instruction if the indulged intruder deviated one inch from the showman's wake. If I lived there as the owner, the sight of all the people of Dunkeld in my grounds every day would only enhance my enjoyment of them.

Perth, Sunday Night, 24th April 1842. — Moncreiff rejoined me here. We were in Court all Friday and yesterday; and this has been a well-spent day. For I have been round the North Inch, I cannot tell how often; and on the top of Kinnoul Hill, and had a pleasant quiet dinner of eight, and have enjoyed this rose of country towns, from morning to night, from the dewy grass before breakfast, to the serene moon at twelve at night, and even processed to the East Church and heard a discourse by Dr. Easdale, saturated with morphia. The day was so warm that the windows were all open, and it was really delightful to see so many people asleep in so pure an air. Of the 700 who I suppose might be present, 300 at least were in Elysium. Of the public authorities I observed five elders, two sheriffs, three magistrates, and one judge, all under the gentle influence at once. I don't recollect being here on a Sunday before, and hence I have perhaps been the more impressed with the Calvanistic grimness of the place, from its being so unlike what might have been expected. I thought that the beauty which God had given to it would have led all the truly pious out to enjoy His works. But no! I don't believe that there have been 100 persons, and certainly not 200 on the North Inch this whole day. It has been an utter solitude, in the morning, between the two public services, and even in the evening. It produces a very painful feeling of the sourness of mind that can think such sullenness against nature a duty. That plain of green velvet on which the very sun seemed delighted to repose, edged by the silver Tay, and surrounded by all the appearances of vernal life in the finest condition; bounded towards the one end by distant blue mountains, some snow still lingering on their loftier summits; and towards the other, by the beautiful bridge, and its comfortable little city, ought to have been swarmed over by the young and the old, the cheerful and the pensive, but especially by the pious, on this their day of thought, from the morning to the evening twilight.

But what can be expected? For since I came here, I learn that even the extensive and comparatively secluded grounds of Dunkeld, are now, for the first time, absolutely shut against everybody — even the few and well-ordered inhabitants of that quiet village — during the whole of Sunday. This is another of the already too many examples of matters being so managed by

100

what terms itself the religious world, that that large class, being the great majority of the people, which will positively desecrate, as it is called, are not allowed to do so in the purest and most intellectual way, but are driven to find their recreation on the streets, or in the pot-house. Fanatical masters and mistresses are very apt to excuse their hatred of a smile upon the Sunday, by ascribing their intolerance to consideration for their servants, and I dare say that this exclusion of the villagers of Dunkeld will be said to be for the purpose of letting the guides go to church. But they surely need not gloom in the church the whole Sunday, and though they did, the visitors would be much the better, and the grounds certainly not the worse of their absence.

Bonaly, Saturday, 30th April 1842. — We finished at Perth yesterday about eleven in the forenoon, and were in Edinburgh to dinner.

I never have been so much struck with the beauty of Perth as during this the only week I ever passed in it. It requires nothing to make it perfect except a great old building. The Cathedral of Glasgow, or the ruins of Elgin, would give it all its wants, — the dignity imparted by time, or by the palpable vestiges of history. It is lamentable to hear some of its best citizens envying Dundee for its trade; that is, for its steam-engines, its precarious wealth, its starving, turbulent population, its vulgar blackguardism. Long may their foolish efforts to deepen the river fail, as they recently have done. We must have manufacturing towns. But there is no necessity for their being made out of the ruins of natural beauty, or of retreats of academic learning. Who can doubt that it would have been better for Scotland, and even for Glasgow, if trade and the loom had been encouraged to fasten their black claws on any other part of the Clyde, and left Glasgow with its College, and its Cathedral, its river, and its Green, alone.

I saw models of two plans for widening the bridge. The one which proposes to raise additional arches for foot passengers on each side, is clearly the best, but the doubt is whether the piers on which these side arches must rest be sufficiently strong to bear them. It is a very handsome bridge as it is, and it is to be hoped that the authorities will not fall into the usual error of letting everything depend on the ignorance of some local ass, ambitious only of an opportunity of disgracing himself, which he calls employment.

I saw my first 1842 swallow on the river, on the morning of Monday the 25th.

We had 84 cases, the greatest number, I am told, that has ever been at any one Circuit town in Scotland, except once at Glasgow, where there were 85. Most of them were from the said enviable Dundee. There was no capital sentence, and only one transportation for life. Nor was there any case worth recording, — except one — too horrid, however, to be mentioned. The dark roll was filled with the ordinary, and scarcely varied repetition of robberies, assaults, sheep and cattle stealing, fraud, conspiracy, forgery, fire-raising, night poaching, bigamy, and above all of theft, which now forms fully a half of all the criminal business in Scotland. There is certainly a fashion in crimes. There was far less transportation than usual, long imprisonments in the recently-opened penitentiary at Perth being the substitute.

Moncreiff and I went and visited this establishment, which, though only opened about a month ago, contains already about 150 inmates. It is a very humane and well-considered experiment. But except upon the youth, I am not sanguine of its success. They who are generally guilty from ignorance, are never to be despaired of, till the effect of knowledge shall be tried; the knowledge not merely of reading and writing, and the rules of morality and religion, but of a trade, and of the practical consequences of misconduct. There is a considerable class too of otherwise well-behaved people, who have got into a first scrape, who if not corrupted in jail, will probably never get into another. But with the true, regular, professional, middle-aged criminal, who requires a change of nature — reformation — I don't expect much from comfortable living, though in confinement, nor from steady occupation, even though combined with considerable solitude. I fear that such criminals must be given over, and that, after all, there is nothing for it but to get rid of them by exportation. The prison is in beautiful order. But like all other prisons, it is far too small. The 400 cells, being all that are now built, will be full next year.

Our business closed by the best Circuit address from Moncreiff that I have ever heard on such an occasion. It had no nonsense in it, and besides being judicious, was benevolent, and practically useful.

During the whole Circuit we have not had one single drop of rain, and scarcely even a cloud.

My book was *Barnaby Rudge,* a novel of which any other author might be proud, but which is, perhaps, the least admirable that Dickens has produced. But still it is excellent. I must, however, except the hangman, who, with his professional jokes, is disgusting and unnatural. Scott, in his *Quentin Durward,* has a couple of hangmen too, and, in his *Heart of Midlothian,* he has a mob. And in neither do I think that he suffers by the competition even of Dickens.

WEST CIRCUIT

Ardrossan, Friday, 9th September 1842, 7 A.M. — I left Edinburgh on this West Circuit, on the morning of Tuesday last, the 6th, with Maitland and Archibald Davidson, the former of whom

Sir James Wellwood, Moncreiff, Bart

was going on a case to Stirling, the latter to Dunira. Circuitising though I was, I went to Falkirk by the railway, but then I had secured the *coupé* (I wish they had given us an English word for it), which is a private carriage and secures the learned lord from contamination with witnesses, parties, jurors, and the world. We got to Falkirk at 8 a.m., being one hour from Edinburgh, posted to Stirling in an hour and a half, breakfasted, and I was in Court at quarter-past ten.

The business lasted two days. Commonplace cases. The weather after five months of unbroken excellence, warm and dry, was moist and foggy. However, I performed my pilgrimage through the streets and round the castle before breakfast. The people are recovering their quasi rights in the beautiful turf pleasure-ground, below, and to the south-west of the castle, of which the Woods and Forests, from ignorance, lately deprived them. These Commissioners put this ground, with all the green and regular mounds which marked its ancient uses as a place of royal and public pastime, into a farmer's lease, and the plough had begun its devastation, when public clamour instructed the Commissioners, and they are now in the course of getting their error corrected.

I observed two things, one was that the apex of a modern (at least not an ancient) porch over the door of Cowan's Hospital, covered one-half of the old square stone which records the virtues of the founder John Cowane. The other was that the two or three public wells are so constructed, having only one spout each, that (as in the High Street of Edinburgh since I remember) the poor people are obliged to stand idle and shivering for hours before they can get their vessels filled, to their great discomfort, and not at all to the improvement of their manners or morals. I counted above 200 tubs, pails, pitchers, etc., ranged on the street, with the owners waiting their turns from the solitary spouts. I told the provost that if I was in his place, both of these evils should be remedied in a month, the one at the pumps by simply multiplying the spouts at the existing drawing places. The answer was that the porch was soon to be taken away for other reasons, that the facility of putting a spout at each of the four sides of a pillar, instead of only at one, had never occurred to them, though they had often lamented the people's delay, and that if it should be found to cost nothing or very little, it would probably be done.

Maitland and I left Stirling at seven, breakfasted at Cumbernauld, and were in Glasgow by eleven. At one, my daughters, Jane and Elizabeth, and my old companion Frank, joined us there, having left Edinburgh by the railway at eleven. At half-past one we all left Glasgow by the Ayr railway, and were here by three, where Maitlands' family has been living for some months.

Lord Mackenzie has gone to Inverary, and we don't begin at . Glasgow till Thursday next, the 15th, and my object in coming here is to get over to Arran, where I have never been, and to pass some days in its solitudes. But the window I am writing at looks across the water, and Arran is invisible, the waves surly, and the air showery. My contemptible stomach almost turns at the look of it, and is not made steadier by the pitching of a sloop a mile or two out. So my long desire to be in Glen Sannox, or on the top of Goatfell, may probably not be gratified to-day.

Ardrossan, Friday, 9th September 1842, 11 P.M. — It was not. We went to the end of the pier here, and saw the steamer set out, and she grunted and heaved so, that I was thankful I was not in her. But then, as usual, she probably landed by half-past eleven at Brodick, so it would have been all over in an hour and a half, by which time it turned out an excellent day. Still it was only excellent for this side, for Arran was only seen like a ghost, through mist, occasionally. But to-morrow!

We took a carriage and went within a mile of Fairlie, and then got out and walked about.

Fairlie is the best village of the wealthy in Scotland. Excellent houses, capital gardens, umbrageous trees, the glorious Clyde, backed by Arran and its dependencies stretched out before them, a gravelly soil, and a mild western climate.

On our way home we went up the high ground on the left side of the road, in order to try if we could find out a waterfall, of which the minister gives a grand description in his statistical account of the parish (old edition), but which the parishioners, or such of them as we fell in with, knew so little about, that none of them could say exactly where it was. After a long and wettish scramble we at last discovered the fall of Southannan. A poor affair. For the guidance of future travellers, I may mention that it lies about a mile and a half on this side of Fairlie, and about half a mile up the hill to the left.

Brodick Inn, Sunday Morning, 11th September 1842. — Yesterday was so little bad that we resolved to tempt the deep. But we lost Maitland, for just before embarking, a letter from Mrs. Cockburn, who is in Edinburgh, announced the death of her and Mrs. Maitland's only surviving brother. The event was expected, and in his wretched and incurable state of suffering not to be deplored. It induced Maitland, however, to go to Edinburgh to give directions, and made his wife stay behind. So Helen, George, and James Maitland, Henry Davidson, my Elizabeth and Francis, and myself came here.

We left Ardrossan at ten. I took precaution of lying down flat on the deck and shutting my eyes, from the very first moment of going on board till we reached Brodick, with the effect, which I had experienced before, of a total exemption from sickness. The voyage is about an hour and a half long.

The clouds said No, to our question whether we should ascent Goatfell. So George Maitland, H. Davidson, and I proceeded and explored Glenrosie, the outlet of which is within a mile of this, and the valley not above three or four miles long. There is, fortunately, no road, and the upper part is so stony and so cut into holes by streams, that it makes rather a severe scramble. But it is a valley well worth passing a day in. All gushing with the clearest water tumbling over granite; deep sides, browned with chocolate-coloured autumn fern, many dark rocky peaks, and the upper end enclosed by as striking an assemblage of black and picturesque precipitous mountain-tops as is often to be seen,

Not wishing to return the same way, we climbed to the top of the range which forms the left boundary of the valley, and came home over it instead of round it. It was a tough pull, and took us apparently more than half up Goatfell. The prospect was extensive, but there was too much islandless sea.

On the way home Davidson and I went into Brodick Castle, — a strong thing, with antiquity, site, and trees, sufficient to have enabled its noble owner, if he had chosen to spare a little of the gilding he has wasted on the weavers of Hamilton, to have easily made it a fine place. The gardener, who took us to the top of the house, when we asked him to point out the way to the top of the hill, did so, but added, with something like a boast, that though he had been living at its base for sixty years, he had never once even attempted to ascend it.

I have walked this morning to the opposite (or south) side of the bay. It is by far the best of the two, at least when warmed, as it was an hour ago, by the morning sun, and in full prospect of the castle rising over its respectable wood, and of the craggy summits of Goatfell. Every one of the neat white cottages that are scattered about round the whole bay is let to people who come here in summer for health or idleness, and it was delightful to see so many comfortable breakfasts laid out, in small, but very clean, well-papered, cottage rooms. The church bell sounded, I don't know why, as I was told that there was to be no service, but its sound added greatly to the charm of the tranquil scene. The day is balmy, clear, and calm.

Brodick Inn, Monday, 8 A.M., 12th September 1842. — The guides don't practise their profession upon Sunday, even when there is not service, and therefore practised their established pious fraud, of assuring us that yesterday would be a bad day, but this is a good one. We therefore got a boy with two horses, on which we put Helen and Elizabeth, and having packed a little refreshment into a basket, we all set out on the ascent. The horses could only get about half-way up. The girls then dismounted, and tried their own proper muscles. But Helen soon failed, and was established on the lee-side of a rock till our return. Elizabeth went to the very top. After lingering there a long while, we picked up the one we had left, recreated ourselves out of the basket, put the ladies on their beasts, and were all safe here in about five and a half hours from our setting out, which had been about eleven.

The guides proved so far right, that soon after our reaching the top, we, and all our world, were covered with mist. But it did not come on till after we had seen everything, and cleared off three or four times. And it was only the Argyleshire side that it ever entirely hid, leaving Clyde almost constantly bright. It was not therefore a perfect day for Goatfell, but it was not a very bad one. We saw everything, but only not long, or steadily, enough. With the exception of this partial misfortune on the summit, the whole ascent and descent were absolutely perfect, and the day, in every respect, was delicious.

In point of mere climbing, the ascent, except over a few rocks near the top, is not at all formidable. A mule could go to the very summit.

I have a taste for the tops of hills; but making allowance for this failing, it is certainly well worth the while even of a lover of flat ground, to mount Goatfell. It gives him a splendid prospect, both of land and water. Nature has rarely been more fortunate. The elevation of nearly 3000 feet of granite, in an island, placed in the wide bay between Argyle on the west, and Renfrewshire and Ayrshire on the east, and near the openings of Loch Fyne and the Firth of Clyde; from which eminence all the adjacent seas, and firths, and lochs, and sounds, and mountains, and islands, are distinctly visible, was one of her happiest achievements.

I have been on a good many Scotch hills; but the competitors for the first prize are only four; Ben Lomond, Goatfell, Demyet, and Swanston (but neither this nor Cape Law is the correct name) (Cairketton), the eastmost of the Pentlands. The claim of Ben Lomond rests chiefly on the stupendous mass of boiling mountains behind it. In point of beauty Demyet is perhaps to be preferred, because it is very low, and holds a delightful district of striking objects, particularly Stirling, within its eye. Goatfell bids defiance to them all, in the bright and varied splendour of its many, and islanded waters, contrasted with the hard and generally dark Argyleshire peaks, by which these waters seem to be guarded and looked upon. But still, considering the beauty of Edinburgh, and the dignity imparted to scenery by objects of importance, I am rather inclined to give the palm to that Pentland.

For prospects, Ben Lawyers, Ben Ledi, Ben More, and Ben Nevis, are to be altogether discounted. Ben Nevis however, has an indisputable superiority of interest, of a different kind to every other height in the British Islands. No other mountain is nearly so grand in itself.

I am sorrier now than I was last September, that I did not ascend the hill in Skye. And, from what lies all around at its feet, I can't conceive how Ben Cruachan (which I have never yet ascended), can avoid holding the spectator up to a prospect of first-rate magnificence.

This is another beautiful day, but not for the hill-top, and I rejoice that we did not wait for it yesterday.

Brodick Inn, Monday Night, 12th September 1842. — This forenoon was given to Glen Sannox. Elizabeth, Eliza Maitland (who came over this morning from Ardrossan with my daughter Jane), H. Davidson, George Maitland, and I, got in, and upon, a car, and drove the seven miles from this to the lower end of the glen. The whole of these seven miles are beautiful, both in their marine prospects, and their fringing of rock and wood, down to the very shores. The girls walked up the glen, till they reached a queer manufactory (not going) of Carytes. I went on a good deal further, but was obliged to return for them. Maitland and Davidson went up the whole of Sannox and down Glenrosie, — a severe, but admirable walk. These two glens — hold Goatfell in their arms — are of the same character; rough with marsh and rock, roaring with water, and gloriously hemmed in by black splintered peaks.

It has been a calm delicious bright day, and Davidson and I retire for the night, resolved to be once more on top of Goatfell, if the weather pleaseth, to-morrow. We should have been there to-day, if the morning had told us that after eleven the summit was to be so clear as it has been. I again walked, between four and six, round this bay. The south side is, beyond dispute, the best. But my exploration was suddenly stopped by discovering that a letter which I had written, addressed, and sealed on the 4th inst., to the Provost of Glasgow, announcing the Circuit, and requiring him to process within his own burgh, on Thursday first, was still in my pocket. I was too late for the post, and had just time to hasten home, and give the letter, crumpled as it was, to a person who was stepping on board the steamer, and was to be in Glasgow to-night. I rather suspect that I would have stormed if anybody else had done this.

Ardrossan, Tuesday Night, 13th September 1842. — To-day was another yesterday, so far as concerned the enjoyment of the seashore regions, but warm lazy clouds lay on the hill-tops. After lounging therefore on the beach till two, Davidson and I set off and walked to Lamlash; after viewing which, we embarked on the steamer, — went back to Brodick, but did not land, took in the rest of the party, and, bidding adieu to Arran, were here by seven.

Lamlash is quietly placed, and this is its only recommendation. No, it has also a more gravelly beach than Brodick, the only defect of which is, that a line of paltry swamp is interposed between the beach and the houses. In every other respect Lamlash is far inferior to its rival capital; particularly in want of wood, want of high hills, and want of scattered cottages. These last, the humble but clean, white cottages, that are tossed

108

about, each occupied by a comfortable idler, form the peculiar charm of Brodick.

Glasgow, Wednesday Night, 14th September 1842. — I went this forenoon to Lochwinnoch, to attend the funeral of my brother-in-law, Lieut.-Col. Laurence Macdowall. After which I came here, where I found my colleague, Lord Mackenzie, who has been at Inverary. And so nothing of this Circuit remains, except the comfortable prospect of having to try about one hundred criminal cases, besides some civil ones, and to dispose of some appeals.

But I have forgot Ardrossan. It is above, or about, thirty years since I last saw it. It was then a sort of poor fishing-village, with no harbour, and no fashion as a bathing place. The late Earl of Eglinton was just beginning the attempt to realise his vision, of glorifying and enriching his family, by carrying a canal from Glasgow, by Paisley, to this part of his property, and thus making Ardrossan Tyre, and Saltcoats Sidon. The canal, after being bankrupt, reached Johnstone, and now, with its railway rival, it will certainly never advance an inch further. But his lordship succeeded in compelling the sea to submit to be a small port, and in alluring genteel invalids, by a large bad inn, and small bad baths, to resort there in summer. So Ardrossan is a town, and has a harbour.

There is no beauty in its own immediate neighbourhood. But no place on the Firth of Clyde can ever be without charms and interest, and until Arran shall be covered again by the waters, it will always be delightful to look from Ardrossan. It consists at present chiefly of a single line of small houses, curving with the line of the beach; in front of the houses is the public road or street, and next the street the sea, which ebbs very little. The summer population consists mostly of strangers, few of whom have what, in Scotch Irish, are called self-contained houses, most of them cramming into the small, but clean, upper flats, which are let for bathers by the poorer people below. The whole place is respectably clean.

The ladies' bathing is conducted on the genuine Scotch principle of not being at all ashamed of it, as why should they? Is it not pure? and healthy? and ordered by the doctor? and anything wrong in it? So the ladies emerge, in full day, from their flats, in their bathing-dresses, attended by a maid, and a sister or aunt, the maid carrying a small bundle containing a towel and some dry clothes, the friend tittering. The bather crosses the road, and goes to the sea, which is never more than a few yards, or inches, beyond the road's edge. She then enters the water, and shivers, or splashes, according to her taste, conversing or laughing or screaming all the while, with her attendants ashore. But it is on coming out that the delicate part of the operation begins; for, as they don't walk home wet, and then dress in their own rooms, they must change their whole raimant before

109

the public. For this purpose the maid holds a portion of the dry vestment over the dripping lady's head, and as the soaked gown descends to the heels, the dry is supposed to descend over the head as fast, so that the principle is, that, between the two, the lady is never seen. Ignorance is sometimes bliss, and it is very wise in the assistance never to tell the patient anything about it. But I wonder how, when they happen to be looking at a fellow-exhibitor, and observe the interest taken from every window, and by all the street, in the proceeding, they can avoid discovering that such feats are seldom performed without revelations, and that a single fold of wet linen adheres too accurately to the inner surface to require any other revelation.

But I never saw bathing performed by ladies in Scotland even with common decency. Why the devil can't they use bathing-machines, or go into retired places, or wall or pale off enclosures? There was one bathing machine on the beach at Ardrossan, which was rarely used, and two in the inn court, which the landlord told me were never used at all. Portobello, however, (the most immodest spot in Scotland), shows that machines may be used so as to be no protection, but the reverse, for there they are used, nearly touching, by men and women indiscriminately.

Bonaly, Saturday 24th September 1842. — We began at Glasgow on the morning of Thursday the 15th, and ended yesterday at four o'clock P.M. We had exactly 99 cases to dispose of, being about 15 or 20 more than were ever on the list at any of our Circuits, and, one way or other, every one of them was disposed of. None, I mean, that could have been tried were not tried. There was no capital case, and the whole batch was utterly uninteresting, the great majority being commonplace thefts. The exile of about 60 of our fellow-creatures is upon our souls.

One of our days was a Sunday, a very serious thing in Glasgow. To avoid its horrors, Lord Mackenzie spent the day at Possil. But I rather think I fell upon a better scheme. Because the Court having risen at six on the Saturday evening, I got into the seven o'clock train, and found myself here (Bonaly), at tea and an egg, before ten. On Monday morning at seven, the impatient engine, after grunting and hissing to get away, was set free; and at nine exactly I was back in Glasgow, and, after a leisurely breakfast, was in Court when it met at ten. I remember Jeffrey offering to speak till a writing could be brought from Glasgow, though the shortest journey then was five hours going and five coming, rather than his cause should be lost. Few orators will restrict themselves now to a run to Glasgow.

Mr. Charles Neaves was our Depute-Advocate, a sensible man, agreeable, literary, and an excellent compounder of clever humorous verse, chiefly in the line of songs, which he also sings well.

Lord Mackenzie is a very old acquaintance, and one of the best possible colleagues. A weak, awkward, and apparently timid manner, gives him an outward appearance almost directly the reverse of the real man. For beneath this external air of helplessness, there works an acute, resolute, and original understanding; combined with great intelligence, and a very amiable heart. Not very practical, and wanting tact, he seems to be constantly engaged with his own speculations, the intrepidity of which make an amusing contrast with the feebleness of his manner. He is a most excellent man, a singularly agreeable companion, and an admirable judge; except that, on the Bench, whenever there is anything to be done which requires force, or impressiveness, his poverty of manner makes him necessarily fail. But in private life this outside awkwardness makes him only picturesque.

I see that I have forgot to do justice to the inn at Brodick. I had heard all my life, and particularly this very summer, that one of the difficulties of a pilgrimage to Arran was that it was impossible to go to the inn, as it was abominable, and choke full of Glasgow weavers every time that a steamer arrived, and that there were no attainable lodgings to make up for this. All nonsense! Lodgings it would clearly be difficult, or impossible, to get for a few days, and at this season. But the inn — for there is only one — is excellent, for a Scotch country inn most excellent, well-placed, clean, retired, with a good larder, and much kindness. The widow landlady, Mrs. Jameson, is a nice, respectable, motherly person. There is at present only one steamer daily, which sails from Ardrossan, and when we were there it landed no passengers whose existence was known to us; we had the upper flat of the house.

I was one morning admiring a very handsome boy about six years old, dressed as a Highlander, and whose fate will probably fulfilled by his being landlord of the inn, or a shepherd on Goatfell. Mrs. Jameson told me he was her son, and said she would like to consult me about what she should do with him. After various schemes on my part, none of which ever went beyond his being landlord, or a waiter or a shepherd, or a poacher, she, a decent, sensible widow, with not a joke even in her head, said, with the most perfect gravity and sincerity: "If I was to send him to Edinbro, do ye think they wad sune mak him a joodge?" (judge). I had not cruelty to cloud her maternal visions in assuring her that birth, whatever influence it once might have had, had little to do with it now. Whereat she seemed considerably pleased.

WEST CIRCUIT
1843

Tarbet, Thursday Night, 20th April 1843. — I ought to have

gone the South Circuit this spring, but I have contrived to avoid it, because John Hope, the Justice-Clerk, the most uncomfortable of all possible companions, would have been my colleague. But I could not have escaped him had it not been that it was a more convenient Circuit than any other for poor Moncreiff, who being obliged to go to London for medical advice for his wife, who is alarmingly ill, wished it to be late and short. I had attempted all sort of manoevres to get rid of our chief; but they were all defeated, because I found that all my brethren were manoevring for the same object. A curious fact for the head of a Court.

But I have got Meadowbank, who has been at Stirling. I am on my way to Inverary, and we meet at Glasgow.

Elizabeth (my daughter), Graham Maitland, and I, left Edinburgh by the railway this morning at eight; reached Glasgow ten minutes before ten, breakfasted there, left it at twelve, and were here by four.

There must be an end of engraving the same lines, so I have nothing new to say.

It was a dull rain nearly the whole way from Glasgow to Tarbet. The young grass and the bright larches were not the worse of this, but it is impossible to forgive the sun when he does not shine on Loch Lomond. I retract as to Kilpatrick, which to-day had rather a blackguard appearance; a distinct west-country manufacturing blackguardism. And oh! how abominable is the whole course of the Leven! Pure enough, I suppose, in Smollett's time, but now a nearly unbroken track of manufactories, which seem to unite the whole pollutions of smoke, chemistry, hot water, and squalid population, and blight a valley which nature meant to be extremely beautiful. No "mottled parr" now, unless they are mottled by the refuse of dyes. It is only when the loch opens, and we cast Glasgow and its feculence off, that the region of beauty and magnificence begins.

We walked about a couple of miles up the loch before dinner, and now (ten at night) the water and the mountains are dark and silent.

Dalmally, Sunday Night 23d April 1843. — We left Tarbet on Friday at eleven, and after much lingering and sauntering in Glencroe, and the considerate aid of a lame horse, reached Inverary at four.

The day though never bright, and occasionally showery, was mild and calm. I have only two things to record this time about Glencroe. One is that the stone tablet at Rest-and-be-Thankful, which used to attest the merits of General Wade, who, about eighty years ago, had made this, as he had made other Highland roads, has recently been chipped and rendered utterly illegible, for which it is fortunate for some people that man's curses are often fruitless. The other is, that in the whole glen I could not find a primrose, even in leaf, though I have seen miles of it brightened with them nearly forty years ago, and in this very month. Possibly May may evoke them. But there is something strange in the localities of this delightful flower; for I am satisfied that there are places where, after being planted and after settling themselves and spreading for years, they die out; and no one can traverse the Highlands without finding other places where it is difficult to suppose that they can have been planted, and yet where they abound. Since they are tossed profusely over several parts of the banks of Loch Lomond, over all the neighbourhood of Inveraray, and over the shores of Loch Awe, — and they flourish best amidst moisture — why should there be intervening districts with the very same surface and climate, which ages have never made them reach, or from which they have decayed? Do sheep extirpate them? If they do, this fact would go far to explain their apparently capricious eradication; for it is only, or at least chiefly under the shelter of old spongy copse, or the drippings of rocks, that they seem to domesticate.

The business at Inverary began on Saturday at ten, and was over that day by five. No case worth mentioning. A jury of fifteen stots acquitted a most aggravated assaulter, in spite of the clearest possible evidence, to make up for which they repeatedly and obstinately tried to convict him of another offence, with which it was over and over again explained to them that he was not charged. One does fall in with a bad drove occasionally.

I gave the usual festival in the evening (for a breakfast, I find, won't go down), with claret jolted last week all the way from Leith, as the landlord said, for the occasion.

I had been over all the grounds in immediate connection with the castle on Friday, before and after dinner, and to-day David Milne, the Advocate-Depute, and I went to the top of Dunaquaich, and other places, before breakfast. In the churchyard, which lies hid behind a horrid wall, about half a mile north of the town, Milne found the following gallant epitaph on the tombstone of "John Stewart, Lieutenant in the 21st Regiment of Foot," who died in May 1820, aged 29:-

> Farewell, vain world! I know enough of thee,
> I value not what thou can'st say of me.

After this preparation (and a breakfast of most admirable sea trout) I went canonically to church. A procession must necessarily be imposing to a public whose magistrates heading it are sixteen in number, while their constituents are only twenty-eight. It was a neat, clean little church, and a discourse very strong in the water. There certainly were not 150 people present. I could only count 132. Nor was there a single kilt, or blue bonnet, a plaid, or yard of tartan. All Saxon and apathy.

But this was the temple of the aristocracy; which at Inverary consists of writers and the Duke. The Gaelic was going on at the other side of the wall. For a town population of about 1200, and a country population attending church of far less than 800, that is for 2000 people, they have six services, three English and three Gaelic, every Sunday, one of each being in the evening; and of the two ministers, dull though he was, the provost assured me that the one I got was by far the liveliest. God help the natives, both for the quality and the quantity.

I have been acquainted with Inverary since I was a lad, and I never saw it without feeling that it was unworthy of the great reputation it has contrived to get. It is plain that Sir David Wilkie thought so too. The castle is abominable. And it and the town are so conspicuously near, that each hurts the other. The head of the loch is too narrow. Except Dunaquaich, which is certainly picturesque, the hills are all insignificant, and those which bound the east side of the loch are utterly paltry. Except in being strewed over by some very fine trees, every one of which, however, is dying of moss, there is nothing in the laying out of the grounds. A brilliant sun gilds anything, but in its ordinary state, Inverary to me is a scene of heavy dullness.

We left it to-day after church, and came here. I have not been along the east side of Loch Awe since I missed old Lord Meadowbank, with whom I was going this Circuit as Advocate Depute in 1808 or 1809, and had to walk from Dalmally to Inveraray. I had not forgot it; but my admiration of this noble loch is greatly raised by to-day's view. Its islands, though mostly small, are more numerous than those in most of our lakes. Not one of our lakes has such irregularity of shape (I speak only of this end), or variety of outline. And which of them can boast of a Ben Cruachan? So far as I have seen our sheets of fresh water, the competition for the second place clearly lies between Loch Awe and Maree. The first is indisputably due to Loch Lomond.

Tarbet, Monday Night, 24th April 1843. — A successful day.

We took a car before breakfast and went to Kilchurn, of which, besides seeing it, I wanted to have a bit, for my long contemplated, and seemingly never to be executed, old castle chessmen. It is a very fine ruin, grandly placed. There are larger and far more beautiful and interesting fragments of religious architecture in Scotland, but I cannot recollect the ruins of any greater castle. And this one has still enough of turret, and window, and ivy remaining to render it perhaps in as perfect a stage for preservation, as a ruin, as it ever has been or can be. But what murder it is undergoing! There is little neighbouring population, and therefore there is little of the usual Scotch sheer filth. But except this, there is every other atrocity. Not one sixpence of money or one moment of care has ever been bestowed on either of the two duties of protecting or

Marquis of Breadalbane

115

of cleaning. The whole rubbish has been allowed to accumulate exactly as it has fallen; and not one trowelful of lime has ever been laid out to prevent the descent and accumulation of more. The consequences are that the inside is almost utterly inaccessible, and that time has made, and is making, innumerable obvious preparations for undermining and throwing down more large and important masses. Whole walls seem to depend in some places on the crumbling of a small stone. The boatman who rowed us over (for though it be on the mainland, boating is the driest way of reaching it) defended his master, the Marquis of Breadalbane, to whom it belongs, by saying that "Something had been dune til't a while ago, as ye wad see by a stane abune the door." And no doubt there is a clear cut lintel above the door, with the date of 1693; for the repairs of which period the castle, after standing since the 13th century, it is to be hoped was grateful. But has there been a shilling laid out since 1693, in mere protection or clearing? It is scandalous, and to me utterly incomprehensible. Here is a noble Marquis with an estate of the highest class, and no children, who can afford to entertain the Queen, and to cover the country from sea to sea with gamekeepers, and to exhaust all the powers of decoration on his residence at Taymouth, but cannot give a mite or a thought for the decency or the perpetuation of a great historical relic, in comparison of which, in reference even to the dignity of his own estate, queens and upholsterers are nothing. It is not avarice, nor is it ignorance, at least not in his case. It proceeds from want of thought, which creates the habit of being reconciled to what ought to be felt shameful; till at last he who would give £500 for a hearthrug, or £5000 for a Gothic diary, stares at the idea of expending a shilling on arresting the decay of the only thing he may happen to possess which painting or poetry think worthy of their notice.

In going to Kilchurn we saw several swallows, the first of the year.

We left Dalmally about eleven, went to Tyndrum, then to Inverarnan, 12 miles, and here, 10 miles more. There is a good deal of hill, though the whole road is excellent, but we walked and loitered, and our day's journey of 34 miles was only ended by the carriage at about five, and by me, who walked the last stage, at about six.

All I now say of Dalmally and Tyndrum, and of their ranges, is that I adhere to all I have said already. What can I say more?

I never came down by the head of Loch Lomond except once before, and this was about twenty years ago, and while the old road was in its full adventurous impassableness. Two of that party, Mrs. Richardson and Sir Charles Bell, are no more, but I often saw them to-day.

The new road has greatly changed, and greatly improved the general scenery. It would not be easy to find twelve more beautiful or picturesque miles than those between Glenfalloch and Tarbet. The descent towards Loch Lomond is not quite completed, when the hills are observed to have lost the whole of the unbroken massiveness which had marked those in the region above, and to have become rocky and ridgy. And there is a very striking succession of them visible along the whole way, from Ben Oss, at the upper end of the valley, to Ben Lomond, which though far below, is seen to more advantage, because deprived of its lumpiness, than in any other aspect. The whole district is as fully wooded as perhaps is desirable; and the copse has been sprinkled with unusual liberality higher up the hills than I can recollect to have seen it. I was alarmed by observing a great collection of sawn wood, and of large cut forest trees; because seeing no new plantations or enclosures, and recollecting that insolvency is essential to a Scotch laird, I anticipated that next time I was here there would not be an old stem left, if there was a sawmill. But I found that there was not, and that this was a depot of wood cut about Taymouth, and on its way to the Clyde. The whole sides of the hills are engraved by torrents, all rushing to contribute their mites to the treasury of Loch Lomond. The day was cloudy but fair, and the tops of all the hills, though sunless, were quite clear. There are a few patches of farming, which, by contrast, rather improve the picturesque sublimity of a valley in which there is nothing soft except the surface of the lake, and the young leaves.

About eight miles above this I saw a large rock, which had plainly fallen from a hill behind, standing by itself about 100 yards off the road, with a wooden door placed in its front. I waited till the carriage came up and asked the driver what it was, who said it was a church. We sent to a house about half a mile back for the key, when it was all explained. It is not a church, but a pulpit. The place is in the parish of Arrochar, but far from the kirk. So the people have made a very striking kirk of their own. This stone seemed to be about as large as a three-storied house. I took it to be about 40 feet high by 40 wide, except towards the top, where it rounds off, thus —

It is one single stone, and stands quite alone. Its top is covered with growing heather. The whole end where the door is, is perfectly smooth, a face of clear whin. And this end is not quite perpendicular, only because it projects a little forward. It is called the Bull Stone, from a tradition that it was shaken and dislodged from its original position by two bulls when they were fighting.

Well, as the movable wooden pulpit which is usual at field preachings would have but a poor chance amidst these rocky and shivered solitudes, they have picked and blasted an excellent covered rostrum out of the solid stone. The hole inside is about 8 feet high, 6 feet wide, and 5 deep. There are ten rude stone steps up to it. A wooden bench is fixed in the back part, the door is cut across into two divisions, and during service the lower division is kept shut, and a movable desk being hooked upon it, the minister is seen about 16 feet above the ground, exactly as in an ordinary pulpit, except that he is closed in on the sides and overhead. There is room for one elder, or any other of the aristocracy, on the bench on each side of the preacher. The congregation sits (if it chooses to sit) on rows of seats fronting the pulpit, these seats being made of lines of low dry stone wall, cushioned with turf. Humble as all this is, it is not too humble for charity. We found two ladles under the bench. I put the whole silver I had into them. It was only a sixpence for each. But no one can give more than he has. Paper would have rotted before the next angel visit.

I cordially agreed with Graham Maitland, when she said that she would like to hear Guthrie preach from that pulpit. Now that Chalmers, who is incomparably his superior in knowledge and in genious, is on the wane, Guthrie is our greatest preacher, and though never courting vulgar popularity by fanaticism or any other unbecoming art, and always observing good sense and good taste, he is pre-eminently the orator of the poor. It would indeed be glorious to hear him under the inspiration of this scene; the dark and pinnacled hills all around; the lake, scarcely rippling, in front, the remnant of Presbyterian mountaineers under the open sky, and he addressing them from his living rock, amidst the very haunts where their forefathers bled, in order that they might hear the same doctrines, preached in the same forms! If Guthrie will preach this sermon, I shall willingly go all the way from Edinburgh to hear it. I think I see the tall dark man, with his singularly graceful action, and hear the full sonorous voice, and the strong natural eloquence, all applied with simplicity, assuredness and success, to soothe and elevate the poor by all the hopes and comforts which they peculiarly require.

Garscube, Tuesday Night, 25th April 1843. — We came here today, through wind and rain, from Tarbet. I have been invited to this hospitable house for above thirty years, but never made it out till now. A very comfortable place, with the air and the reality of luxury, in everything about it. Considering the odious manufacturing country that surrounds it, its principal excellence is its singular seclusion within the dressed ground of the place. A stranger could never suspect while admiring its trees, beautiful grass, well-kept walks, its garden, stream, and mansion-house, that if he ventured to raise his head above the slopes that enclose him, he would see groves of chimneys, the obelisks of manufacturers, polluting the atmosphere on every side.

Bonaly, 3d May 1843. — Meadowbank and I left Garscube on the morning of Wednesday the 26th of April, and processed into Glasgow. Whether it was our error or theirs I do not know, but the magistrates and we took different roads, and for about half an hour we chased each other, to the great diversion of the people. We had our public dinner on that day, and were quiet, though not absolutely solitary, every day afterwards. On Saturday evening I came to Edinburgh, and went back on Monday morning.

There were 82 indictments and 142 prisoners. Some of these cases were so long, that if they had all gone on, they could not have been disposed of till the end of this week. But a doubt occurred about the citations of about twenty of the longest of them, which prevented these being proceeded with, and it has had a similar effect at Perth. This misfortune, for it is wrong not to dispose of all the business, and it generally recurs at some less convenient season, liberated us suddenly yesterday at two, and at five we were in Edinburgh.

There was one capital sentence, a murderer's, a brute, who after fatiguing by beating his half-drunk wife, at last sharpened a knife on the hearthstone, and stabbed her, all because she would not give him breakfast, which his blows made her incapable of doing, but which was done for her by another woman. She was an intolerable wife, insomuch that he had often said that "one of us would certainly swing for the other." But they had gone out this morning about nine on good terms, and had returned in about an hour, both more than stupefied than excited by whisky; and after taking all his blows without any other resistance than an appeal to "Charley, dear." the wretched woman was bled to death by a fierce cut of the femoral artery, on no other provocation than that of being disabled by his violence from feeding the beast with her own hands. This scene occurred on a Sunday; a day sacred, with a part of our population, to whisky and brutality. The convict's name was Charles Mackay.

There was also the case of a woman accused of murdering her husband, but it was one of the twenty, and did not come on. It will be a famous case in its day, however. She first committed the capital offence of giving her husband a dose of arsenic, which very nearly killed him, but he survived it. Thinking (truly) that it was her unskilfulness in administering that made this dose fail, she resolved to improve herself by a little practice, and then to renew the attempt. She therefore experimented upon a neighbour, whom she killed. And having now ascertained how to proceed, she gave another dose to her spouse, and killed him too. She was indicted for the two

119

murders and the abortive administration, an awkward accumulation of charges. It being in her case that the motion to put off all trials was made, she was brought to the bar; and, whether it was fancy or not, struck me as having a very singular expression. She was little, apparently middle-aged, modest and gentle-looking, with firm-set lips, a pale countenance, and suspicious restless eyes. Her name is Mary Macfarlane or Taylor.

A band of five horrible women, — real Glasgow faggots, — incorrigible devils, were sent to Botany in a batch, for a ferocious robbery, committed on a decent stranger they had inveigled into their den. I was greatly diverted by overhearing the account which one of them gave, in a soliloquy, of her learned judges, as she was leaving the bar, "Twa d____d auld grey-headed blackguards! They gie us plenty o' their law, but deevilish little joostice!"

My books were the 156th No. of the *Edinburgh Review,* and Allan Cunningham's life of Sir David Wilkie. The last is made dull by sheer protraction. Instead of three large volumes, one moderate one would have been enough. Wilkie seems to have been a modest, amiable, industrious, and contented man, but without much originality or strength of mind. His life does not impress me with a favourable idea of the position even of a successful artist in this country. In Wilkie's case it produced little money and constant anxiety about patronage.

WEST CIRCUIT

Rothesay, Sunday Night, 10th September 1843. — My two daughters, Elizabeth and Mrs. Stewart, and I, left Edinburgh yesterday by the one o'clock train, and were in Glasgow before three. At four we left Glasgow by the train, and got to Greenock by five, and then, embarking in a steamer, were here by seven.

I never was at this famed place before, or indeed below Dunoon, except crossing from Ardrossan to Largs. It far exceeds all my expectations.

There could not possibly have been a more perfect evening. Such a September, so far as it has yet gone, has rarely been seen or felt in Scotland. The temperature was about 70 in the shade, which, at this season, implies a cloudless sky. The Clyde was glorious! Whether is it the bright waters of the Firth, or the dark masses of the Argyleshire hills, or the bays and the promontories, or the long lochs and the islands, or the holiday gaiety of little sea towns devoted to idleness and enjoyment, or all of them, that constitute the peculiar charm of all this district? Before our voyage was over, the southern sides of the Argyle mountains were in the shade, the glow of the sunset was fading even from the opposite shores of Renfrew and Ayr; and at last the moon, nearly full, had quenched the few remaining streaks of day, and was shedding its magical lustre over this beautiful bay and its delightful little town. Our landing, with the people lounging under the mitigated air, and the lights in the semi-circle of windows, was striking and pleasing. Henry Davidson (who was waiting for us) and I, walked along the beach for nearly an hour before retiring to rest, and indeed even after the night-shirt was on, it was not easy to refrain from taking always one other gaze at the trembling water, the bright houses, and the silent masses of the hills.

Last night the whole population was abroad. This was not quite so good a day, being grave, hazy, and pensive, but still it has been warm, calm, and pleasing. But, being Sunday, the population has been all dead. I had always heard that a smile upon the Lord's day was a sin in Rothesay, and now I have found it to be so. The landlord and landlady of this public inn (no less than "The Bute Arms"), refused to let Davidson and his brother have their dinner in the house two years ago, because it was Sunday. They were driven into a temperance coffee-house, where their stomachs were filled with solids; but not a drop of wine were they allowed even to bring in, and they only got it by the good nature of a compassionate apothecary, who sent them in a bottle of sherry, wrapped up and labelled, with all the laboratory marks, as Bitters. Last night I said I wanted to see the ruins of the castle this morning. "No power on earth will get you in to-morrow, it's Sunday." I then asked if the garden of Mount Stuart was shown. "Oh, to everybody, my lord, but not upon Sunday." And conformably to this mode of making Sunday amiable, except on the way to and from the Established Church, and the Free Church, and the Seceders, the people have been literally dead. Not a foot has been heard on the pavement, no working man's dusty skin has been refreshed in the pure sea, no boat has skimmed from the shore, no eye has performed the pious homage of raising itself to observe glories which God does not veil upon Sunday.

However, Davidson and I contrived to get a car, and to give ourselves a general notion of Bute, the Montpellier of Scotland. We first went to Mount Stuart. No admission to the garden. We strolled through some part of the grounds, but thought little of them, possibly because we were angry. If I had been autocrat of Bute, I would have erected my castle at this (the Rothesay) end of the island. But every station near any part of its shores is good.

We then drove to Kingarth — a mere name, with two or three cot houses, an inn, and a church, most beautifully situated, so as to look upon the sea on both sides of the island, at least by going a very few paces.

After driving a few miles homeward by the inland road, we left the car, and walked along a succession of heights, to the top of the highest ground in the island; spelt "Ben Varogen" by MacCulloch, but pronounced by the natives "Ba-rone", leaving out the Ben. I should doubt its being higher than Arthur Seat. Yet MacCulloch says, "Arran is here a peculiarly fine object, the whole of its mountain district being displayed in a magnificent manner, and conveying a more perfect idea of the grandeur of this tract than can be obtained from any other position." I suppose this means that a better idea of the grandeur of this district is to be obtained from Barone than from Goatfell. This is an example of the different eyes, though in the same head, with which it is possible to see things in different states; a good or a bad day, good or bad humour, fatigue or strength, patience or impatience, make all the odds in the world; insomuch that they can render the prospect from Barone as magnificent as that from Goatfell. We did not see it well, because the extreme distances were invisible, and nothing even of Arran was to be seen except a part of its dim ghost. But the whole of Bute, and all the near seas and lands, were within our view; and occasional abatings of the warm haze, aided by some bright streaks, disclosed enough of the distance to show that under a clearer sun the unobstructed panorama must be both beautiful and grand. The interior of this island, however, is paltry. Its cultivation is the best of it. The portions still in a state of nature consist of poor, flattish heath, and of the four or five fresh-water lochs, none have any beauty except Loch Fad, and it not much. The only striking feature in the internal scenery is this town of Rothesay, which lies delightfully between two little hills, with its bay, round which it is extending its arms in front. The people still try to make a sight of Kean's cottage, merely because it was lived in by that ranting liquor-loving player, and seemed surprised that we would not go to look at it.

On the whole, this famous Bute is plainly worthy of its reputation. For though there did not seem to me to be a single inland spot which seemed to say, "Place a cottage here," there was no part of the shore which did not give such an invitation. The sea, and the absence of great heights, account, I suppose, for the undoubted softness of the climate. But it is this town, with its quiet bay, its Argyle hills, its idle holiday population, its active steamers landing and removing sight-seeing crowds, that is the real charm of the island.

Rothesay, Monday, 9 A.M., 11th September 1843. — We have been this morning to the castle. I have been wrong in calling Kilchurn the largest of our Scotch castles in ruin. Robert Bruce's, at Rothesay, is a much larger, and must have been a noble edifice, but its being placed where it is seems odd, for it has no natural defences of rock or of situation. It was cleared out about twenty-six years ago, and though not at all as it ought to be, is in a far better condition than most of our ruins. It will crumble, however, sooner than it need do, under the mass of universal ivy which is encouraged to eat into its bones.

A good day for our sail through the Kyles, clouds and sunshine playing on all the hills. But the wind is far too high for the chyle of my stomach.

Ardpatrick, Tuesday Morning, 12th September 1843. — We lingered about Rothesay yesterday till near twelve, sauntering up its heights, and round its bay. It is really beautiful; and at this season, on a fine day, enjoyment seems to be the sole business of the inhabitants. Going in cars, boating, sitting on the rocks or at open windows, bathing, sewing or reading on the shore, looking through telescopes, or basking in luxurious idleness, — these are the occupations of a community composed of strangers who resort there for pleasure, and of natives who let their houses to them. The bathing is conducted on the primaeval and innocent principle of seeing no difference between water and air, and of living with the same freedom in both. It is more socially done than at Ardrossan, where the ladies come forth in their marine robes one by one; whereas at Rothesay I counted a single group of about forty, all in company, and indeed in contact, and very merry. And it wants the profligacy of Portobello, where men intermix, with an obvious but disregarded sense of its impropriety; while at Rothesay such is the universal simplicity that there is no consciousness whatever that, in point of decency, there is any difference between wet clothes and dry, or even between clothes and no clothes. Men and women, ladies and gentlemen, proceed with their respective visits to the sea, close together, and apparently even in arranged parties, with exactly the same ease and absence of ceremony that they would feel in walking and conversing together in a ball-room. I had been told that this was always the case at Rothesay, and it did not require more than a few hours of one warm day to show that the report was correct. A single fact indeed attests it. The edge of the bay is lined for at least half a mile by dwelling-houses standing close together. These houses are not 100 feet from the water, and all the bathing is in front of them; yet, except one private one, there is not a single bathing-machine or covered bathing-house of any kind in the whole place. So simple is the purity of this little island; it refines even strangers who come upon it from the mainland.

Davidson returned to Dunoon, where he is living with his brother Archibald, and the rest of us embarked in the Inveraray steamer about twelve. We reached East Tarbert about three, took a car across the mile to West Tarbert, got on board the Islay steamer there, sailed down Loch Tarbert, and were landed in about an hour at this house, presently inhabited by the Campbells of Kilberry, to whom we are consigned on a visit of three days.

The whole journey from Rothesay to this was new to me, and aided by novelty, and by a calm, warm, splendid day, it was most delightful.

The chief beauty of the sea being the land, the narrower the sea the better. Therefore there can be few better sails than round Bute. In themselves, most of the individual features are insignificant, but it is pleasant to sail through comfortable-looking Highland farms, almost within the sound of the sickle, and within hand-shaking of the people on the shore. The Kyles proper are far more rugged and picturesque, and get so narrow and so involved in rocks, that it is frequently a puzzle to find out where we are to thread next.

But Tarbert! East Tarbert! How is it that I had never even heard of that curious little bay? I can't recollect that I ever saw it mentioned in any tour. I was never more surprised than in sailing into that quiet sort of a natural wet dock, apparently not containing above 10 or 20 acres. There it lay, calm and silvery, deeply set all round, except at the narrow entrance, in ridgy hills of hard rock; a curve of about 20 or 30 small houses drawn round the upper end, all comfortable looking, and, except three houses and seven hovels, all bright with fresh whitewash; a great number of herring-boats floating at anchor, with their brown tanned sails hanging to dry; the ruins of an old castle standing on a rocky knoll at the left side of the entrance, and the whole scene of peaceful and secluded industry crowned by a respectable church, which looks down on it from a little eminence behind the rim of habitation, — a striking and beautiful spot like a scene from a theatre.

Nor had I ever heard Loch Tarbert praised, or even talked of. Nevertheless, many a worse has excited many a pen and many a pencil. It is about 10 or 12 miles long, perfectly straight, about a mile wide or less on an average, lined by black, rocky, but not very high, hills, very jagged along its whole edges by rough promontories, which, however, are softened occasionally by patches of cultivation; a very picturesque piece of water.

Inverary, Sunday Morning, 17th September 1843. — We remained at Ardpatrick all Tuesday, Wednesday and Thursday. During these days we drove and boated, and ate oatcakes, and drank whisky, and slept, and were very kindly treated, and by no means stinted in sleep. The weather was beautiful, both under the sun and under the moon. My chief pleasure was in getting up any knoll from which I could see the heights of Jura. Our host's property of Kilberry extends from the sea opposite Islay on the west, to Loch Tarbert on the east, about 7 or 10 miles or so in all. It is at present mansionless, and he must build. Loch Tarbert tempts him by the finest possible sites, on a range of rocky hills, covered with wood and rattling with burns, and rich in little haughs and knolls, all washed by the loch. Yet though he admits that that is infinitely the most convenient situation, he is nearly resolved to set himself down on his western extremity, which consists of a bare, flat, featureless, half-reclaimed moor, made only the uglier by some turnips and barley. And why? Because it was the family place! That is because some savages practised rapine there 550 years ago, and built what they called a castle and a religious house; of neither of which does a single organised fragment now remain. I scarcely know a greater sacrifice of sense of folly.

On Friday (15th) at about one we came away in his carriage to East Tarbert, thus seeing the loch by land as we had formerly done by water. And we got another visit to the village. I went up to the castle, which must anciently have been a very large stronghold. There were about 200 boats in the bay, with their tanned hanging sails. And I observed, which I had not noticed before, that the bay, small though it be, has three islands, one of them cased in masonry, about 30 feet square and flat on the top, and used for hanging nets upon over rude screens. It is really a delightful nook. But the Sheriff tells me that it is a profligate place. Nonsense! I don't believe it. The brawls, which are his only facts, must proceed from the stranger fishers who nestle in it. I won't believe anything bad of the natives of that little Virgilian port.

This Sheriff — a worthy, ugly, sensible, cart-horse of a man, hideously ugly and with a coarse, high-keyed idiotical voice, at which the very stots stare. Sir Walter Scott once amazed us all by taking this strange, good, and most illiterate creature to Paris with him, — the most incomprehensible fact in the history of either man. It is commonly accounted for by ascribing it to Scott's great neighbourly kindness, but many of the anecdotes brought back by the novelist made it plain that his chief enjoyment consisted in observing the effect of foreign things on his rustic and simple associate, who seems to have glowered and munched, and to have been free in all quarters, with what he meant to be French, and to have rolled his large white eyes, and to have made "unwieldy mirth", in all sorts of ways, to the poet's entire satisfaction. An English lady, who had just arrived in Scotland, with her head full of enthusiasm about everything Scotch, had the good luck to be seated at Abbotsford next R———. She happened to ask him the name of the stream she had seen joining the Tweed. "It was the Ga-a-ala Ma-a-dam." "The Gala! Well, I am so delighted at that! Because I know the song of 'The Braw (brae) lads of Gala (Gay-la) Water', and I should so like to see one of them." "Ou! joost lok at me, Madam; a'm ane o' them masel'". Nevertheless, there cannot be a worthier or more sensible man.

We had got horses and an open carriage (for this Circuit I had no carriage of my own — it is an incumbrance in this district) sent from Ardrishaig to Tarbert, and we went along the western shore of Loch Fyne to Inveraray, which we reached about nine at night. Knowing that it would be under cloud of night that I would enter, I had dispensed with the attendance of the provost and his poor tail.

The stage from Tarbert to Ardrishaig was the only one that was new to me. And it is extremely beautiful, and would be so even without the aid of such an evening as we had — quite calm, the water and the sky contending in unbroken blueness, and the air so soft that it was a luxury to let the hands and face bathe themselves in it. I left the carriage and took a look of the new house of Barmore. It is Playfair's work, and seemed worthy of its author. The place, too, is beautiful. But I hope that it is not true that the house cost about £30,000, and that, after selling an estate to pay it, the laird has only about £3000 a year left. Probably, however, it is true, because a proprietor ruining himself by too large a mansion-house is quite conformable to the Scotch practice. Malcolm of Poltalloch, the Croesus of Argyle, has built a grand hotel at Ardrishaig, of which the ostensible landlord is only his manager. Both this village and Lochgilphead (within a mile of it) looked most attractive, for they were glittering in sunshine.

The moon was rising over Inveraray as we approached it.

We had only three trifles to dispose of in Court yesterday. The last trial failed by a juror's taking a fit in the box while they were considering their verdict, and the rest of the jury having been dismissed, as this was the only remaining case, the trial could not be begun again.

At dinner we had a grand dessert of unripe fruit, brought for the occasion from Glasgow, and no herrings, though they were never more plentiful or better. But I never come to Argyle without seeing that a herring has no honour in its own country.

Strachur, Monday Night, 18th September 1843. — I went to church at Inveraray yesterday, and had another opiate from the same preacher as last April. The Provost and the Sheriff of Bute are both keen Free Churchmen, and were very averse to countenance the Establishment, and were only reconciled by my assuring them that they could only be held to attend officially, which inferred no homologation. But then they could not brook one of the two ministers, who was a rat, and ought to have gone out. They were told that he was from home. So they girt up their loins and processed, and after being fixed in the pew, their friend the rat mounted the pulpit.

After church I took a boat and came here. The day was bad.

This day has been better, but not very good, and so I only loitered about the shore throughout the forenoon. In the evening, people are pretty independent of weather wherever Lord Murray is the landlord.

We go to-morrow by Dunoon to Glasgow.

Glasgow, Tuesday Night, 19th September 1843. — We left Strachur (an open carriage and horses sent from Inverary) to-day about nine, and reached Dunoon about one. The day was excellent. But no sun can make Loch Eck smile. Narrow, straight, and islandless, its unvarying form is seen at once, almost from end to end, without a single village, and with very few houses, and little culture; it is never enlivened by sound, and its dead surface is rarely broken by an oar or a sail. The large and heavy mountains that line it on both sides have one-half of it generally in shade, and even when the sun is in the meridian, depth makes its water dark. It is beautiful, but sad.

We went to Archibald Davidson's, who is living at Dunoon, and remained there till half-past four, when we crossed to Greenock, and were here by the railway before seven.

I heard at Dunoon, for the first time, of the sudden death of George Houston, an irrecoverable blow to his family, of which he was the delight, and the last direct branch. I can scarcely recollect any stroke more utterly crushing than the one that has been inflicted by the early and unexpected removal of this excellent young man.

Bonaly, Sunday Night, 1st October 1843. — I found Moncreiff and two of his daughters in Glasgow on the 19th of September. Next morning we had our usual procession to Court, where 69 cases kept us till the evening of Wednesday the 27th. The 24th being a Sunday, I came here on Saturday evening, and was in Court again on Monday, a few minutes after ten.

When here, I received intimation of the death of my old friend, George Joseph Bell, Clark of Session, and Professor of Scotch Law, and destined to be known to posterity as the author of the book on Bankruptcy. His death was not to be regretted, — old and blind, poor, and getting poorer, and never forgetting the disgraceful treatment which excluded him from the Bench because he would not be dishonest, life for him had lost most of its attractions. There could not possibly be a better man, and he is the greatest legal writer in Scotland next to Stair. It is not, perhaps, too much to say that his work is the greatest practical book on Mercantile Jurisprudence that has been produced in modern times.

None of our cases were of any novelty or importance. An able doctor of medicine, a clever writer in *Blackwood's Magazine,* was transported for embezzlement, and for composing and sending a threatening letter. I was shown (after the case was over) another epistle from the same powerful blackguard to his victim, in which he intimates that at his trial he has nothing to do but plead insanity. I have little doubt that, at present, when the benevolent towards criminals have succeeded in raising a cry against punishing any cuplrit who had, or says that he had, a crotchet which led him to commit his offence (which they call by some technical name), there are very few acts of criminal malice that are not helped on by the idea that this defence may be successful in the time of need.

In another case an honest-looking, generous-hearted Irish lad moved me greatly be repeating, and with equal eloquence and feeling, the proposal of MacCombich in the Court at Carlisle, that they would let him have his head cut off instead of Vich Ian Vohr. He and several of his countrymen were accused of aggravated housebreaking. He was acquitted, but his brother was convicted, on which he entreated, with great simplicity and earnestness, that he might be allowed to be transported in his brother's place. He was grieved and shocked when told that this was impossible, and after a parting at the bar, very painful to see, they were separated, probably for ever; and for the moment at least he by far the most severely punished of the two. The misfortune is, that, though attached to his brother, his only attachment to others was to their property.

There has been a strong desire for years past to avoid the necessity of transportation by trying long imprisonments in properly regulated prisons, and the whole system and apparatus of prison discipline in Scotland has been changed in order to give this benevolent experiment fair play. I grieve to say that as yet the results are not encouraging. Those who have come out of an eighteen months' or two years' confinement seem to revert to crime, at least to crimes against property, as easily as if nothing had ever been done to reform or to frighten them. We had about twenty of them this Circuit at Glasgow alone! I don't see how it can be otherwise so long as convicts are turned out after their term is over, without money, or character, or master. The proposal now is to let them emigrate at the public expense. And I am clear for getting them out of this country in as great numbers as possible. But it may be easily foreseen that even this voluntary emigration won't tempt those who have once fairly tasted the sweets of a life of thieving. Every other criminal, except probably a coiner and a preacher, there may be hope of, and possibly even of a first thief. But after a second conviction shows that stealing has become a trade, be he or she old, middle-aged, or young, I don't at present believe that reformation is possible. Simply because the sport of thieving in its various forms, is the most irresistible of all pastimes. What have the moors equal to it? No licence to pay for, no permission to ask, no close time, total idleness, great risk, frequent success, constant excitement, a community of their own, the whole public their preserve, the delight of eluding the law, and the many chances of escape even after being caught trespassing. If anything could be required to whet the appetite for this game, it would be its contrast with the dulness of a good prison recently left. I hope I'm wrong, but if there be a thoroughly reformed, twice-converted thief, I would rather pay a shilling to see him than to see any other wonder in any living show.

Our Advocate-Depute was Mark Napier, the biographer of the discoverer of the logarithms, and author of other good Scotch works. He is better known as an author than as a counsel, but he is a sensible industrious, amiable man, and

Moncreiff and I agreed that we had never seen the business better done.

I came here on Thursday (28th) forenoon, somewhat stricken with cold, and have been mostly in bed till now.

I read nothing except some articles in the new *Quarterly*.

It will be long before I can cease wondering at the folly of the Butes in not removing Rothesay when this was possible, and laying out their money, and such taste as they had, upon a place near its present site. They would have had finer prospects, an historical ruin, better shelter, and might have brought Loch Fad and some others within their grounds. At present the lochs are lost.

There is a passage, I think, in one of Scott's novels in which he makes somebody, who is lamenting the encroachments of civilisation on Highland solitudes say, but only as an extreme result, that he should not wonder if the mail-coach horn should one day be heard in Glencoe. Alas, alas! it has been heard all this summer. A romantic tourist pinched for time can now be hurried from Fort William to Edinburgh in one hot long day. A coach left Fort William all this season at about six in the morning, and after blowing away to Ballachulish, up Glencoe to Kingshouse, and from thence to Tyndrum, and down Glenfalloch to Tarbet, which it reached about two, its passengers could get into a steamer there and reach Glasgow in time for the five o'clock train, which landed them at Edinburgh about seven. Spirits of Fingal and of Rob Roy! what say ye to this?

GLASGOW CIRCUIT
1844

Bonaly, 8th January 1844. — I left Edinburgh by the half-past seven o'clock train on Tuesday last, the 2d, and was in time for the Winter Circuit procession at ten. Medwyn was my colleague. The job lasted till Saturday evening the 6th, sitting generally from nine till about eight. There were 64 cases, and we left not one untried that the prosecutor could proceed with.

My strolls, whether before breakfast or after dinner, being all in the dark and generally under heavy rain, I saw nothing.

The cases were a mass of commonplace trash.

It seems to me to augur worse and worse for the effect of long imprisonments. We had about twelve thieves, all of whom had been imprisoned by the Court of Justiciary for at least one year, and several more on whom the benevolence of long and religious incarceration had been wasted by Sheriffs. I suppose that, including the last Spring and Autumn Circuits in Glasgow. I have seen about fifty such cases in the last ten months. One handsome-looking young woman, called Mary Boyle, had been in the Penitentiary in Perth, the very school of penal virtue, and had come out with a great character, a thoroughly reformed creature, their best swatch. Well, after being a month free, and employed, she engages in a daring burglary with a gang of male villains; and then on being sentenced to transportation threw off in an instant the decorous air which had made people first doubt the evidence, and then pity her, and broke out into a paroxysm of the most cordial fury I ever saw at the bar; cursing prosecutor, judges, jury, her own counsel, and all concerned, in the coarsest terms, and in the manner of the best brimstone, and dealing effective blows on all the enemies within her reach, not omitting even the poor macer, who had nothing to do with it. But crime — nay, the particular sort of it — runs in families like everything else, and this lady belongs to a race of thieves. She has a father and mother and two brothers or sisters already in Australia, and the only two that remain have already gone through what seems to be the first stage of the transporting process — a short imprisonment. It is to be hoped that the strength of the hereditary tendency saves the reputation of Perth.

I was stuck with two copies of the printed indictments which had been served on two lads, incorrigible and now transported thieves. One of them was covered with verse, partly from Burns, and partly original, the last better than any jail verse I ever saw, all about his sad separation from "Betsy". The other was adorned by the pencil, the drawings (by quill) describing the artist's own feats, particularly the one which, added to many others, was taken advantage of to get him out of the country, picking the pocket of a tall gentleman whose nose was in the skies, while the boy and his comrades were dealing with the tails of his coat. It was a very spirited sketch.

A Lanarkshire Justice of Peace was examined in two cases of bigamy, who admitted that he carried on a sort of trade of receiving declarations of marriage, for which he was paid by half-crowns, which failing, by drams, and that he believed that he might have done so 100 times in one year. We, as recommended by the jury, referred his case to the Lord Advocate, who happened to be in Glasgow, and next day a register, which the Justice stated that he had kept, was got, from which it appeared that in the last ten years he had married above 1200 pairs! Whether he will be allowed to marry any more or not will not be seen. Meanwhile his name is Hugh ——, and such a number or irregular marriages, not over all Scotland, but in one place and by one man, is a curious fact in reference to the law, and to the habits of the people of Scotland.

David Mure (Caldwell) was our Public Accuser; a most excellent youth, well educated, judicious, gentle without weakness, and firm without any intemperance, incapable of being misled by professional keenness into any want of candour, and, in feelings as well as manners, a gentleman. He is one of the Tories at our Bar who ought to have been a Whig. He is one in reality, although he does not know it.

Thank God, no other Court will ever be held in the abominable structure which, for above thirty years, has disgraced Glasgow, and impeded the administration of justice, to say nothing of its smiting judges, who were exposed to its bitterest gale, with lumbago, sciatica, and all manner of colds. The wit of no devil could devise a more atrocious composition. Posterity will scarcely believe that so recently as about the year 1810, a large sum was expended in a great city on a Courthouse so constructed that the judges sat (literally) on top of a staircase, and separated from the street only by a folding door, that their only room for robing or taking refreshment was a closely adjoining water-closet, that there was not a single apartment of any kind for cousel, or anybody, except two, that were got for the occasion each Circuit, one for the jury to be enclosed in, and one of about 15 feet square, for as many of perhaps 1000 witnesses as could be squeezed into it without respect to age, sex, or station, and that for all concerned, except judges, and witnesses, and prisoners, that is, for counsel, agents, jurymen, and mob coming and going, there was only one door, and it placed at the greatest attainable distance from the greatest number of people. This cursed door made the Court just a street. There was a constant stream of jostling comers in and goers out, whose noise, from tongue and from feet, the thumbscrew itself could not have checked. The court is still to be held in the same place, but totally changed in all its arrangements. How these will turn out will be seen in September. A good Court-room must have innumerable apartments close at hand, a separate place, and each place with a separate access, for each class of the members of the Court, judges, counsel, agents, jurors, witnesses, and distinguished spectators, and though there ought to be due and comfortable accommodation for the public, it is an error to suppose that it is necessary to admit the whole public at once.

Of all the judicial spectators in Scotland, those of Glasgow are the worst. They are the least attentive, and by far the most vulgar. But I observe that the attention is always in proportion to the facility of hearing.

The only bad fact that I know for the new Court is, that John Hope, has taken the chief charge of the plan, and declares it to be perfect.

NORTH CIRCUIT

Dunkeld, Monday, 15th April 1844. Night. — North again, after two years' interval. Creeffy is to be my colleague; my daughter Elizabeth, and my niece Mary Fullerton, my companions.

Meaning to proceed the whole way by the ordinary old road, I can have nothing to say.

We left Edinburgh this morning at eight, and were here by four. Rain, of course, over Kinross-shire, but everywhere else, a respectable Scotch Spring day.

Dunkeld never looks so well as in the evening, and particularly in its approach from the south; it was extremely beautiful to-day. Spring is much more advanced here than it is about Edinburgh, and there are few places where spring is more pleasingly marked. The gardens, and villas, and cottages, and cultivated haughs, for about two miles down the Tay, were all in the most perfect order, dry, weeded and sown; and, by bursting larches, fresh green hedges, and daffodils, made delightful to old and to young.

I made an inward vow last time I was here never again to degrade myself by entering the grounds of Dunkeld, as if I were a maniac and his keeper. But the girls having never seen the place, I was obliged to go through the ceremonies for their sakes. The velvet walk up the river is certainly very fine. We went into the cathedral, which I had not done for many years. Its keeping — absolutely within the ducal shrubbery — is most disgraceful. Letting one end of it be made into the parish church, and the other into the parish burying-ground, is scandalous, but perfectly natural, for it saves the heritors from providing other accommodation. The worthy lady who showed the cathedral apologised by saying that it had always been so — at least ever since the Reformation. Dunkeld having been one of the Catholic religious edifices, for the cleansing of which from all vestiges of popery there was a special order, this is possibly true. But what defence is it to dukes who can afford to give £5000 a year of their estate to the deer?

Kingussie, Tuesday, 16th April 1844, Night. — Left Dunkeld this morning at ten, and reached this at seven.

A day of dull leaden clouds, but calm and dry.

We walked through most of the Pass, and gave nearly an hour to the Falls of the Bruar. These falls were beautiful, even though not yet embowered by Burns's foliage. The ravines through which the water tumbles are so narrow in proportion to the size of the stream, that there can never be any apparent deficiency of water.

It was (at least in this late spring) a month too soon for the Pass. The whole valley from Dunkeld to Blair loses half its glories in being leafless. And of all trees the birch, especially when seen in masses, on a slope, from the whiteness of its stem, reminds us the most of the absence of its leaves. Some of the hillsides looked, to-day, as if they had been stuck full of white-painted poles. There was very little of a spring feeling either on branches or on fields, or in the air. A thrush — the only bird that we heard — attempting a note, struck us all. Drumochter was heavy with clouds, and with innumerable patches of snow. But after getting a little down Speyward descent, we came again to a milder and clearer region. My admiration of this whole, long solitary track, especially after actually reaching the Spey, and returning to rock and birch, increases every time I see it.

My old friend the inn of Pitmain I found converted into a farmhouse, and we are now in the Gordon Arms Hotel at Kingussie, with the loudest bells and the strongest teethed rats I have ever encountered. Old Pitmain! an abominable hostel, but it served the public, I suppose, at least one hundred years, and all this time had received that sort of welcome which is given by a vessel in distress to the only port it has repair to. In the days in which the traveller had to pass two nights on the road between Edinburgh and Inverness, even when going by the fastest public coach, Pitmain was his second house of refuge. And what a scene! when the enormous vehicle disgorged a cargo of beasts, clean and unclean, greater than what loaded the ark, and, knowing by experience the advantage of first possession, every monster rushed in and seized whatever he could lay his claws upon — meat, drink, the seat next the fire, the best room, the best bed — and awkwardness or timidity were left to shiver or starve! The moment of the arrival was quite well known, yet the savages of the house, partly from Sawney's natural want of tidiness, and partly from knowing that they had the defenceless wretches in their power, never had anything ready or arranged, but considered the hubbub as showing the importance of the house. Yet the merriest night I ever had was there — with Macbean and Dr. Gordon — the evening before breakfast at the Bridge of Carr. It was on that night that an experienced quartermaster, who was missing at the public supper, was found to have secured himself a bed by having taken real, corporeal and actual possession of the first that came, drenched but undressed, and having thus appropriated the prize by spoiling it for anybody else, ate his morsel and drank his jorum as he lay in peace, leaving one dry and well-fed fellow-traveller, who had been sneering during his damp friend's cramming, to sleep on the floor.

Inverness, Thursday, 18th April 1844, Night. — We left Kingussie on Wednesday about ten; got to the Frasers at Laggan, four miles beyond Inverness, at five; dined there; and came here before twelve at night.

I have nothing more to say; for the course is unchanged, and I have said it all already. Yesterday was a beautiful day, more sunny than cloudy; rain we don't dream of; and the air was soft. And these Cairngorms! I got out of the chaise, without stopping it, by the (front) window, and sat (as I often do) for an hour or so, after leaving Aviemore, on the cap box, and gazed at them for the twentieth time in undiminished delight. There were parts of the road from which the whole plain between us and the base of the hills lay visibly below us. The larch was only in its brown, bud-bursting state; but its leaflessness left the heather visible, which, though not in flower, brightened the dark verdure of the Scotch fir. Through that sea of pines, the blue, full Spey was sweeping; and beyond stood that noble range of mountains, singularly marked by corries and valleys, variegated by streaks, and patches, and fields of snow, of all sizes, positions, and forms, all softening under a mild southern air, the unsnowed parts standing out in deeper darkness; the whole masses clear to their very summits, but hovered over by racks of gorgeous clouds, which seemed as if anxious to show that they could be as magnificent as the solid matter before them.

The prospect of the Moray Firth and the coast of Ross-shire, from the height between Inverness and Freeburn was as good as ill-placed but (thank God) ill-growing larches allow. It is a very fine scene. But I can't say that I discover the resemblance between it and any views I have ever seen of the Bay of Naples, with which the worthy people here are very apt to compare it. No two things can be less like, except that there's salmon in both. But every beautiful sea view in Scotland is said to be like the Bay of Naples. The Firth of Forth is, and the Firth of Clyde, and many parts of the Solway, and above all, Loch Lomond is. Except in climate some of them are perhaps better, but the habit of comparing them is mere homage to the fame of Naples.

There is a strange wild place called Glen Truim on the left hand (going north), between Dalwhinnie and Kingussie, the progress of which I have been marking since ever it began a few years ago. It is the work of a Major Macpherson, an Indian officer, I believe, who, no doubt from his having run about in a torn kilt here in his youth, has adventured on the rather bold attempt to make a habitable residence in apparently the most savage position of the whole strath. Everybody laughs at him, and he has certainly set his mansion too high; but since he has courage to begin, and to live there, I predict its one day being a fine and not uncomfortable highland place. It will depend entirely on the wood he will be able to coax into life.

Kilravock, Sunday, 21st April 1844, half-past 7 A.M. — We finished our insignificant dozen of cases on the evening of Friday the 19th.

Next morning (yesterday), Moncreiff and I went to inspect a road on the estate of Leys, in reference to a civil cause, and saw what is called "The Druidical Temple", said to be the most complete remains of one of these constructions in the north of Scotland. I never saw one anywhere (but I have not seen Stonehenge) so entire. It consists of the usual outer and inner circles of large stones. One of the outer stones is about 8 or 12 feet high; the rest are lower, but not perhaps less, for they are mostly large lumps. Both circles are nearly entire; and if the owner would only clean them, so as to let them be distinctly seen, they would be very striking; especially as their position on a knoll, with a very good prospect from it, is excellent. But they are half-buried in whins, and open to all cattle.

Moncreiff and his two daughters went yesterday to Fochabers. We came here.

I am sorry that I did not stop within two or three miles of this, and walk up to Dalcross — seemingly a good ruined castle — standing on a table-land eminence, with a good view of the Moray Firth. But laziness, or indifference at the moment, is the sin which besets some travellers, of which they are always sure to repent after it is too late.

After looking about this place, which has for fifteen years been tenanted by Mrs. Campbell and her daughter — English people — we were driven by Miss Campbell, a great equestrian in all forms, to Cawdor Castle, about two and a half miles off. It is a long time since I saw it. There is a deal of good wood, and everything about the place has a secluded rustic air. But the castle is the thing. And a strong, venerable castle it is, well situated, a little above the Cawdor, a respectable stream; and if living poverty of purse and of spirit had been kept away, time and Shakespeare would have dignified all about it, inside and out. But, O these miserable nobles! The edifice, though pretended to be still maintained as a place of residence, is all in the most humiliating condition of paltry disrepair. There are a number of curious, old, clumsy, carved stone chimney-pieces, and there was probably one in every room formerly. But the peer has repaired several of the apartments, among the rest the one which has the reputation of having had Duncan murdered in it. And such reparations! New floors — quite right. Cleaned walls — quite right. But such floors! and such cleaning! Fir deals ill-laid by the village carpenter; size by the village painter; furniture by the village upholsterer; the old chimney-pieces taken away, and bits of plank and plaster put into their places. Yes, the carved chimney-piece which saw Macbeth stab Duncan has been probably broken for a dyke and replaced by 1s. 6d. worth of ill-sawed larch and bad Cawdor plaster. The whole castle is in the same scandalous style of bad taste and beggarly penury. There is no Findhorn fishcurer or Nairn grocer who would not have done it better.

The parish church close by is one of the very best (outside) in Scotland. Part of it is plainly in its old state of Catholic village architecture. Corstorphine, however, is better.

We dined yesterday at this place, and are still here. I had been long wishing to see Kilravock, which I had never heard described except as an interesting old place; and I have not been disappointed.

The castle, as they call everything here, consists of a square tower about four centuries old, with the usual later, but still not very modern, additions; They all harmonise well enough; not the worse that the maker of each addition never thought whether it would harmonize or not, but left them all to make the most of it. The tower is perfect. High, massive, plain, no regular window in it, but only a few very little holes; a small round turret in a sort of half relief at the top of each corner, and a steep-roofed house on the summit.

All this is placed — not on a rock as I had been told — for there is no rock in the place, but on the edge of a bank about fifty or seventy feet above the river Nair, which flows through an unpicturesque valley below. It is a good position, and, seen from the valley, the building looks admirably. It is an excellent house inside, with no want of broad wooden stairs, queer closets, and old family pictures.

Close beside the house, at one end, there is a most beautiful flower-garden — unwalled, unhedged, but surrounded by a cheap trellis fence. The spaces for the flowers are cut in the usual way, and in all forms, out of the turf; and there is a good mixture of evergreens and trees. This garden, like everything else about the place, is in perfect keeping, and there are a number of very fine trees — walnut, chestnut, oak, etc. In an admirable wood of about eighty acres, full of heather and juniper, and undergrowth of all kinds, there are a number of the very finest Scotch firs I have ever seen. They are spread and tossed about in the branches like forest trees, and have the true, but rare, bright brown barks, on which the slanting rays of the evening sun were shining beautifully.

Altogether it is an interesting place, even as we saw it, nearly leafless. When the trees are out it must be excellent.

We have had the kindest possible reception, and passed a quiet but merry evening yesterday. When I observed that one and a half bottles of wine far more than sufficed for four ladies and three gentlemen, I could not help thinking of the very different days that the tower had seen. For it was at Kilravock, as old Henry Mackenzie, who was related to the family, used to tell, that a sort of household officer was kept, whose duty was to prevent the drunk guests from choking. Mackenzie was once at a festival there, towards the close of which the exhausted toppers sank gradually back and down on their chairs, till little of them was seen above the table except their noses; and at last they disappeared altogether, and fell on the floor. Those who were too far gone to rise lay still there from necessity; while those who, like the Man of Feeling, were glad of a pretence for escaping, fell into a doze from policy. While Mackenzie was in this state, he was alarmed by feeling a hand working about his throat, and called out. A voice answered, "Dinna be feared, sir; it's me." "And who the devil are you?" "A'm the lad that louses (looses) the neckcloths."

Fochabers, Sunday 21st April 1844, Night. — We left Kilravock to-day about half-past ten, and reached this by six; a beautiful day.

We first went to Forres, seventeen miles. Walked through

136

the silent city; went to the Pillar; called on the Tokes, who are at Colonel Fraser's villa — all at church, and the house without a servant; so, after loud and vain ringing, we pinned our cards to the door and retired.

I then fulfilled a vow I had often made, and often broken, never to be in this quarter without seeing Pluscarden. We went four miles round, and saw the abbey on our way to Elgin, by an excellent road.

It is a more paltry situation than most old religious houses, beside shabby hills — modern larch wood, no rock, and no water beyond a bad muddy rill.

But it is a most beautiful ruin, — not large, but well proportioned, and its whole original structure distinctly shown. Placed on a well-kept lawn, it would be an exquisite relic. The main square tower is mellowed by a reddish lichen which combines excellently with the fresh ivy. But this ivy, if not kept in order, will soon eat up the whole concern.

But what a mercy it is that Lord Fife became bankrupt some years ago! Long may he continue so! An old abbey still in adequate preservation may, innocently, and even with good taste, be kept up as a residence, if this be done properly. But this poor, insensible, ignorant wretch was making Pluscarden into a shooting-box! He had got a great part of it roofed and slated, and several portions cut into two stories, and new floored, and made comfortable with register stoves. The jambs for his kitchen range are put up. In another year the monster would have had sportsmen and lacqueys drinking and snoring and smoking in Pluscarden Abbey! But Providence interfered. It is in execrable taste, though not just so execrable, that he allowed a part of the abbey to be fitted up and used as a preaching-place. And since he made up his mind to do so, why could he not have got it done properly! Even the presence, nay, the being actually surrounded by, the pillars and arches, and tall windows of a beautiful Gothic building, cannot seduce a Scotch laird, even when still solvent, to abate his paltriness and abominations. The modern chapel, though used every Sunday, would be scunnered at by any congregation of pigs.

However, give the devil his due; he has done one thing well. He had given the use of this chapel as a relief to the parish of Elgin. The minister went out. But his lordship, who is tolerant of dissent, lets him and his people continue; and it is now a chapel of the Free Church.

We passed an hour amidst the ruins of Elgin. Since I was last there, the Woods and Forests have preserved two important fragments of the buildings by judicious, but rather smooth, under propping.

No epitaph for John Shanks yet. I believe I shall make and set up one myself.

I found the following epitaph to-day, which is new to me at least:-

Heir is the burial-place
Appointed for John Geddes, glover,
Burgess in Elgin, and Issobel
Mckeian, his spouse, and their
Relations.
This world is a cite
Ful of streets.
And Death is the mercat
That all men meets.
If lyfe were a thing
That monie could
Buy, the poor could
Not live, and the rich
Would not die.

On coming away I overheard Mary Fullerton saying, I thought to herself, "What a shame that these things" (old cathedrals, she meant) "should have been seen entire by people long ago and not by us." A just and natural remark. But I don't see how they could have been preserved IN ORDER, under Presbytery.

Our evening here has been distinguished by a most diverting theological discussion between her and Moncreiff. He is a stern Presbyterian, and a resolute adherent of the Free Church; she an Episcopalian and a Puseyite, and of course with no horror of Catholicism. The subjects handled were Puseyism and Episcopacy as against the Free and Presbytery — the worship of angels — the expediency of a liturgy — the propriety of prescribing set forms of prayer, and excluding all others — and the merits of the Bishop of Exeter. In confidence in their own views, and contempt of all other opinions, they were pretty well matched, but the gentle firmness, and calm brevity of the young lady, had a conspicuous advantage over the vehement dogmatism of the learned lord, who in vain attempted to crush the weaker vessel by mere texts with his own construction put upon them. None of the three listeners, who formed the public, gave the slightest interruption, except when I roared with laughter, which the combatants were too keenly occupied to notice.

Aberdeen, Monday Night, 22d April 1844. — We came here to-day at five, by Huntly, from Fochabers. A bright day. I adhere to my admiration of Aberdonian skill and obstinacy in subjugating nature to their will.

Arbroath, Friday Night, 26th April 1844. — We left Aberdeen to-day at eleven, and, in spite of many pauses, were here at six.

We were in Court most part of Tuesday, Wednesday, and Thursday. Nothing particular. Bad thefts, and plenty of transportations, but no glorious murder. No earl's son of worth and irregularity, of great courage and beauty, and abominably used by an old hunks of a father, or a vindictive stepmother, driven to forgery, by the necessity of protecting a clergyman's daughter, whom he had deceived. No theatrical apprentice despising honesty, and delighting the club by his account of his cheating his master. None, in short, of the poetry of crime; all prosaic theft — aggravated by house-breaking, habit and repute, and previous conviction. The truth is that the suppression of the gallows deprives modern Courts of half their charm. I did not keep an exact list; but, out of twenty thieves, I I have no doubt that at least twelve had been formerly convicted in the Justiciary, and had all laughed at long imprisonment. So far as thieves are concerned, it plainly won't do.

I retract, or at least qualify, much of what I have formerly insinuated against Aberdeen. It is an admirable provincial capital; and to strangers, who necessarily see only the smiling surface of things, a kind cheerful, and happy place, though, no doubt, it has its miseries and dissensions.

Their cross is now settled in its new site at the upper end of Castle Street, — all repaired. It is now the handsomest thing of the kind that I know of in Scotland.

A statue has also been erected in Castle Street, and near the cross, in honour of a late Duke of Gordon; a base and despicable, but, from manner, rather a popular fellow. It is of grey granite, the design by Campbell. A bad statue, but still very ornamental of a street. There are two parties in Aberdeen, one praising, the other abusing, its position. It is a little too high up in the street, but, on the whole, the railers could not show me any site that was not clearly worse. So far as I am aware of, this is the first granite statue in Scotland. And, whatever such a statue may effect for the general decoration of a city, for sculpture as exhibiting the human figure, I don't think it will do. The freckled face, if the granite be grey, or the pimpled or blotched face, if it be red, are insuperable objections. This duke's visage looks as if it had been rubbed over with oatmeal. The pedestal is too thin.

Steell had made me promise to see and to report upon his lately erected statue in white marble of Provost Blaikie — reverenced in Aberdeen as a citizen and magistrate. It stands in the vestibule of the West Church, and is very respectable, though for £1000 sculpture can't be expected to yield its finest fruits.

This church, or rather the building which contains it and another church, has been excellently repaired; and including its burial-ground and handsomest facade of a railing along the street, is a great honour to the place.

I was much struck with the view, from the bridge down towards the infirmary, of a rude cathedral-looking mass, which contains three Free Churches. Seen from that distance, it has really a tolerably Gothic air.

I visited Mrs. Elmslie's Orphan Hospital; a new institution founded, and as yet managed, by a living lady of this name. The edifice is greatly admired by the natives. They say, among other things, and I think truly, that it is the best specimen they have of the possible fineness of jointing the granite. But still it is clear that granite must always join ill, unless its edges be polished, as they never will be for architecture. The tidiness of the whole establishment, outside and in, was perfect. It was satisfactory to learn that they meant to avoid the usual folly of rearing these poor destitute creatures for governesses and other fine things, and were training them as domestic servants. It struck me as likely to be an excellent place to get a servant from, and I asked the matron to show me the one who, by first reaching sixteen, would be first turned out. She sent for the girl, aged fourteen, who appeared, with a sensible Aberdeen face, her stout arms bare, and all glowing from washing a stair. They intend to receive boys hereafter, but at present have only about twenty orphan girls.

I also visited a set of rickety garrets in which a school was taught on an excellent principle. It was solely for the children of the poorest of the poor, who, without this aid, would beg and go to ruin. They take them all in who choose to submit to the condition that, after coming there in the morning, they don't get out till the evening, when they depart to their homes, such as they may be. They are taught to read, write, work, and sing. They get three meals daily — two of porridge and one of broth and meat. This is produced at 2½d — yes, at two pence half-penny — a head per day; and of this the children's work repays about one-half, and the balance, if there be any, goes to themselves. The result is that these infants (for they keep none after fourteen), of raggedness get education, heat, food, and pocket yearly from 20s. to 40s. I don't suppose that any establishment ever cost less. The master of the working department, who seemed to me like an ordinary labourer, gets but 12s. a week. Nothing with the object of preventing juvenile delinquency seems ever to succeed, but this seems as plausibly calculated for it as anything.

The market, which I left in spring 1842 just about to be opened, is now in full operation. It has its defects — the chief being that the tables are all of lousy-looking wood instead of pure stone; but in spite of all this, it is by far the grandest covered market, or rather bazaar, in Scotland. Nor has Scotland such a fountain. But, like many other concerns which benefit the public, it does not reward the subscribers.

The girls had two dances, which I honoured. Both excellent, easy, merry parties, with abundance of liquid and of solid refreshment, and got up in a style of offhand readiness, good humour, and success, which certainly could not be imitated in Edinburgh.

This has been a charming day. The sea, both in the distance and in the bays which so indent this eastern coast, has been beautiful, and all the little beach-placed sea-towns looked calm and respectable.

140

We crossed a field by a footpath, which distinctly invites the traveller, and got to Dunnottar. But strong gates prevented all access without the key; and the key, we found, was kept in Stonehaven! We saw the general nature and position of the castle; and I, who had been in it before, think I did not deceive my companions when I consoled them by saying that the interior was nothing. It is the strange, savage, sea-girt pedestal of puddling-stone that is the wonder.

Arbroath, Saturday Forenoon, 27th April 1844. — Another day of blue sky and of still bluer sea, both variegated, however, by passing clouds.

We have been to the cliffs, the abbey, and the harbour. All excellent.

But Fairport is getting too large and too public. It was a nice respectable place while little and secluded. But, like all spots of the kind that they touch, the railway has smote it. It is now within half an hour of Dundee, the palace of Scotch blackguardism, unless perhaps Paisley be entitled to contest this honour with it. And I grieve to say that wherever we have been between Edinburgh and Inverness, the aspirations is for steam. Every town worships the volatile god. I venture to predict that if I be on the North Circuit in 1854 (alas, alas!) I shall be able to go the whole of it without horses. The effect of the railways in drawing people, all by fixed routes, to fixed stations, is, so far, good. It clears the country of them, and, in some places, leaves Nature more to herself. But it also extinguishes inns, and pours greater mobs over such glens, and loch, and rocks as happen to be within the reach of a steamer or an omnibus.

Meanwhile, Arbroath is what they call rapidly advancing, that is, its steam-engine chimney-stacks are multiplying. But its character is disappearing.

And so we will be off in a little by its railway to the said Dundee, from whence, having to-morrow free, I mean to pass on and meditate amidst the fragments of St. Andrews.

St. Andrews, Sunday Night, 28th April 1844. — And a delightful meditation it has been. We got here yesterday in time to mount St. Regulus, which soon gives a stranger an idea of the whole place, and to view the cathedral; and I have passed the whole of this, the day of peace, amidst the relics and the scenery of this singular spot. Both days have been beautiful.

I have only been twice here before, and am thankful that I had utterly forgotten everything about it, except its general character. The first time was about thirty-two years ago, when I came as counsel before the presbytery for Principal Playfair, under the scandalous persecution by which his old age was troubled; a persecution carried on in the name of the local Church Court, but suggested, kept up, and conducted solely by his rival principal, George Hill, the most graceful and externally elegant, but the meanest of political priests. I never abused any man with such cordiality as I did him for about four years. Professor Fergusson, then in his 90th year, lived here at that period, with whose family I was very intimate. He was then the most monumental of living men. A fine countenance, long milk-white hair, grey eyes, nearly sightless, a bare, deeply gullied throat gave him the appearance of an antique cast of this world, while an unclouded intellect, and a strong spirit, savoured powerfully of the next.

My next visit here was a few years after this — I can't remember exactly when — but I came to see some priory acres, about which there was a litigation. I only stayed one evening. And on neither occasion had I time to see, or leisure to feel, the place.

I have now, partly alone, and partly with Professor Jackson, seen and felt it all, outside and inside.

There is no single spot in Scotland equally full of historical interest. A foreigner who reads the annals of Scotland, and sees, in every page, the important position which this place occupied in the literary, the political, and the ecclesiastical transactions of the country, would naturally imagine the modern St. Andrews, though amerced perhaps of its ancient greatness, to be a large, splendid, and influential city. On approaching it, he sees across an almost treeless plain a few spires standing on a point of rock on the edge of the ocean; and on entering he finds himself in a dead village, without the slightest importance or attractions, except what it derives from the tales that these spires recall.

There is no place in this country over which the Genius of Antiquity lingers so impressively. The architectural wrecks that have been spared are in themselves too far gone. They are literally ruins, or rather the ruins of ruins. Few of them have left even their outlines more than discoverable. But this improves the mysteriousness of the fragments, some of which, moreover, dignify parts of otherwise paltry streets, in which they appear to have been left for no other purpose except that of protesting against modern encroachment. And they are all of a civil character. Even what is called the castle was less of a castle than of a palace. It was a strong place, but not a place chiefly for military defence. They all breathe of literary and ecclesiastical events, and of such political transactions as were anciently involved in the Church. There is no feeling here of mere feudal war.

And the associations of ancient venerableness which belongs so peculiarly to St. Andrews are less disturbed by the repugnance of later ages than in any place that I can think of, where the claims of antiquity are opposed to those of living convenience. The colleges which, though young in comparison with the cathedral, the tower, and the castle, are coeval with the age of the Reformation, instead of interfering with the senti-

ment of the place, bring down the evidence of its learning into a nearer period, and prolong the appropriate feeling. The taste of some of their modern additions may be doubted, and the thing called the Madras College is at present a great blot. There should have been no commonplace, vulgar, bare-legged school here. Very useful, in one sense, probably, as bruising the towers of Oxford, and making its pillars and oriels into Mechanics' Institutions, would be useful. But, unless ingratiated with more circumspection than has operated here, all such inventions of what is now called useful knowledge, a phrase which generally means useless ignorance, are horrid to the *genius loci.* But the old academic edifices are in excellent keeping with the still older ruins. And these colleges, when gone into, display many most interesting remains, especially the general university library, a far better collection of books than I had any idea they possessed.

The town itself, though I would rather have no town at all, is less offensive than might be at first conceived possible. I don't speak of that detestable Bell Street, which, like everything else connected with the Founder of the Madras College, has an inharmonious, contemptible new freestone look. Neither do I speak of a few villa sort of things which have set themselves down on the edges of the city, and have too often been allowed to steal bits of ancient walls and gardens. But the proper town — the true St. Andrews — is in good character. It is still almost entirely surrounded by its ancient wall, and is said never to have been larger than it is now, a statement which the absence of all vestiges of ancient buildings beyond the wall makes very probable. Its only three considerable streets all radiate, at a very acute angle, from the cathedral westward. There has never been any attempt at decoration on the houses, which are all singularly plain, though often dignified by a bit of sculpture, a scarcely legible inscription, a defaced coat-of-arms, or some other vestige of the olden time. There are very few shops, and, thank God, no trade or manufactures. I could not detect a single steam-engine, and their navy consisted of three coal sloops which lay within a small pier composed of large stones laid rudely, though strongly, together upon a natural quay of rock. The gentry of the place consists of professors, retired Indians, saving lairds, old ladies and gentlemen with humble purses, families resorting here for golf and education, or for economy, or for sea-bathing. Nobody comes for what is called business. Woe be on the ignorant wight who did! He would die of lethargy the first week.

For all this produced a silent, calm place. The streets on Saturday evening and all this day were utterly quiet. The steps of a passenger struck me, while sitting in this Black Bull parlour, as if it had been a person moving in a cloister, or crossing some still college quadrangle, amidst the subdued noises of a hot forenoon. I remember when I was in Dr.

Fergusson's long ago, observing a young man on the street, in August, with a grand blue coat, a pair of splendid bright yellow leather breeches, and glorious boots. I asked who he was, and was told, "Oh! that's the boarder." He was an English Lord Somebody, who had been at the college in winter, and was sentenced by his friends to remain here till the classes met again, being the only visible student who remained. I felt for the boarder — solitary wretch.

It is the asylum of repose — a city of refuge for those who cannot live in the country, but wish for as little town as possible. And all this is in unison with the ruins, the still surviving edifices, the academical institutions, and the past history of the place. On the whole, it is the best Pompeii in Scotland. If the professors and the youths be not studious and learned, it must be their own fault. They have everything to excite their ambition — books, tranquillity, and old inspiration. And if anything more were wanting, they have it in their extensive links, their singular rocks, and their miles of the most admirable, hard, dry sand. There cannot be better sea walks. The prospects are not very good, except perhaps in a day such as this — a day of absolute calmness and brightness — when every distant object glitters, and the horizon of the ocean, in its landless quarter, trembles in light, and the white sea-birds stand on one leg on the warm rocks, and the water lays itself out in long unbroken waves, as if it was playing with the beautiful bays. The water, however, though clear enough for the east coast, is no match for the liquid crystal that laves all our western shores.

Nor are the philosophers here disturbed, like some other naturally quiet spots, by being made a thoroughfare of. The town leads to almost nothing. Few can say truly that they went to any place by St. Andrews. St. Andrews itself must be the object of the pilgrimage.

But though, to a stranger, tranquillity seems to be deeply impressed on the whole place, the natives are not solitary. On the contrary, among themselves they are very social. Except those who choose to study they are all idle; and having all a competency, often humble no doubt, but sometimes considerable, they are exactly the sort of people who can be gregarious without remorse, and are allured into parties by the necessity of keeping awake. And they have a local pleasure of their own, which is as much the staple of the place as old colleges and churches are. This is golfing, which is here not a mere pastime, but a business and a passion, and has for ages been so, owing probably to their admirable links. This pursuit actually draws many a middle-aged gentleman whose stomach requires exercise, and his purse cheap pleasure, to reside here with his family; and it is the established recreation of all the learning and all the dignity of the town. There is a pretty large set who do nothing else, who begin in the morning and stop only for dinner; and who, after practising the game, in the sea breeze, all day, discuss it all night. Their talk is of holes. The inter-mixture of these men, or rather the intermixture of this occupation, with its interests, and hazards, and matches, considerably whets the social appetite. And the result is, that their meetings are very numerous, and that, on the whole, they are rather a guttling population. However, it is all done quietly, innocently, and respectably; insomuch, that even the recreation of the place partakes of what is, and ought to be, its peculiar character and avocation.

If St. Andrews contributes little to knowledge, what college contributes much? What have been the direct products of Oxford? The chief use of the academic bowers is, to preserve the taste and the means of learning. And in this view, though other Scotch colleges may be better fitted for professional education, there is none of them so well suited for a lettered retreat.

Yesterday and to-day I have explored all the outsides of things, and as much of the interiors as Sunday would permit Mr. Jackson, the Professor of Divinity, to show me. I walked eastward with him this afternoon to the Spindle Rock, about two miles off; a beautiful sea-beach walk, ending with that tall and singular cliff standing apart on the shore — the best of many specimens of the same kind.

We went to his at seven to tea, where we found Connell, the Professor of Chemistry, and his wife, and Dr. Haldane, the Principal of St. Mary's. At ten, the tea became an excellent supper. Two of the fattest hens I ever saw. They must have been fed by the monks for their own use. We came home under a brilliant moon, which ruins like.

Bridge of Earn, Monday Forenoon, 29th April 1844. — Having seen St. Mary's College yesterday, we went this morning, before breakfast, and saw St. Leonard's and St. Salvator's, and the churches. Jackson and Connell and their respective spouses attended us.

St. Mary's has been all repaired within these few years, and is in a state of respectable comfort. The library — which is that of both colleges — is far better than I had supposed; and, with their £650 (or thereabouts), in lieu of their former Stationers' Hall privilege, it ought in time to form a great collection. But they are sadly in want of binding and repairing; and if they don't attend to this soon, the mischief will become irreparable.

The United College is more interesting in antiquarian remains; but, on this very account, it is in a melancholy state of disrepair. They have rashly laid out about £12,000, being all they had, in a wretched new building, containing only four class-rooms. If they ever get more, I anticipate a brief surviv-ance of the remaining old portions of the college. They will all be torndown, not repaired, in order to make way for some poor substitute by the Burn or the Reid of the day — the two masons who have had most of the recent spoiling of this venerable place. There are many things well-deserving of preservation; but what can be expected of poverty too great to keep even the monuments of Bishop Geddes and of Archbishop Sharp in order?

After a pleasant useful exploration, we all went and had an excellent breakfast at Dr. Haldane's. We then visited the garden of an Indian Major, the Provost. It is a nice garden, and he is an active and useful provost. But the childish and elaborate gimcracks that deform the garden show that a man may be sensible in some things, and a fool in others.

Sir David Brewster! He lives in St. Andrews and presides over its principal college, yet no one speaks to him! With a beautiful taste for science, he has a stronger taste for making enemies of friends. Amiable and agreeable in society, try him with a piece of business, or with opposition, and he is instantly, and obstinately, fractious to the extent of something like insanity. With all arms extended to receive a man of whom they were proud a few years ago, there is scarcely a hand that he can now shake.

We reluctantly left this place at eleven, and have come by Cupar and Newburgh here. There is nothing worth looking at this way except a little broken, hillocky ground near Newburgh, and the Tower of Abernethy. The last has that interest which attaches to anything said to be 1000 years old, but is less worth going a mile to see than most sights, chiefly because it is so absolutely simple and so easy to be described.

Moncreiff has gone to Cavil, and I enter Perth alone to-day at four; and having reached this two hours too soon, I am sitting in this nice English-looking inn bringing up these notes. The day is bright and warm.

We saw a swallow on Saturday near Arbroath, and yesterday they were skimming the St. Andrews bays in great numbers.

Bonaly, Sunday Night, 5th May 1844. — We were at Perth from the evening of last Monday, the 29th of April, till yesterday, the 4th of May, at three; that is, we had four days and a half of business. We got away yesterday at three, and came to Edinburgh.

There were only about forty-four cases, none of which were at all interesting, except a female fire-raiser, and a mad murderer. She of the fire burned above £1000 of a farmer's grain and outhouses, because he gave evidence against her in the Small Debt Court; and he cleft the heart of a constable who attempted to apprehend him. His total insanity was made quite clear, both by evidence and by his conduct at the bar. She, according to the present fashion of all great criminals, claimed an immunity from responsibility because her intellect was rather weak; that is, because whe was not a strong-minded woman. She was sentenced to transportation for fourteen years. Of the mob of thieves, above a dozen had been already convicted in the Justiciary, and purified by long incarceration. I fear that it may now be deemed certain that thieves, especially if young, cannot be reformed by being shut up in a box.

Mark Napier was our public accuser. Our most sensible counsel for the accused was Mr. Arkley of Dunninald — a judicious and worthy youth; but too gentle, I fear, for the rough work of the law. Our orator was a good soul, who ekes out the humble competency with which he is content by keeping boarders, and rises at four in the morning to read Plato in Greek, and is a good Whig, and though otherwise judicious and very modest, is a nearly perfect specimen of the extent to which the voice and the language of rhetorical declamation, particularly in the pathetic line, may be combined with absolute, and even ludicrous, nonsense. We had an appeal on Saturday to the feelings of a jury on behalf of a resetter of stolen goods, of which I hope that Whigham, the Sheriff of the county, who seized his pen and wrote as soon as the sentimental passage dawned, has a good report, for its serious, well-composed and well-spoken absurdity was perfect. No small part of the comedy consisted in the way in which this awkward attempt to wheedle them out of their senses was taken by the fifteen plain men to whom it was addressed. They first lifted up large agrestic eyes and stared, then looked sulky, and at last confounded the orator by hodges of loud laughter. Yet all the words and thoughts were excellent, the manner, though heavy and formal, was not bad, and the voice was good. There was nothing wanting but common-sense, as applicable to the subject in hand. But he is a worthy man, and so good-natured and simple, that when somebody, as we were all crossing the ferry together, asked him, in joke, to recite the conclusion of his speech to the ladies, he was very nearly doing it. If I had a small but respectable office to bestow I would give it to this excellent man, who will probably be neglected because he is too modest.

My due feet never failed to walk the North Inch, in the morning and at midnight. The South Inch deserves more praise than it gets. The ten gardened houses on its west side are beautiful. I never discovered till now that Perth has one of the very sweetest chiming bells I have ever heard, even in the villages of England. I am told it is very old. I heard it, for the first time, at twelve at night, when I was at the west end of the North Inch. It would have been difficult to say whether it, or the Tay, or the moon was the softest.

I grieve to say that the Perth heads are all full of railways, and new streets and depots. They are not aware how very little would extinguish their city.

My nocturnal peregrinations have made me know that the washer-women here are distinguished from all their Scotch sisters that I am aware of, by having a police of their own, or at least for their own protection. I have often been surprised at seeing their clothes left out on the Inches all night. But I never went near the white plain without perceiving a man at my side, and I find that the nymphs of the tub have guardians of their own who watch all night while they are otherwise occupied.

From the day we set off till the day we returned we had not one hour of rain. Nothing but bright, mild, vernal days and nights — weather which says, ''Go to sleep in peace, and don't disturb yourself about to-morrow.'' The only exception was on our approach to Edinburgh. We left Perth amidst sunshine and warmth; but as soon as we approached the Forth, we found everything clouded by the icy breath of that blighter of springs — haar.

I read little except the recent numbers of the *Edinburgh* and of the *Quarterly Reviews*. The great article of the day is Macaulay's ''Life of Barrère,'' in the *Edinburgh*. It is a power-ful, indeed an exterminating, exposition. But I see no use of such force for such an object. It is like setting a mastiff to worry a mouse. To my feeling, too, Macaulay is always ponderous. In the two one-things-needful — thought and knowledge — he never fails to be admirable. But his mere style I cannot approve of. I know no great English writer whose style is so dangerous to youth. It is more so than even Gibbon's, because his other qualities are more attractive than Gibbon's. His elaborate brilliancy, constant antithesis, and studied quaintness of manner, are all wearisome. But these faults, though still gross, and even still paraded as his peculiar excellences, are diminish-ing; and if the progress shall end in simplicity, he will then be a good writer. Simplicity ought to be his aim. All that is bad of him may be traced to the want of it.

SOUTH CIRCUIT

Cumpston, Saturday, 14th September 1844, Noon. — Mrs. Cockburn and my two daughters, Elizabeth and Johanna, left Edinburgh with me on the morning of last Tuesday, the 10th, and got to Dumfries for dinner. A good day, which that dull road requires, and almost defies. Even Moffat, however, looked comfortable.

Moncreiff joined me at Dumfries next morning from Jedburgh, where he had five cases to dispose of. We had one prisoner, and he for only stealing a greatcoat at Dumfries; and transporting him for ten years finished the business of this innocent district. Had he not been sentenced to be transported before, he would have been sent to the Sheriff now, and left Dumfries without a Circuit indictment. Moncreiff has gone home, and I am on my way to Ayr.

My love of Dumfries — at least of its beauty — increases. A most respectable country town, it wants nothing but an old cathedral. However, its church and churchyard, its nice, half-

Anglified, reddish houses, with their bright windows, its clean streets, paved with small stones, its most beautiful river and green, and the memory of Burns, give it all a blessing and respectable air. I am not sure that there is a more perfectly beautiful village scene anywhere — even on the North Inch — than on looking up the water from the lower end of the green. The spectator must be so far down the green as to lose all the paltry part of Maxwelltown, and to see only Dumfries, lined by the Nith, softened by a few trees, and the prospect bounded by the bridge. Notwithstanding a few black coal sloops, and the pretty constant din of a cursed manufacturing mill at the lower end of the green, it is a singularly serene and pleasing prospect.

There are just, if I recollect right, three country towns of the kind in Scotland — Dumfries, Inverness and Perth. I mean country towns lying on the verge edges of considerable and accessible rivers, and with large spaces of open recreation ground in connection with the town and the stream. The Tweed at Melrose is usurped as private property, the Jed at Jedburgh is only to be enjoyed from the highway, the Green of Glasgow, and the Clyde, too, are but the breathing courts of a hot and smoky workshop. (But query — as to Peebles and Kelso?). At these three places the mind is literally led ''Through pastures green, the quiet waters by.''

I was delighted to see some comfortable iron seats placed on different parts of the green, near the infirmary, marked ''for the sick poor.''

Our public dinner, as it is called (Commercial Hotel), was the worst I ever beheld, even at a Circuit. I record it as a dinner of unexampled abomination.

After getting quit of our solitary thief we went and called at Terreggles, where we saw a recently-made flower-garden. It is extremely beautiful. Good flowers, shrubs, and trees, adorning but as usual, more adorned by pure, regular walks, bright, smooth turf, and well-kept stairs, urns, and terraces. But there are three errors. First, no water. They are going to bring it for the house soon, from a hill a mile off, and then they promise fountains. But at present they are dry. Second, they have put lines of gravel walks alongside of most of the flower-pots, cut out of the grass, instead of leaving the plots to be bounded by the grass itself. Thirdly, and chiefly, they have employed a professional rock-maker, from London I believe, to manufacture masses of fantastic rock-work. This in Scotland! a country full of the best productions of the great rock maker, Nature! Fech!

After coming back I renewed my acquaintance with Lincluden and with the kirkyard of Dumfries, and went, for the first time, into Burns's house — the house in which he lived and died, and out of which he was taken to his long home. The two poor apartments are just as he left them; but the only things within them that were there in his day are two bells in the kitchen. It is a shame to Scotland that that house is not bought and preserved.

It is now occupied by a seemingly very poor journeyman painter.

That night Elizabeth, having found a friend in Miss Thomson, went with her to Allanton, to stay till Monday. The next morning (the 12th) Johanna left Dumfries with her cousin, George Maitland, and came here. That day (the 12th) was spent by Mrs. Cockburn, Mr. Macbean, whom we had met in Dumfries, and me, at Allanton.

It is a nice little place, seven miles up the Nith, occupied by Mr. Norin, who married a daughter of my very oldest, and still living friend, Dr. Anthony Tod Thomson, of London. The Doctor promised to meet me there, but failed. His wife — formerly Miss Byerley — was there; the author of many books, yet a natural, unobtrusive, and agreeable woman. She is meditating lives, or biographical notices of the leaders in our two Jacobite rebellions. I told her that in so far as the Scotch ones were concerned, she must either be false or represent them as a set of as paltry, foolish, and selfish fellows as ever dishonoured a cause, which nothing but disinterested heroism could have dignified. A hero of Lovat, Lochiel, or even Balmerino and Kenmure! What a fancy!

We went to the top of a hill near Allanton, from which we had a splendid prospect of the whole valley of the Nith, from Drumlanrig to the sea. There are few finer inland scenes.

We returned to Dumfries at night; and came here yesterday to dinner, calling at Gelston on our way — one of the ugliest of places.

I go towards Ayr tomorrow.

Blairquhan, Monday Morning, 16th September 1844. — Leaving the rest of my party at Cumpston, George Maitland and I came on here to-day, by Newton-Stewart and the Rowan Tree — the longest way, but said to be the best worth seeing, and new to me.

We set out amidst heavy rain, which had been going on for two days, and had deluged everything. But it brightened up for about two and a half hours after leaving Gatehouse; and we had this gleam from Gatehouse to Newton-Stewart, and through the wood, beyond that of Penninghame. These twenty-three or twenty-four miles are beautiful. Till we turn inland at Newton-Stewart the road runs close by the sea-shore, and passes through several wooded private properties. Of these, the one I would accept of with the least hesitation is Cardoness; but there are others that I would not rashly reject. Gatehouse is clean and comfortable, but too visibly the village at the Great Man's Gate. Creetown and Newton-Stewart are beautifully situated, and seen at a little distance amidst their sheltering trees, look like capitals in Arcadia; but oh, oh! when they are entered!! Not even the peat-flavoured air — whispering the approach of a Highland village so agreeably — can save them. Styes for human swine. The opposite coast of Wigtown Bay is too flat; but still, an expanse of bright water is excellent, though certainly not entitled to the extravagant admiration of being perhaps the most beautiful in the south of Scotland, by which it is sometimes misinterpreted. And Loch Cree, which I have so often heard complimented, is, as a loch, nonsense. It is no loch. A loch one hundred yards across! It is a widening of the River Cree; the river being only so much the worse of the widening. But in so far as either loch or river are within the Penninghame woods, the combination is very good.

Immediately on leaving the coast and turning northward, the scene is entirely changed. From Penninghame to Blairwham, a distance of about twenty-eight or thirty miles, it is all one world of unbroken desolation. And the traveller has no pretence of not having leisure to observe it, because he has to ascend the whole course of the brawling Minnick, which gives him about twenty miles of a continued rise. Had it been bright, I have no doubt that a region of such utter solitude and wildness would have been extremely pleasing. But fog sat upon every knoll; and while rain prevented walking, the horses had to drag the carriage slowly up, hour after hour, till its swinging creak became provoking. Nothing but philosophy and Burke's *Correspondence*, interspersed by occasional slumber, made the tediousness endurable. At last we reached the Rowan Tree — a solitary hovel — where, whatever there was in some former state, no tree now is. There there were no horses; so we had to rest the ones we had, and to take them on twelve miles more; the first three of these miles being the steepest of the whole, and showing themselves in a long dull sweep over a heavy lumpish hill. In order to be ready to fall at once on the Blairwhan banquet, we dressed here; but despairing of it, allayed the inward monster by oatcake and kebbock. The natives were kind and merry; a single Adam and a single Eve, who, in that paradise, had produced children enough soon to people the whole garden. These three miles exhausted fifty minutes; but we were now at the summit, and after a very rapid descent we got here at seven. The banquet had begun; but we soon made up to them.

Shewalton, Monday Night, 16th September 1844. — And a pleasant quiet banquet it was.

I rose early (I mean at seven) this morning, and surveyed the beauties of Blairwhan. It deserves its usual praises. A most gentlemanlike place, rich in all sort of attractions — of wood, lawn, river, gardens, hill, agriculture, and pasture. The house (by Burn) is too ostentatious and too large for the place, and, architecturally, is nothing. But still it proclaims itself the mansion-house of a gentleman, and a thing that does not intend itself to be taken for a common affair. The long approach, mostly by the side of the Girvan, is well conceived and well executed. There is, as usual, a cruel aversion to the axe. Part of it arises here from the anxiety for underwood for shooting. A fair object, but too often made a pretext for neglecting the trees. But whatever pheasants may like, the Dryads love a lover of the hatchet.

Sir David Blair and I began our acquaintance in the same class at the High School. He is an excellent man; and I was glad, at this my first visit to his seat, to see him comfortably and respectably placed.

We drove in the forenoon to Ayr, from whence George Maitland, Mark Napier the Advocate-Depute, and I, walked to Craigie House on a visit, after which Napier and I came on here to the Lord President Boyle's. We were in time for a two-hours' walk before dinner, and have passed an agreeable, though not a very merry, evening; for it is a heavy house. The only persons who have been here, besides the family, Napier and I, have been Alison, the historian, and his spouse.

Shewalton is a mere farm; but is a very good one. Quite flat, with good land, and much capable of being made so, all in excellent order, chiefly in clean, well laid down pasture, not unlike an English farm, except that there are no decent trees, and which worse, none that time will ever make decent. The President is an honest, kind gentleman; and it was very agreeable to find a Chief-Justice enjoying his vacation in check trousers, thick shoes, and a grey jacket; with a weed-hook in his hand, health in his stomach, and jolly good humour in his face. The river Irvine gives little, if any, mere beauty to his place. But he partakes in common with all the coast of Ayrshire, of glorious Arran.

I again paced the rhododendron at Craigie, to see which Rutherfurd and I performed a pilgrimage from Edinburgh last year, when it was in flower; and I again ascertained that it was positively about eighty feet in circumference.

We go to Ayr to-morrow.

Cumpston, Wednesday Night and Thursday Morning, 18th and 19th September 1844. — Napier and I, and Archibald Boyle, went to Ayr accordingly before breakfast; this being the first time I was ever in that burgh judicially.

A very shabby procession for such a place landed us at an inn worthy of the procession. The judges should always have their own lodgings.

There were only five cases. Of these, one was disposed of by a plea of guilty, another by the absence of a witness, and a third by the prisoner's challenge (purposely) exhausting the special jurymen. So there were only two trials, which, however, occupied about ten hours; and in one of these the jury convicted the accused of what another part of their verdict, as recorded, acquitted her; and this ended in a certification to the Court, so that a three months' imprisonment for a gentle homicide was the only penal result of this part of the Circuit. There were no appeals. The distinction of jurymen into special and general, as we use it, by having a proportion of both in every jury is absurd. It was introduced about twenty years ago when the horrid power of "picking" every jury was taken from the presiding judge and given to the ballot-box, the notion being that this invention secured juries from having no "respectable men" in them. The common are just as respectable as the special, and I expect to see the blot of this aristocracy removed from the box, though the qualification of the whole had better, perhaps, be raised.

I used to be a great deal at Ayr formerly, especially when I lived with my long-deceased friend Robert Kennedy of Underwood, very soon after I came to the bar. It was then filled with the families of gentlemen, from the country, from India, and from public service, and was a gay, card-playing, dancing, eating and drinking, scandal-loving place. There seemed to be a dinner or a tea and card party every day at several houses of Kennedy's, and Boswells, and Crawfords, and Dalrymples, and lots of old colonels, and worthy old ladies. And to get up a ball, nothing was wanted but for somebody to set it agoing and they would be footing it away in a few hours.

The taste for scandal and for guzzling probably remains, but all the rest is gone. There are more people in the town now than then, and they live in better houses. There was no Wellington Square, and scarcely a single suburban villa in my day. But the sort of gentry who formed its soul exists no longer. The yellow gentlemen who return now from India take their idleness and their livers to Cheltenham or Bath. The landowners don't reside even in the shire, or at least very few of them, but leave their seats cold under a very general system of absenteeism. The Municipal Reform Act has deprived the burgh even of the wretched political importance of its regularly bribed Town Council. The individuals whose station, age, habits, or characters gave respectability to the comfortable county town, are gone, and their very families — the scenes of such mirth, beauty, kindness, and enjoyment — have entirely disappeared. The fashion of the Ayr world hath passed away. The great family of Cassillis had formerly a large mansion, which was standing ten years ago, for their winter residence in Maybole! The meaning of this was that the clustering together of the adjacent families made even Maybole agreeable, or that the inconvenience of living in that village was less than that of going ten miles further and reaching Ayr. These were the days of no roads and of detached communities. All things are now melted into one sea, with a strong Corryvreckan in it sweeping everything towards the metropolis. And this has been the process in all provincial capitals. Improved harbours, railroad stations, better trade, and larger masses of migratory people have succeeded, and those who prefer this to the recollections of the olden time will be pleased. As to me, my reason is with the

154

modern world, my dreams with the old one. And I feel that as to the ancient days there is much of their enchantment that arises from distance.

I went to the point of the pier, along the links, round the edges of the town, and through most of the streets, yesterday, before breakfast. Except Wellington Square, the Court-House, and a few half-country houses, it is all very unchanged. The old kirk steeple has been rebuilt and modernised, and of course amerced of its chief beauty and interest; and the unpardonable and irreparable Vandalism has been committed of removing the Wallace Tower, to which Ayr owed its chief dignity. The shore westward of the pier, though far inferior in firm, dry, purity of sand to that of St. Andrews, is excellent for the recreation of man and horse, and the whole bay is washed by a very respectable sea. There are some ugly symptoms of visions of building on the "Laigh Green," a tempting, but fatal proceeding for the seashore expatiation of the people. The greatest improvement on the mere town would be to take the vermin of the Newton off its phylacteries, and to put a terrace of neat, bowery houses above the old bridge, on the right bank of the river. The great deduction from the comfort and respectability of Ayr proper is this horrid Newton, and the squalid lines of wretched over-crowded hovels, stared out of by unfed and half-naked swarms of coal black and seemingly defying inhabitants, that form its eastern approaches. They have a very Hibernian air.

I found that Ayr still boasted of its peculiar female beauty. I scarcely ever knew a provincial town that did not. Ayr is not behind; but though on the lookout, I can't say that my eyes were particularly dazzled. There was one fair figure, however, that haunted my memory; that of her who, in the former days, was Marion Shaw, and is now the widow of the late Sir Charles Bell. Beauty, such as hers, was enough for one city. That portion of it which belonged to the mind is as bright and as graceful as ever, and there are few forms with which time has dealt so gently. But the place knows her no more.

George Maitland and I left Ayr yesterday (18th) after breakfast, and got here easily to dinner. Having got enough of the Rowan Tree on Sunday, we came by Dalmellington, Carsphairn and New Galloway.

I cannot compare the two routes, any more than a man can take the same view of things before dinner and after. We endured the one through heavy fog, anxious not to be too late in reaching a house called a castle, and impatient with a road of unexpected and unchanging steepness; the other we enjoyed under a friendly sun, with plenty time, and a good road, sloping down as much as up. In these circumstances I greatly prefer the Carsphairn way.

Some of it of course is better than the rest, but the whole track is really excellent. It is all rich in extensive inland views, bounded and varied, not by wide plains which because they are high above the sea are said to be hills, but by real, plainly marked, sticking-up mountains. There are a great many beautiful places, and the whole country is alive with streams. I am not sure that I have seen any better specimen of our Southern Highlands. I wish I had Barbeth. When the time shall come (as come it will) when English cottages or English neatness shall be introduced into Scotland, what a village Dalmellington may be. A few old trees, irregular ground, tumbling burns, a spire, and a mill, — what more is wanted? Loch Doon, like Loch Cree, is scarcely a loch. It is an aneurism on the river. The lately detected lead-mines near Carsphairn, instead of marring, to my taste improve the scene, and even increase its wildness. It looks like a colony of solitary strangers who were trying to discover subterranean treasures in a remote land. The finest part of the way is about New Galloway, particularly before reaching that place.

N.B. — I beg Newton-Stewart's pardon. It was not it that I meant, but another very small village, the name of which I forget. However, the purity even of Newton-Stewart is certainly not exemplary.

Cumpston, Monday Forenoon, 23d September 1844. — Still here, and shall be so for a few days longer. It is an excellent and respectable place, with a competent portion of old wood. There are not many seats in this country with so well-managed young wood, and not one that I know of with better turf. The pasture might be contended for in England. But, in general, the turf of Galloway has not the poor yellow verdure of the turf of ordinary Scotland, but is good, firm, clean, green turf of the south. There is a delightful variety of surface here, and some very good prospects. The defects of the place are the want of level ground — though properly conducted walks might abate this — the absence of water, and the presence of the paltry puddle of ebbing and flowing mud, which the natives flatter themselves is the sea.

I have revisited Dundrennan Abbey, and claim the principal merit of its being in the state it now is. The objurgation which I have recorded in 1839 was freely administered verbally. This roused Thomas Maitland, now of Dundrennan, and he roused Lord Selkirk and others; and the result is that the Commissioners of Woods and Forests have cleaned out the rubbish, and drained the ground, and made some judicious repairs, and cleared away the abominable offices of the manse, and enclosed the whole. It is still far from what a reverenced ruin ought to be, because its preservation requires much more pinning and cementing, and purity; but compared to what it was, it is humanity to barbarism. It is another of several examples, that none of the hallowed architectural remains of Scotland, except those belonging to the Crown, will ever be kept in decent order. Something may always be expected to be done by the Woods and Forests, as Elgin, Arbroath, and Dundrennan attest. It is plain that every private ruin is destined to disappear. Mr. Maxwell of Terregles, the owner of Lincluden, a most liberal gentleman, and whose taste for old relics is excited by his Catholic faith, complained to me that he could not get that building preserved from the mischief of tourists and Dumfries picnickers. And what had this man of fortune, residing only two miles off, done to preserve it? Put a wall round it, or planted a keeper there, or prosecuted any profane hand, or commanded reverence for that beautiful and beautifully situated fragment by the order in which it has been kept? No, none of these. But he leaves it unenclosed, and may see the tenants' cattle in it any time he may choose, and lets spoliation proceed unchecked, and leaves every new ton of rubbish to lie, for the nettles, where it may fall. What can he expect from a broken placard, intimating that Mr. Maxwell of Terregles "requests" blackguards to do as little mischief as they like? Does he do no more for his pheasants?

I have also been at Cally again, and I retract much of what I have formerly said of that house. It is not too small; and, indeed being in just proportions, size is not very material. The joining of the stones is almost entirely concealed by the angular groove in which they are set. And, on the whole, it is a beautiful portico; and Papworth's taste may be observed in all the internal details.

Cumpston, Morning, Wednesday, 25th September 1844. — After another of many visits to Kirkcudbright and other places, George Maitland and I enclosed the day by a pilgrimage on foot to the monument raised a few years ago to the covenanting martyrs in the Glenken Hills. We found it about seven miles from this, — a small, and rather ill-built, granite obelisk, placed beside the spot where James Clement and four others were murdered in 1685, and Clement buried, in a hollow, well suited by its seclusion for the concealment of the persecuted, yet equally suited, on rising a few steps, to inspire them by a splendid prospect of still, solitary plains and mountains. The funds for the erection of this testimony were produced by a sermon preached on the spot upon the 11th of September 1831, to which, notwithstanding the month and the elevation, about 10,000 people listened. So unchanged are the religious feelings of the Scotch; so unextinguishable is indignation of persecution and admiration of courage. Yet this is the people whom an ignorant Government lately thought would submit quietly to a greatly increased interference of patrons and Civil Courts with their spiritual concerns. The Free Church is the pillar to this folly.

Cumpston, Thursday Morning, 26th September 1844. — Yesterday given to an expedition to the lighthouse on the island of Little Ross, about six or seven miles below Kirkcudbright. Some rode and some drove, and George Maitland walked till we all came to the alehouse on the peninsula of Great Ross, where we took boat, and after about a mile's sailing, were landed on the island. It is one of the lesser lights. All its machinery was explained to us by a sensible keeper. I never understood the thing before. The prospect from the top, and, indeed, from every part of the island is beautiful. But I was more interested in the substantial security and comfort of the whole buildings, both for scientific and for domestic purposes. No Dutchman's summer-house could be tidier. Everything, from the brass and the lenses of the light to the kitchen, and even to the coal-house, of each of the two keepers, was as bright as a jeweller's shop.

Eleven people lunched at the alehouse on our return upon the oat-cakes, cheese, butter, and ale of the house. In a frenzy of generosity I resolved to pay the bill, and was rewarded by finding it only amounted to one sixpence. There's a hotel for you! I shall tell this to William Clerk, and he'll take up house there.

George Maitland and I walked home — a tough tramp. But it lay all the way along the shore, and mostly through — Woods. Admirable woods most scandalously mis-managed. He is one of the poor creatures who have become the slaves of their own vermin. His pleasure is in death. He must be perpetually killing something. And when his existence reaches any unhappy season in which there is nothing killable at home, he goes to Sweden or Norway and torments the unprotected fishes of these countries. There is one other rising youth in Scotland at present who soars far beyond what is called game, and, for mere pleasure, kills sheep and poultry, and particularly swine, the shedding of whose blood is his especial delight. These are Young Scotland. ———, grovelling in his own tastes, sacrifices everything to the creation of game. For them, and for hares and pheasants, everything else is neglected. The worse state his woods get into, he thinks it the better, so as they may be only suffering from growing into tangled masses of branches and of underwood. Tall jungles are his object. I could overlook the meanness of his taste, for it is his own loss; and I could almost endure the cruel war which he and his mounted patrols of game-keepers carry on against the people, because he gets properly cursed for it; but it is impossible to forgive the selfishness which bequeaths the beautiful scenery which has the misfortune to call him master in a state of decay to the next generation. We passed to-day through miles of the finest sweet chestnuts — all under sacrifice, in order that, during his hour, he may boast of his battues.

Cumpston, Friday, 27th September 1844, 4 P.M. — Yesterday was (almost) wasted on a voyage from Kirkcudbright to a place about six miles below, on the east side of the bay, called Dirk Hatteraick's Cave. The party consisted of George and

James Maitland, a Captain Dun, with whom, when he was in the Kirkcudbright Militia, I, a gallant captain of volunteers, was quartered in Leith, in the year of our Lord 1807, the present provost, Mr. Gordon, the old provost, Mr. Macbean, and myself, and four of a crew. Like all other aquatic expeditions of pleasure, the only pleasure was in getting out of the boat. A squally, dull day, a leaky boat, bad oars, and no captain, completed our comfort. The only thing that diverted me was the constant advices and entreaties of each provost to the other how to steer. The old one was clearly the best seaman, and indeed was admitted to be the best on the river. But then he was out, and a Whig. So, out of respect of the Tory, who was in, the ruling authority on shore took, and though plainly unfit, was allowed to keep the helm on the water; and if the point had been out or in at the Council board, the altercations could not have been more keen or frequent. "Keep her head up!" "Keep her head down!" "Keep off yon bank, can't ye!" "What the deevil are ye doing now?" "Oh, man, gie me less of your advice!" "Hullo! we'll be all swampt in a minute." "I wish you would try the rudder yourself." "Na, faith; keep it, since you've got it; only keep her head up," etc.

And, after all, the said cave is perfect nonsense. A narrow, wet, dirty slit in a rock, produced by the washing away of the loose matter between two vertically laminated rocks, and answering Scott's scenery in no one respect, either outside or in. The coast is rocky and bold.

To-day I went to Tongueland Hill to have another view of Kirkcudbright. I doubt if there be a more picturesque country town in Scotland. Small, clean, silent, and respectable; it seems (subject, however, to one enormous deduction) the type of a place to which decent characters and moderate purses would retire for quiet comfort. The deduction arises from the dismal swamps of deep, sleechy mud, by which it is nearly surrounded at low tide. It is a dreadful composition. And what fields, and streaks, and gullies of it! The tide rises at an average about twenty or twenty-five feet, and often a great deal more — sometimes thirty-five. This great flow fills up all the bays making a brim-full sea for three miles above the town, and for six or eight below it. It is the a world of waters. But what the sea, ashamed of its advancement, shrinks back, what a change! It becomes a world of sleech. It is worse than even at Chepstow, where the abomination, though deeper, does not cover so extensive a surface. I believe that painters don't dislike this substance, which they don't require to touch. It is not unpicturesque. Of a leaden grey colour, very shiny, in the sun even in appearance; utterly solitary, except to flocks of long-billed and long red-legged sea birds, and to occasionally a heavy fisherman working at a stranded boat in huge boots; and its dull plains interspersed with odd streaks and pools of shallow water, it has hues and objects enough to afford subjects for many pictures. But, Lord, how horrible it is for real life! Think of being surrounded by a dirty substance, impossible to be touched, and most dangerous to be gone upon. A town surrounded by a lake of bird-lime!

It is only at full tide, or nearly so, that Kirkcudbright is to be viewed therefore, or at such a distance that the difference between water and watery mud is lost. And then, how beautifully does it stand! With its brown ruin of a castle, its church spire, the spire of its old town-house, and the square tower of its new one, all seen above its edging of trees, and the whole village surrounded by wooded hills and apparently glittering sea. There is no point from which it can be viewed, whether high or low, and I have seen it from all possible points, at which it does not present the same appearance of picturesque peacefulness, of intermingled wood and water. From several aspects it is the Venice of Scotland.

So I must go and pack up. For we plan being in Bonaly to-morrow, but only by being off soon after five in the morning.

But I have forgot the two humble and very rustic churchyards of Christkirk and Senwick, both on the western or right bank of the river; Christkirk nearly opposite Kirkcudbright, Senwick about five miles lower down. If the Scotch keep a churchyard decent, the positions and solitude of these two would make them beautiful. Few of their epitaphs are old, and not one good. Mere names and dates.

By the way, I may mention in reference to the epitaph I found in 1843 at Inverary, beginning, "Farewell, vain world," that I found the same thought, and in somewhat the same words, in Dundrennan, and also a few weeks ago in the two Herefordshire churchyards of Ross and Goodrich.

Bonaly, Monday, 30th September 1844. — And we made out our journey well. We left Cumpston on Saturday, the day before yesterday, at half-past five in the morning; reached Ayr by Dalmellington, before one; left Ayr by the railway at two; got to the hotel at Glasgow by half-past four; left it by six; and were here by half-past nine.

I have nothing to observe. It was a dull, wet day. But I should have observed before that the owner, who is now Lord Kenmure, has been pleased to white-wash his castle. That old, grey, tall, feudal keep is now as white as milk. The only thing let alone is the piece of ruin abutting to one side of the tower, which is left in original darkness; and the contrast makes both the white and the black more ridiculous.

Captain Dun told me that as he was walking last year with this worthy peer, his lordship happened, by awkward step to come against a large and well-placed tree — of which he has certainly not too many. He was not in the least hurt; but the touch brought the temper out, and he instantly called to some workmen, "Down with it! Down with it instantly!!" and stood for some hours till their hatchets laid it low. It was a tree that had certainly seen his ancestor "on and awa'" in 1715.

My book was Burke's recently published Letters. I took it because Jeffrey, who is in England, wrote to me on the 4th instant that he had been reading it, and that it is "to me full of the deepest interest and delight. The greatest and most accomplished intellect which England has produced for centuries; and of a noble and lovable nature." The "centuries" cannot go beyond two, because three would include Bacon and Shakespeare; and even one includes Newton: with any one of whom Jeffrey could not mean to compare Burke. But no doubt the person he was fascinated by when he wrote these words was great and accomplished, noble and lovable. Nevertheless, for the public, his correspondence must be a dull book. For a person writing a history of England during the last half of the last century these letters may probably be invaluable, because they are chiefly occupied by parliamentary details, and by statements about the political manoeuvres of the great political families. But what is all this to a general reader? Nothing can be more wearisome than vague allusions, or than even precise statement, touching bygone Court intrigues, counterjobbings of Whig lords against Tory lords, and parliamentary movements, which, however absorbing in their day, left no permanent traces on the surface of the waters they ruffled. *Macauley* is meditating an article in the *Edinburgh Review* on this correspondence, and there can be no doubt that he, the future historian of Burke's time, will make it the finest thing in the world. But, to others, he may be assured that he will never make it have an atom of interest that will attach to the review.

And surely Burke's whole thoughts and days were not given up to party politics. Did he never write of literature? or to ordinary friends? One could scarcely guess from reading these letters that he had any literature, or was intimate with Goldsmith or Johnson, or that a thing called "the people" existed in this country. It is all Lord Rockingham against Lord Somebody else, or the king against them all. Did he never philander or go to the Literary Club? Certainly he did. Then as certainly he wrote about these things, and why are they all kept back, and little given except the party proceedings, which he himself declares that he wished chiefly to forget. It is refreshing to come to his two letters to Arthur Young about carrots and swine. I cannot conceive how so many letters could be extracted from the correspondence of a man so immersed in life, without almost a single description of a man, or of a scene, an anecdote. or even a graphic account of any of his favourite House of Commons occurrences.

The letters are all well written. But not as letters. For these they are far too formal and didactic. Still, as expositions of principles, and of his own views, and a few on other matters, they are admirable.

Bridge of Tilt, Friday Night, 11th April 1845. — Here again, with my daughter Elizabeth, and my niece Graham Maitland. I meant to have varied the route the whole way; but this has been prevented by being forced into bad arrangements, and by a very backward spring. So the old round is before me. I shall vary this journal by saying nothing about it. Not that I'm at all tired of it; but, for the nonce, I am tired of describing it.

Aberdeen, Friday Night, 18th April 1845. — But I must, after all, record days and places.

From Tilt Bridge we went to Aviemore last Saturday, the 12th. A clear and very cold day.

On Sunday we went to Cantray, Mr. Davidson's. The way is the ordinary way towards Inverness till the river Nairn be crossed, which is at Craggie; after which the left bank of that stream is descended about ten miles, when Cantray is reached. We got there about two. Cosmo Innes and I immediately got into a gig, and drove to Cawdor, three miles, and walked up Cawdor burn about half-way. I had never seen it before. We had a very merry dinner, with a few neighbours and a large domestic party.

Next day after some further accession to the party, we again proceeded, and got partly in carriages and partly on foot to the top of the burn, and walked all the way down, about two miles.

It is very original. I know nothing like it. It is all one narrow ravine of pudding-stone, about, at an average, I should suppose, from 150 to 200, or even 300 feet deep. The ravine is probably not broader, and often not so broad, as George Street, sometimes not 50 feet; while the perpendicular cut is from 15 to 300 feet deep, reckoning from the walk on the upper edge of the rock to the surface of the stream. If the whole bank above the walk be included, it may be 400 or 500 feet. I say perpendicular height, because the sides of the gully are, in general, literally perpendicular, or very nearly so, so nearly so, that no path has been, or could be, formed at the water's edge, or lower down than the existing walk. It is a deep slice of rough-edged rock. And the whole rock, on both sides, is worn into the endless picturesque shapes into which pudding-stone is so apt to be rubbed. The whole scene is not merely woody, but entangled with wood. Old undisturbed shrubs and trees have rooted themselves in every fissure; and where they have not room to grow upwards, they grow outward, and project, and hang, and twist, festooned by all sorts of wild trailing plants, so fantastically, that wonder never ceases. And what masses of ivy! What lichens! What skins of bright verdure closely to the inaccessible rock! How the deep, dark water tumbles, and foams, and roars, and whirls! The trees overhead, and to the very summit of each bank! The old, dotard oaks dying dimly in their own white moss! The brilliant worlds of holly bushes! If I were a bird, Cawdor burn should be my country. There might be, and I dare say are, a hundred thousand nests in that dell, which all the boys in Christendom might be defied to discover.

> "A steep wilderness, whose hairy sides
> With thicket overgrown, grotesque and wild,
> Access denied."

We looked into the castle on our way home, and also at Kilravock, and passed close by Holme. We had a still more numerous and hilarious party in the evening. Our most excellent and unostentatious host indulges in the full Celtic garb. Odd enough, at this time of day. But another respectable and middle-aged gentleman, who, though called Mackenzie, is, by birth, education, and residence (till lately), a Middlesex Englishman, does the same, merely because he has shootings here, and is pleased to fancy himself a Highlander. A strange taste for ordinary life, in its quiet state. But it is a beautiful dress, and I trust that neither it, nor the language and manners it represents, will ever be extinguished.

The flattish strath of the Nairn used to be called "The Happy Valley", not from any particular felicity of climate, scenery, or seclusion, but from the harmony that long united the six families it belongs to. These are — The Macintosh at Daviot, Davidson of Cantray, Rose of Holme, Rose of Kilravock, Campbell of Cawdor and Macintosh of Geddes. The devil has got among them in modern times, though not more than among the rest of the sons of Adam. But he was a long while, it seems, of finding out the Happy Valley.

On the morning of Tuesday the 15th we went to Inverness to breakfast, having joined Moncreiff and two daughters at Cantray. The paltry business occupied all that day and a part of the next.

On the next day (Wednesday the 16th) Moncreiff and I were honoured by a grand academic banquet. For above half a century Inverness has been so distracted by local dissensions, that when the directors of their Royal Academy had to elect a Rector about seven years ago, the only thing they could agree upon was a resolution that they could agree about nothing, and therefore they concurred in a request that we too would elect for them. We did so, and got them a capital man, Mr. Gray, who was promoted last spring to the Professorship of Natural Philosophy in Aberdeen. On this vacancy they found that they were as discordant as ever, and they had just the sense to repeat their application to us. We again acted, and think that we have got them another good Rector. For all which we were requested to inspect the school, which we did, and also to submit to be banqueted and complimented, which we did also. So at four we sat down at a long table, with forty or fifty, in the museum of the Academy. The table was gorgeous with cold meat and spring flowers, and there was no want of ice or champagne. The chairman of the directors drank us and the Queen. Moncreiff replied. I asked a holiday for the boys. And at five it was all over. A very well managed affair.

I and my comrades then left Inverness, and went to Nairn, leaving Creeffy and his there. Next morning (Thursday the 17th) we went to Knockomie to breakfast. Knockomie is a villa — or rather a comfortable cottage with a farm — about a mile from Forres. It stands upon a sort of low knoll, and has a beautiful prospect of that little, venerable old city, and of the Moray Firth, and of the Ross-shire hills, all of which were sleeping in calm, clear beauty. Except that it had no lake or stream, the place is perfect. A most excellent house, in the cottage style, bright grass, a profusion of evergreens and flowering shrubs, and a capital varied, half-flower and half-vegetable garden. And the owner, Miss Smith, is just as perfect herself. An aged maiden, cheerfull, sensible, well-bred, kind, and very quiet. She took Cosmo Innes, Mr. Baillie, Mr. C. Robertson, and Mr. Irvine, the night before, within her wooden and ivied porch without any warning and without the slightest disconcertion. And that morning she had a first-rate breakfast for us three, Mr. Davidson of Cantray and another, besides nieces and a governess in the house. Yet this is all handsomely done out of her own two farms. The only peculiarity at breakfast was "Brodie Cockles" — a dish new to me. They were merely boiled in the shell, and were excellent to the taste, with a fresh sea flavour. But I felt them clustered together in a ball all day in my uncockly stomach.

After breakfast we proceeded up the Findhorn, a river I knew well when the Lauders lived at Relugas, but had not revisited for about fifteen years. I never saw it in greater glory at this season. The birches and larches were just opening their first soft leaves; the haughs had on their greenest herbage; the water was at an average fulness, and as blue as the sky, or as the distant sea; the dry pebbly channel seemed, by its purity and brightness, to invite us to play with it and the stream; and the day was calm and balmy. Some of the party loitered about Altyre. I went up with two or three of the quiet to the Heronry — a royal burgh, and an ancient one, of these civic birds, nobly placed; to the Pool of Sluie, deep and eddying, and set in glorious rocks; to Logie — deserted and in disorder; and to Relugas! the scene of many a happy day, and perhaps happier night. It was also in bad order, and "a stranger inhabits the mansion of peace". But the two rivers — the Divie and the Findhorn — the banks, and the rocks, these were the same. And what a combination! I hold the Findhorn to be indisputably the finest river for scenery in Britain, and Relugas the most delicious spot in the Findhorn. But it was sad. Neither the shake of Sir Thomas's hand was there, nor the eternal light which shone from his window — the Pharos of hospitality, nor the white frocks playing on the green, nor the joyous family, nor the kind welcome, nor the reluctant, lingering farewell. Yet I am glad that I went.

We returned to Knockomie to a lunch that most dinners might envy, and left the worthy lady about four, and reach Fochabers at seven, where we found Creeffy, not just impatient for dinner, but plainly thinking such patience as he had great virtue.

I stopped a moment at Elgin to see to John Shanks. When I came home from the North Circuit in April 1844, finding that nothing would be done by the Elginites voluntarily, I set about getting him a monument myself. On this they promised to provide and erect the stone, if I would furnish the epitaph. This I agreed to, and after nearly a year's delay and manoeuvring I was lately told that the monument was up. I wanted to be sure of this, and so stopped and saw that it was so. A plain slab, fixed (by permission of the Woods and Forests — which permission I had to procure) to the outer angle of the cathedral, with these words on it:-

Here lyes
John Shanks, Shoemaker in Elgin, who died 14 April 1841,
aged 83 years.

For 17 years he was the keeper and the shower of this Cathedral; and while not even the Crown was doing anything for its preservation, he, with his own hands, cleared it of many thousand cubic yards of rubbish; disclosing the bases of the pillars, collecting the carved fragments, and introducing some order and propriety. Who so reverences the Cathedral will respect the memory of this man.

I've seen worse epitaphs. It is very ill engraved — the words, instead of being run all together like a piece of fact-stating prose, being divided into absurd lines.

Mr. Baillie, Mr. Robertson, and Mr. Irvine dined with us at Fochabers which we all left together, and got to Aberdeen by about five to-day (Friday, 18th April 1845).

Arbroath, Tuesday Night, 22d April 1845. — We were at Aberdeen all Saturday, Sunday, and Monday — the 19th, 20th, and 21st. We left it to-day and came here. Near this I saw two things new to me.

One was Brotherton, about four miles on this side of Bervie. It is a private residence very near the seashore, with a garden which has scarcely any merit in being excellent, for, with a dry, sandy soil, a low elevation, and a sunny exposure, what else could it be? I saw one fuchsia with a stem three inches in diameter, and another fully ten feet high. There is a slope from the house to the flat below, which is divided into three terraces, each backed by a strong wall, forming capital lines of ornamental garden. But the house is, to my eye, the most interesting. It is very old, as indeed the whole place is, very low, very irregular, and altogether not unlike an ancient fortress. The rooms are delightful, odd places cut out of thick walls, and small, but comfortable, and very diverting. The whole house seems to be panelled, and most of the compartments of panelling turn on hinges, and being opened, disclose deep holes and presses, dry and commodious, where arms, kegs, or captives could be safely and comfortably disposed of. We were urged to stay all night, and had it not been for breaking tryst with Moncreiff, whom I engaged to rejoin here, I should have liked to have done so.

The other novelty was Den Finella; that is, the den of the burn called the Finella, within half a mile of this side of Brotherton, and close by the public road. It is a waterfall of about seventy feet high, the stream, after its descent, flowing away down a deep rocky dell, buried in poor trees, and rich in ivy, ferns, and wild-flowers. Nothing with these elements can be bad; but the paltriness of the water makes it all somewhat insignificant.

The defect of Brotherton, even when in leaf, is that it is too bare. It is a beachy place. It is difficult to understand how, with its obvious generations of care, it is without almost a single evergreen.

Perth, Monday Morning, 28th April 1845. — We came here from Arbroath on Wednesday the 23d, and shall be home tomorrow.

Our cases, here as elsewhere, have been mere dirt. And, on the whole, the weather has not behaved as well as usual. Though with some delightful days, it has been cold and too showery.

The Advocate-Depute gave us a concert and ball on Saturday evening. There were five ladies and seven gentlemen — the latter consisting of two judges, two sheriffs, and three advocates, with one pianoforte; many a waltz, polka, and quadrille; abundance of ice and negus, and no want of laughter. An excellent precedent, not to be forgotten. Public Circuit balls were constant, at certain towns, formerly. I must say something about them some day.

We processed to church yesterday. A discourse by a lately-placed youth called A_____, who, if he does not soon get more sense and less ambition, will settle into an eloquent ass.

I went afterwards with Whigham to Dupplin and Invermay, at which last we dined. I had never seen either place before, and it was not a favourable day. The place of Dupplin I was not struck with. But indeed the contemptible little miser that owns it keeps it so ill, that the sun itself could scarcely gild it. The house, however, both inside and out, is excellent. One of the few modern Scotch houses not absurdly large, and well filled with pictures and books. It seems to me to be Burn's best.

Invermay, in foliage and in a good day, must be delightful. A very contrast to Dupplin in keeping, it has excellent distant prospects, wild natural banks, the rugged ravines of the May, and constant vestiges of age. But the trees, by their white moss, call out, "Drain our roots." The laird and his brother seem a couple of the most comfortable bachelors I have almost ever seen. But woe be to the survivor! I missed a petticoat much.

Bonaly, Tuesday Night, 29th April 1845. — We got quit of our criminal friends yesterday about one.

In spite of a drizzly day, we all went to Kinfauns, which I had not gone into, or over, for many years. The late peer, whom I remember a happy and independent man, with scarcely £500 a year, having got a good estate, of course died largely in debt, insomuch that some of his pictures and knickknacks were sold by public auction. I was glad therefore to find the place in good order, and the house, for which he chiefly ruined himself, not at all displenished. The whole concern is an excellent condition. And an excellent concern it is. The only misfortune is that there is too little level ground.

We then went and dined with Captain Scott, at present tenant of Seggieden. A very nice place; a kind couple; and a cheerful evening.

To-day we came home.

From Edinburgh to Inverness the whole people are mad about railways. The country is an asylum of railway lunatics. The Inverness patients, not content with a railway to their hospital from Aberdeen, insist on having one by the Highland road from Perth. They admit that there are no towns, or even villages, no population, and no chance of many passengers. But then they will despatch such flocks of sheep, and such droves of nowt! And in furtherance of this shares are actually up for a railway through Killiecrankie, and by Dalwhinnie and Aviemore! And any one who puts in a word for the preservation of scenery, or relics, or sacred haunts, is set down as a beast, hostile to the "Poor man's rights," "modern improvement", and the "march of intellect." At Perth the magistrates, fancying, as usual with these civic guardians, that money and crowds are happiness and importance, are eager for giving up the South Inch for four railway stations! After what has been done by their brethren of Edinburgh they need not despair. I visited the ground with their leader, but could not make him comprehend how turf or trees could be of any use to a town. The misfortune is that railways have come too late; they should have put in their claim before the country was made up.

Our Depute was Charles Baillie. I began with a prejudice against him, thinking him a stick. But I ended with a prejudice in his favour, thinking him sensible, candid, and a gentleman, dry certainly, but only in manner.

My studies were the last number of the *Edinburgh Review* and a novel called *Foreman*. The pillar of this number of the *Review* is Stephen's account of Gregory the Seventh. *Foreman* I have not just finished yet. It is good, but wants spirit.

I see I have forgotten to mention ⁺hat Mr. A's text began "What are these which are arrayed in white robes? and whence came they?" Though the words refer to certain models, and not to the Lords Commissioners of Justiciary, yet as there is a good deal of white on our gowns, all eyes were on us for a moment.

It is possible that the selection of this passage was accidental, but it certainly was not so when a clergyman preached at a stiff grim blockhead of an Advocate Depute, called Samuel McCormick, somewhere about thirty years ago. His text was, as he read it, "And Samuel went from year to year in circuit to Bethel, and Gilgal, and Mizpeh." These three places meant Jedburgh, Dumfries and Ayr. The Justice (Boyle) and Samuel, who were stuck up in the front gallery, were visibly much offended, which did not diminish the smiles and winks of other people.

Any minister who prostitutes the pulpit by such personally punning texts should be thrashed on the spot. This would be the true practical commentary. Even the text puns that are not personal, but expound the subject, are reprehensible, though some of them have been very witty. Swift, Sterne, South, and Sydney Smith have all given excellent specimens of it.

When Moncreiff was at Glasgow, judicially, for the first time, he went, as he generally does, and heard his friend, the pious and venerable Dr. Brown, preach. He was unwigged, but perfectly well known in that congregation. The worthy doctor was not dreaming either of this judge, or of Circuits, or any modern thing of the kind, but his text began, "There was in a city a judge, which feared not God, neither regarded man". He had only uttered these words when the turn of all heads made him see the learned Lord, and he could hardly proceed from confusion and horror. The text has stuck to Creeffy, the most religious among us, ever since.

WEST CIRCUIT

King's House, Sunday Morning, 7th September 1845. — I got into the railway train for Falkirk at seven in the morning of Thursday last, the 4th, with my son Frank, my daughter Elizabeth, and Lizzie Thomson, a daughter of my very oldest living friend, Dr. Anthony Tod Thomson, physician in London.

Moncreiff takes Stirling, and I take Inverary; and we unite at Glasgow.

The only part of my intended route that will be new to me will probably be from Ballachulish to Oban, through Appin. I shall therefore say little or nothing of places already mentioned, but as to these shall only keep the log, unless where anything new happens to occur.

We breakfasted at Stirling on Thursday, and then spent some hours in that delightful little royal city. I never saw the interior of the castle so well before. Seeing it thoroughly now we owed to the politeness of Sir Archibald Christie, the deputy governor, whom I knew a little, and called upon at his official house. He showed us everything, and explained everything — both inside and out. There was a little too much haze; but it was a beautiful day, and clear enough for all objects not very distant.

Except St. Andrews, I can't recollect any other place of such exclusive historical interest. They have both been Pompeiied, saved by circumstances from being superseded, or dissipated, by modern change. It is the old stories alone that still linger in each. Stirling has its buildings and its walks ennobled by its singular position; but still, it is the old tales that adorn it.

How disgraceful it is to the nation, and particularly to Government, that the scenes of its history should be converted to such base uses! The place where the Parliament met a barrack-room! And every other sacred spot equally debased! I have been often and positively assured that about the beginning of the last war, 1804, the Government of the day wished virtually to obliterate the castle altogether, by giving it up as a fortress, or as public property, and getting it all disposed of by a statute, if necessary! I have reason to believe that had it not been for a few of the neighbouring families, chiefly the Abercrombies, this would actually have been done, and that we should have had it all made into a manufactory. Anything is credible after the unquestionable fact that only three years ago Government actually gave up many of the historical fields and green mounds, including, I believe, the tilting-ground, to be ploughed by a farmer under a lease. This error was corrected, no doubt; but even yet, not entirely. The fearful fact, however, is, that such errors can be committed.

Sir Archibald Christie's face had the rare honour of stopping a cannon-shot, and the still rarer good luck to survive that feat. But the ball has had its revenge. For the convexity of the one cheek, and the concavity of the other, with their effects, in twisting eyes, mouth, and nose, have left as hideous a countenance as war ever produced. Yet, such is the result of kindness and good manners, there are few more agreeable persons than this gentlemanly old soldier.

In passing, we looked into the Cathedral of Dunblane, which I had not seen for many years. A very interesting relic; and well kept. It belongs to the Crown; and the lairds, having nothing to pay themselves, have generally been clamorous for payment from the public purse. It does the Woods and Forests great credit. And its purity struck me the more from having, only a few days ago, gone into the interior of Jedburgh Abbey. What an abomination! It cannot be described. And under the very lock and key of the noble house of Lothian, to whom it belongs, and who live within five miles of the smell of it! nay, over the very dust and prostrate statues of their own ancestors! They can dine off plate; and they can build Puseyite chapels in Jedburgh; but they cannot lay out one shilling in protecting a ruin, the ownership of which does them more honour than their title does, from pollution at which the snout of a famished hog would revolt. Yet it is no badness of nature that produces this, to me, utterly inconceivable misconduct, but mere want of thought. They sweep their own rooms because they would see the dirt in them if they were dirty, but they never waste a thought on duties and decencies, the violation of which does not incommode themselves. Yet how they can resist the mere romance of the matter I cannot understand.

And, the very next day, I saw about twenty respectable and well-behaved farm-servants ask admittance to Melrose Abbey. Instead of having the door thrown open, and being encouraged to humanise their minds by the spectacle of such an edifice, they were sternly barred out, and those only let in (which to their honour was the whole of them) who would first pay a penny. And this Abbey belongs to the Duke of Buccleuch, to that great duke whose piety is such that he will neither allow Melrose Abbey to be seen on Sunday nor give the Free Church one spot of ground, but compels its adherents to worship God under the open sky. Let no friend say that his Grace knows nothing of the penny. Why does not he? It is a system, and not any casual impropriety by his keeper. Does not he know that the Abbey is not open to all, and that it might safely be so did it receive one-thousandth part of the attention that the ducal kennel does?

We got to Dunira by four. Walked up the Boldercan. Dined and stayed Thursday night. On Friday we mounted as many heights and drove about as many of the valleys of Strathearn as could be done in one day. On Saturday the 6th (yesterday) we came from Dunira to this London made edifice of King's House.

I have already spoken of all this course, and have no more to say. But I trust that though I were to travel it a thousand times I would always have more to think and to feel. My admiration, and even my surprise, increases.

The day was most beautiful, — indeed, for such scenery, perfect. Quite calm; sun enough to leave the highest summits clear, yet clouds enough to let huge shadows repose occasionally on every mountain-side. It is all most glorious! From the soft, still beauty of Lochearn to the lofty cone of Ben More, enriched with scattered foliage full 1000 feet above its base; and from the long inspiring desolation of the Black Mount, made doubly black by the settling down upon it of the shadows of evening, to the detached and stately severity of Buachaille-Etive and his compeers, who, with him, guard the descent into

171

Glencoe, and frown as darkly as if they had just heard of the great massacre, nothing can be more magnificent. God help the poor man whose eyes see nothing, and whose mind feels nothing in such scenes.

This is a very passable Highland hostel, — better than I either expected or wished. I wanted the adventure of another Shiel House.

Twice yesterday did I hear the horn and see the scarlet coat of the guard of the stage-coach which hurries people from Fort William to Loch Lomond and vice versa in eight hours. Och! och!

And not for Glencoe.

Ballachulish, Sunday Night, 7th September 1845. — And a perfect Glencoe it was. A calm, dun day — as a Scotch Sunday should be — but bright with occasional splendour; every ravine, crag, rill, and pinnacle quite clear, though the far distances were slightly veiled by mysterious gauzy vapour; and an irresistible feeling of pleased awe was inspired by a silence so profound, that it was broken by the bleating of a lamb or the hum of a bee. I will not attempt to describe what is so common, and is yet so superior to all description. It is the Switzerland of Scotland. And sublime as are the savage summits that line the glen, we no sooner slide into the more open regions of Loch Leven, than we begin to doubt whether, after all, the beauty of the water bounded by the mountains of Appin, Morven, and Lochaber be not preferable even to the Pass. My decision is in favour of whichever is before me. And, on the whole, I felt no nationality, but only justice, in believing that a candid Swiss could not more fairly describe some of the best scenes of his country than by saying, "This is the Scotland of Switzerland".

Lord Ivory, to whose residence at Fasnacloich we are veering, met us here. We pass to-morrow at Kinloch Leven, the residence of John Stuart, a Chancery barrister, and brother of the Laird of Ballachulish. This will show me, what I have never seen, the upper end of Loch Leven. The still night, and the soft, dark water, streaked by long gleams of trembling light, seem to promise a steady day. The house is asleep; the ferryman's oars no longer move; nothing is heard except the murmur of the stream descending through the delicious nest of Ballachulish from the picturesque mountains that overhang it.

The Ballachulishites are well kirked. That little community of slate quarriers, amounting only to about 600 souls, has an Episcopal Chapel, a Catholic Chapel, and a Government Church. In addition to which — this being a site-refusing district — I saw the Free Church worshipping upon a knoll.

Besides sundry grand commoners, we yesterday passed a brace of dukes and half a brace of marquises — Richmond, Buckingham, and Breadalbane.

Kinloch Leven, Monday Night, 8th September 1845. — We breakfasted this morning at the house of Ballachulish, one of the laird-occupied Highland houses, where, at this season, the hospitality is greater than the accommodation. I can scarcely conceive a more delightful spot.

We departed on our nine miles' voyage about eleven, and reached Kinloch Leven about half-past one, rowed by two strong Celts, and steered by the former reporter of Chancery cases. The day did not entirely fulfil what I supposed to be the promise of last night; but, on the whole, it was a good day, — no rain, plenty occasional sun, the summits mostly all clear, nothing wanting but that general brilliancy, which besides intensity, gives variety of light.

We were all in ecstasies. And no wonder. This Loch Leven (an unlucky name, for it is mistaken by strangers for the Kinross-shire pool) is one of the scenes which nearly defy anticipation. It is narrow — seldom, if ever, a mile broad; but deep and dark in its waters, lined the whole way by noble, detached mountains, full of glorious corries, which, however, though the loch be set in them, have openings enough to disclose innumerable distant peaks, so as to make the traveller feel that it is not merely between two rows of hills that he is placed, but that he is embedded in an universally mountainous country. The upper regions are all black, rocky, and in general peaked; their sides worn into countless gullies and ravines, of course with water commonly roaring and sparkling in them, though too many of them were dry now; and the lower portions on both sides were profusely sprinkled with wood, chiefly ash, alder, oak, and birch, and greened all over with bright grass. Nothing can be more absolutely perfect than the contrasts of the blue water, the rich natural foliage, and the black rock.

And the solitude! After leaving the slate quarries, and Sir Duncan Cameron's modern town house of Callart on the opposite side, there is an end of man and his works. I only observed one little Highland farm after this, on the south side, and I don't think there was even one on the north. And no roads on either side. I don't mean merely no made road; but no road at all on which any wheeled vehicle could be drawn, — scarcely footing for a native pony, a soul-refreshing peculiarity, amidst this iron age of railways. The loch is the only practicable means of access to Kinloch Leven.

Promontories narrow the loch at two places, like necks, giving at each the variety of an apparently new lake, with somewhat new scenes. I observed only three very small islands — two at the lower end, and one near the upper. They are both flat and green, and attract the eye only by their history. One of the lower ones contains the ashes of the massacred in 1692; the other is said to have been sacred once to nuns. There is a fragment of wall upon it, and a solitary tree.

Nothing seems so ineradicable as the recollection of public

injustice. The isle of St. Mungo (as it sounds) is pointed out, after the lapse of 153 years, with nearly as much interest as it was soon after the strange massacre it recalls. And I never knew till now that the knoll close beside the inn was what the sentence calls, "The conspicuous eminence upon the south side of, and near to, the said ferry," on which James Stewart was executed on the 8th of November 1752. I happened to put my foot into a hole, when I was told that it was the hole in which the main beam of his gibbet was erected, and that it was religiously kept open to mark the spot. Why should the people desire to preserve such a spot? Certainly not on account of the man, nor on account of his believed, and now almost certain, innocence, in which respect his fate, though very rare, is not absolutely singular. But because he was unfairly tried. An Argyle and a jury of Campbells, very faintly admonished by Elchies, and rather encouraged by Kilkerran, sacrificed him because he did not belong to their clan. Had his name been Campbell, he would not have been even accused. And had he been fairly tried, his innocence would not have perpetuated the memory of his story. He owes his local immorality to the misconduct of his judges.

There is a dark, conical little hillock which, though part of the mainland, stands like an island in the middle of the loch halfway up on the right hand, and, whatever side it be seen from, is a singularly picturesque object. The position of the Episcopal Church is most beautiful. It stands on a little green plot by the water's edge, near Ballachulish, in the society of a few trees, close beside it. There is nothing peculiar in this. But where is there anything like the mountain right behind it? Almost amphitheatred by a magnificent corrie, reaching from its very summit to its base, on which base the chapel smiles, and tossed all over by trees, while a stream rushes down through it, and only gets gentle as it approaches the temple of peace.

Except the doubtful bit of wall on the nuns' island, there is no fragment to testify that man had ever had possession of this loch. At first I thought that a ruin would have graced it; but this was a mistake. It is far better that there is nothing to disclose that its recesses had ever been occupied. The impression of loneliness which imparts such sublimity to the whole scene, is greatly deepened by its appearing before us now, exactly as it was ages ago.

After landing, Mr. Stuart, Ivory, and I, walked for some hours up the River Leven — a very considerable, and very rocky, boisterous mountain river. We did not go up to the falls, not having time. Both the stream and all the hills, and each partic-ular rock and gully, are softened by that rich and varied wood which seems to delight in Argyleshire, and is, I suppose, to be ascribed to the showeriness, the soil, and the mildness which seems to prevail everywhere in this country near the coast. A few years ago (not twenty-five) the left bank of the River Leven

174

was covered, for about five miles from the junction of the stream with the loch, and high up, with very fine old birch. The whole of this wood was sold by the meanest man I was ever personally acquainted with, for about £80. The purchaser, finding it too expensive to cut and carry away the trees, left them standing, but all peeled; and there are still thousands of them not yet rotted away, but standing dead and grey. Can there be any doubt that the rich brute who could allow five miles of wood, the ornament of a district, to be destroyed for £80, is now suffering for this in a hotter world? Spare him not, Devil. Give him his own faggots.

Fasnacloich, Tuesday Night, 9th September 1845. — This morning I went about a mile up the river Leven before breakfast with Lizzy Thomson — a most indefatigable, but most intelligent and unobtrusive, sightseer. After breakfast our party re-embarked for Ballachulish.

The Stuarts were all agreeable and kind. What good sense there is in selecting Kinloch Leven for his vacation. He has not yet got a long enough lease to justify his building, and therefore the cottage he now lives in, though as nice as English habits can make it, is too small, both in the size and in the number of its places, to suit even a Scotch minister or farmer. But there the resider in a good London house, and the receiver of about £6000 or £7000 a year of equitable fees, retires annually, and is happy with his not much used gun and rod, his solitude and his scenery. It is his native country; and I would believe him to be a good man, were it only from the kindly familiarity with which the elder people all greet him as 'Maister John.''

I am afraid I must confess that the day was bad. Rain and wind might have been endured, but fog robbed us of our heights. Tourists are not children of the mist. It was a ''dark and stormy water''. Our two rowers could not have made it out. But we stopped at the little farm half-way down, and, half by coaxing, and half by the terrors of the ''red Lord'', got other two hands, and the four brought us to our port of destination.

After getting dried, we had to go to lunch at the house of Ballachulish, after which we set forward, we in our carriage, and Ivory, Frank, and Benjamin Bell, whom we met here, in Ivory's car, towards Fasnacloich, twenty-one miles off. The whole drive is beautiful, when seen, especially from Appin onwards. But we only saw enough to let us fancy what we were losing. But, just at Appin, it pleased the sun to make one of those sudden and short bursts that often close a dull day. A splendid flash of about ten minutes. Everything was visible, — the Old tower of Castle Stalker, which rose within a quarter of a mile of us, the bright moss of the little sea-surrounded rock on which it stands, the Morven Hills on our right, the headlands and islands before us, the glittering roofs of the few houses that shone in the distance, all was revealed. And in this paroxysm of radiance the sun expired. We were in our fog again, and reached Fasnacloich at eight, without knowing what like it was.

Fasnacloich, Wednesday Night, 10th September 1845. — A day of perfectly cloudless, unchecked, calm splendour. What a day!

I found that this place is about a mile from one of many heads of Loch Creran. But as no Argyleshire place can exist without a lake, a fresh-water one of about a mile long lies close before it, within one hundred yards of the door. Except at the end, where the fresh and salt waters are within a mile of joining, the place is entirely surrounded by high and properly-shaped mountains, displaying a great deal of wood, which, being all natural, excludes larch. The place is in the usual condition of most Highland places — great once, when retainers made greatness, but now, when rent is the thing, fallen down far, if not protected by a quibble-proof entail, certain soon to fall into the hands of some base but wealthy Saxon. It is all in disorder, wood uncared for, fences mouldering, ditches choked, steading unpaved, gates broken, garden with its espaliers of white moss and wet weedy walks oppressive with a heavy damp odour. The house patched suddenly up for a tenant, and making one wonder how little sufficed in the days of yore for a feudal chieftain. Everything about it depending on man is melancholy, everything depending on nature beautiful and grand. The proprietor, a boy, was here, and rowed us on his own loch.

The best part of the day was given to recover what we had lost yesterday, by a return to Appin. We drove to the house, and had our repast on the turf, a little higher up the bank.

The whole scene — I mean the whole district — is glorious — the finest succession of sea and land compositions that are anywhere to be found. There is no end of the Creran, which pushes its bright waters into innumerable bays, and presents itself in so many and such new forms, that we are surprised to learn that all these are still the Creran. And there is such a confusion, or at least such a mixture of lochs, and such a strange breaking of the land into islands, or promontories like islands, that when seen under such a sun as kindled all this up for us to-day, nothing can be more beautiful. But still, the eye turns even from these islands, or seemingly islands, with their woods and their culture, and their blue waters, to the iron mountains of Morven! What a ridge of stern rock! Apparently as perpendicular as so high a ridge can be; not a tree, or a visible blade — nothing but sheer stone, upon which all the storms may rage for a thousand years in vain. I am not sure that I ever beheld such a composition of land and water as that which is displayed from the lawn of Appin House. It owes much to Stalker's Tower, standing up upon its island rock — a monument of other days.

After a sunset which only shows itself at Fasnacloich by the brilliancy of hill-tops and the darkness of shaded valleys, we had a merry, though rather noisy, dinner. Before tea, the girls stole out by themselves, and rowed on the lake, under a soft moon. Their being discovered and joined by some gentlemen did not improve the effect of the adventure as seen from the land, as it destroyed its peacefulness.

Loch Etive is one of the things I have been wishing to see for half my life; and to-morrow, I am to see it.

Fasnacloich, Friday Morning, 12th September 1845. — And I have seen it, well —

First for the facts. Yesterday was as perfect as the day before. Absolutely perfect. We divided ourselves into two parties. One, consisting of one Miss Ivory, Frank, Bell, and three or four youths, a guide, two ponies, and provisions, went by land to the head of the loch, by Glenure. My Lizzy, Lizzy Thomson, Miss Ivory, Lord Ivory, and I drove to the lower end of the loch and sailed up. The land party had to go about ten miles, we about twenty-six. They went over the hills and we went round them.

We left Fasnacloich at a little after seven in the morning in Ivory's car, and went to a place which sounded like Creagan, four miles off, where there is a ferry across Loch Creran. But as it can ferry no horses or carriage, we should have been at a stand had not Mr. Cameron of Barcaldine tendered his carriage and horses, which, on getting across, we found waiting — an open carriage, strong steeds, and a sensible, handy Celt of a coachman. He drove us, through Barcaldine, to Loch Etive, about ten miles.

On getting there (the Bunaw ferry), my prediction of the risk of not sending word a day before was confirmed, for after wasting an hour and a half entreating, and trying to bribe, and even letting off the red Lord, we could not get a single man to move at the opposite side, where alone tourists boats are kept, and which Ivory crossed to. I thought our expedition ended, when three stalwart quarriers from our own side volunteered their services, and the coachman, doffing his livery coat, volunteered his. They found a boat, our provisions were put on board, and voyage began. I never saw so good a Highland crew. Tall, strong, sensible, cheerful, willing fellows, and excellent rowers, but the coachman clearly the best.

We got up at about two, having taken rather less than three hours to the fourteen miles. We looked eagerly for the land part of the expedition, which ought to have joined us here; but in vain. Every distant rock, and tuft, and stot was taken for them. But they never appeared. So, selecting a well-placed knoll, about half a mile from the very end of the loch, which seemed to have the best view, we spread our table, literally in the wilderness.

After an hour's contemplation and refreshment, we sailed again, homeward bound. Three hours and a half, stoppages included, brought us back to Bunaw. We there parted with our three maritime quarriers, on very good terms on both sides; and the coachman took us back to his ferry, where we, on equally good terms, parted with him. Ivory's car received us at his side of the water; and another splendid moon lighted us to Fasnacloich, which we reached about nine.

It was then explained that the hill party had reached the head of the loch; but, despairing of us, had gone away before we arrived. They describe their whole route, especially Glenure, as very fine, which I believe, for the mountains imply it.

So I have seen Loch Etive. There are few things in this country better worth seeing.

From the Bunaw ferry it runs about fourteen or fifteen miles up the country, is nearly straight, and from one mile to three wide. The boatmen said that for about seven miles up, on the right side, there was, since they remembered, a profusion of birch, which the Bunaw furnaces had cleared away. Whether this be correct or not, there is scarcely one observable stem or leaf there now. No country can be more utterly woodless. There is some tolerable wood for about a mile next the ferry on the west side, and a sprinkling on the same side, very near the top. But these, though aided by a few foliaged ravines, are too insignificant to affect the general character of the valley, which may be described as utterly bare. Not even grass or heather seem to be happy here; at least not the soft green grass, nor the bright purple heather of Argyle. Nothing seems to live, a few oases excepted, but a sort of short, pale, wiry bent. And even this is mixed with stones, which gradually increase in quantity and in size, till, when not kept off by the solid rock, they get entire possession of the summits. These summits stand high and hard, and line the whole loch on both sides.

But there are four of them which the eye can never withdraw itself from. Ben Cruachan rises from the very water at the lower end of the loch on the east side, and its peaks and enormous corries stand all out full in view, after getting a few miles up. Then on the same side comes Ben Slarive, a savage rock. And then the upper end is closed in by the two Buachaille-Etives (Beg and More), and a third of the same character, of which I can't describe the sound of the name by letters.

These mountains are the objects! Seen any way they are grand. But seen, as we saw them, first in the meridian blaze, and then varied by the deep shadows of evening, they are sublime. But both Cruachan and Ben Slarive yield to the three upper giants, not in bulk certainly, but in interest. There is something in the form and in the position of these distinctly separated, conical mountains which made me feel as if I was wasting my opportunity when I looked away from them, though it were only to look at their two rivals.

The general and strongly impressed character of the scene is that of grey, lonely, sublime sterility. It reminded me of some of Roberts's views of the country near Petra. I need scarcely say that there is no road on either side except for about a mile from Bunaw, for there is no village or even toon, and the two or three poor houses that are detectable are only noticed for their loneliness. The only interesting building is an atom, which they call a church, on the east side, about half-way up, with three bothies beside it. It is only a preaching-place. I asked whether it was Free or Established? One of the boatmen answered, "Ou, it's between the twa, for they're fechting aboot it." However, the Established had it yesterday, for a minister of that sect preached in it preparatory to the dispensation of the Sacrament on Sunday first. As we were passing homewards, the people came out. We counted them. Including the minister they were twenty-nine — a large congregation for such a locality. About four or five of them went into the bothies; the rest went all off different ways, in four boats. The whole scene was most interesting. I hope they will have a good day on Sunday. I cannot well conceive any one, whatever his own habits may be, so insensible of the feelings of others as not to sympathise with these poor people in their enjoyment of religious ordinances dear to their hearts, and without which what pleasure or humanity would their situation leave them? I understood it to be the kirk of Inverousken. What cathedral is better entitled to our reverence.

Connected with this, I forgot to mention that I spoke to three very nice-looking children at King's House; and finding that they were the landlord's, I asked the mother what school they went to. "Nae schule at a'! There's nae schules here." "But do you not mean to teach them anything?" "Ou ay; but ou keep a tootor for them." This tutor, I found, was a boy from a normal school, whose salary consisted of his having the run of the kitchen during the teaching months. She seemed shocked at the notion that even her humble circumstances were to leave her children uneducated.

The best way to see Loch Etive would be to sail up, and then to walk to King's House, about ten or twelve miles off, on the other side of Buachaille-Etive. This would show the upper part of the country, which is the best part, better than it can be seen from below. Descending from King's House, and sailing down, would do also. But this implies a tryst with a Bunaw boat — always dangerous; and it is always better to trace water and valleys to their sources, than to go down to their opening terminations. *Juvat intus accedere fontes.*

Oban, Friday Night, 12th September 1845. — We left Fasnacloich to-day at eleven, and got here by five. The Ivorys came with us to Shean Ferry. The whole distance is only about eighteen miles; but it took six hours to devour this space, because we had the two ferries of Shean and Connel, the first of which took nearly two hours to itself. The boat, though bespoke, was at the wrong side. And then the pulling and lifting the poor carriage, by Celtic arms alone, unaided by any machinery, the scolding and directing — all in Gaelic — and no man master! The expeditious passage of a Highland ferry would be a much greater miracle than the passage of the Red Sea. The whole way is beautiful, and in the same style; a succession of sea lochs, deeply set in rocky shores, the flats of which are woody and cultivated, the heights wild. The delay at Shean gave us a more general notion of Barcaldine than we got by driving twice through it. It is a beautiful place. And if not seeing the finest sea views in the world, though close at hand, be an advantage, the modern house has been very skilfully contrived.

A beautiful day.

Oban, Saturday Night, 13th September 1845. — The two Lizzies, squired by Frank and Bell, went this morning at seven to Staffa and Iona, and returned in almost exactly twelve hours. I could not inspire myself for such a voyage. So having seen them off (but only through my bedroom window), I have had a day of solitary repose. But a very bad day it has been. Wet and hazy. But I have again looked at this little capital, and continue to think it beautiful. It is becoming a great steamboat station, — too great. Each landing creates a flutter which disturbs its solitude. It seems fuller of strangers than of natives. But the birds of passage will soon be gone. My voyagers had a better day than I had, but still not a good one. There was rolling enough of the vessel to satisfy them that I was better on land.

Having thus noted all that was new in this tour, I suppose I may consider the chronicle for the passing autumn as at an end.

Dalmally, Sunday Night, 14th September 1845. — We came here to-day by four o'clock, glad to find these nuisances to travellers, the inn-usurping shooters, all gone.

The day has had a battle with itself, as to whether it was to be very bad or very good, ever since morning. After many vicissitudes, the final victory, I hope, is with this clear and steady moon.

I am even more struck than I was five years ago with the country between this and Oban. Only, there has surely been some change of the road, which deprives passengers of a great part of River Awe. We did not pass along its velocity to-day for more than a mile or two. Nevertheless, the whole drive is beautiful. Its elements are, the many-bayed Etive, the River Awe, the loch, Kilchurn, Ben Cruachan, Dalmally, with its church and its own mountains, all enriched by profuse sprinklings of copsewood. Cruachan is, no doubt, grand from this side, but it is only from Loch Etive that his merits are to be understood fully.

Strachur, Monday Night, 15th September 1845. — We went this morning and visited Kilchurn. Much of it has fallen since I last saw it in 1843. Strange that no friend will tell Lord Breadalbane about it, and about his duty. Pinning it all firmly up by using the fallen stones and properly coloured cement, and protecting the tops of all the walls by coping and mastic, and then wheeling away the remaining rubbish, killing the nettles, and laying it all down in pure turf, could probably be done for £500. But suppose it cost £5000. Would not the Marquis spend twice this in defending one of his grouse knolls, or even his marquisite?

Dalmally never looked grander than it did last night under the moon, and this morning. The tower of the church peering over the trees that hid the church itself would be a striking object anywhere, but is particularly so amidst the solitary masses that surround it. But I beg the Circuit Clerk, and the Macer, and my representatives to take notice that I won't be laid in that Kirkyard. Abominable!

We left Dalmally about twelve, and reached Inverary about three. Loch Awe beautiful. We met the Rutherfurds near Claddich, journeying towards Ballachulish. Sir Thomas Lauder was waiting for us at Inveraray with his official cutter, and took us to Strachur in its boat, beneath watery clouds and over a dark sea. And, after such spare fast as oft with Murray doth diet, here I am quite ready for that bed.

Inverary, Tuesday Night, 16th September 1845. — An excellent and a well-spent day, anything that gets one out of the horrid, dull moisture of Strachur being agreeable. I saw the cutter itself — the very Princess Royal, 102 tons, twenty-three men, and a Navy lieutenant — laying to, close inshore, with great pleasure, Aeolus plainly whispering that even I might venture. We all got on board, and, after hours of tacking, got down a little below Minard, and were relanded at Strachur about six, after about seven hours on Loch Fyne. A most agreeable cruise.

I wish I had a sea stomach, since my friend Lauder has the use of such a vessel. I should then have seen, as he has done, every interesting point of the British and Irish, but especially the Scotch, coast. There is scarcely a creek, island, or rock on the shore, that he has not explored, nor an accessible ruin or lake; and all these he has described in several journals written with considerable spirit, and embellished by graphic pencil and crow-quill sketches. I doubt if any one ever saw the coast of Scotland better. Certainly no one now or recently living has. I have read several of his journals. An excellent work could be made out of them. The best part of James Wilson's book called *Voyage round the Coasts of Scotland,* being the account of St. Kilda, is substantially Lauder's. I envy these two months' summer voyages exceedingly. They cost him nothing, or very

181

little; they are dignified by a sort of pretence of public business; and their pleasures are not entirely maritime, for wherever a friend lives within reach of the coast, the herring secretary has only to anchor, to land, and to reach him. Then the gratification of taking friends, including his daughters and other ladies, on board, and giving them trips, and of wearing a blue jacket and trousers, and letting the moustaches sprout; what can be more delightful to a sketching and geological man, whose digestion, and slumber, and reading, Neptune, with his worst lurches, cannot disturb?

After more of the spare diet, I and my party got into a small toy of a steamer, which is hired out at Inveraray, and reached that place at about eleven to-night, after an hour's calm, mild, lunary sail from Strachur. The passage, including sending the steamer for us, only cost fifteen shillings.

Tarbert, Loch Lomond, Thursday Night, 18th September 1845. — The heavy rain of yesterday was avoided by being in Court till five. This disposed of all the district guilt.

Argyleshire stots make the stupidest jurymen. A Bute man was tried on the clearest possible evidence of deforcement. They convicted him, which was quite right, and recommended him to the lenity of the Court, which was quite wrong. On being asked, and indeed urged, to tell on what the recommendation proceeded, they stated and conferred, and stared again, but had not a word to say. They could give no reason whatever; but though they were made perfectly to understand the necessity, for their own object, of my knowing their ground, they all remained dumb, and just glowered. It was suspected that they wished to acquit, but, finding this impossible, that they gave the recommendation as the next best for the excise deforcer; and that they dare not avow that they had no reason except a desire to acquit. An Aberdeen jury who had got themselves into this position would have got out of it at once by a cunning pretence.

We came here this forenoon. A rainy day. But it faired from about two to six, which enabled us to drive seven miles up the loch, during most part of which the Ben was clear to the summit. It was all very lovely, but Loch Lomond should never be seen under heavy dull clouds. To-morrow for Dunoon.

Kilmun, Friday Night, 19th September 1845. — A bright day. We left Tarbet at about nine. Liz Thomson, Frank, and I went a little way up the hill behind the inn at Luss, and had a good view of the lower division of the loch, but not nearly so good as from the top of Inchtavannach, to which island we all sailed. One of the boatmen said he had rowed Richardson and me across to Rowardennan the week in which Lennox the ferryman at Inveruglas's boy was drowned forty-one years ago, and he had also been our boatman when we were here with (alas!) Mrs.

Richardson and Sir Charles and Lady Bell sixteen years ago. I engaged him to meet me here again on the 19th September 1861, when it would be sixteen more, — to which he made a very ingenious answer, that as soon as he saw me there then he would be sure to appear.

After being detained an hour on the water at Dumbarton, where we got into a steamer, having sent the servant and the carriage on by land to Glasgow, and another hour at Greenock, we at last made Dunoon, where Captain H. Dundas told me of the sudden death at Rothesay of John Borthwick of Crookston, his brother-in-law, and in one and a half hours more a car at last landed us here at seven in the evening. The Fullertons are living here, and this is a visit to them.

Kilmun, Saturday Night, 20th September 1845. — A baddish day. We passed it chiefly at Loch Eck — a piece of water grandly bounded but solemn enough without being lowered over by dark clouds. Its gloomy stillness, however, did not prevent an hilarious hour at the public.

Kilmun, Sunday Night, 21st September 1845. — A good day.
A large party went to Glenfinart to Church in a "roomy" chariot lent the Fullertons by a neighbouring cottar-king called Grahame. I took a boat across to Dunoon, and called on the Dundases. On getting home, at one, I went in a car and joined them at Glenfinart, eight miles up Loch Long. My chief object was to see the place, which I knew in its old condition, Lord Fullerton having occupied it as a tenant for four years, since he became my near relation. It was then in its simple state, as when Rogers, who had visited the family of Dunmore there, alluded to it in the lines "written in the Highlands of Scotland"_____

> Glad sign and sure, for now we hail
> Thy flowers, Glenfinart, in the gale.

The new and rich proprietor has changed it a good deal; but, in general, for the better. He has given it a handsome but sensible house on the old site; and a broken, disorderly, and rather offensive foreground has been converted into about sixty acres of excellent lawn. People object to his garden. But since, to a family far away from purchasable peas and turnips, a garden was indispensable, I could not discover where he could have placed it better. But he need certainly have had no wall. Few owners, however, can resist the temptation of souring their mouths, at a great expense, by hard peaches, because they are their own, instead of buying good ones cheaply, and enclosing their gardens with evergreen hedges in place of flaring stone. The worst thing I saw — and it was very bad — was the conversion of an excellent, free, mountain stream into a long, regular canal, with a succession of little two-feet falls; and this abomination only for fresh-water fish!

After getting home at four, Mrs. Fullerton, the two Lizzies, Mary Fullerton, and I, went in a car up Glen Messan, at the head of this loch. It is a wild, rocky, picturesque, narrow glen, any one mile of which might keep the pencils of a thousand sketchers going for a year. But what Argyleshire glen would not?

We got back at seven, had a quiet dinner, and family worship closed the day.

This Kilmun is a delightful retreat from the mill, the bank, and the bench. Its being better than the more open Clyde is perhaps doubtful. Moreover, it is a bad bathing-place, because there is no possible privacy. This is bad enough for ladies, though they have bathing-dresses; and unless men cover their nakedness also, they may just as well walk as they were born in Princes Street, as bathe at Kilmun, where, besides that the beach is lined by a row of houses, there are not even the rocky nooks that roughen the shore of Dunoon.

So, for this bout, Argyleshire, adieu.

If I had at present my choice of an Eden in this delightful shire, I would select Ballachulish.

But, alas! let no one who can delay select now. The angel of destruction is hovering over its finest recesses. It is in great danger of being blasted by railways. See this advertisement!—

Argyleshire Railways

A Company is in the course of formation for giving the benefits of railway communication to the large and important county of Argyle. The principal line is intended to commence at Oban, and to proceed by the banks of Loch Etive to the River Awe; after crossing which it will run along the north side of Loch Awe to Dalmally, where it will fork — one line proceeding by Tayndrum to Loch Lomond, and there form a junction with the railway already projected from Glasgow into Dumbartonshire, and the other by Glen Ary to Inverary, and from thence by Loch Eck to Kilmun, on the Clyde.

The surveys are nearly completed, and so soon as the engineer's report is received, a detailed prospectus and list of provisional committee will be published.

Edinburgh, 19th July 1845.

Britain is at present an asylum of railway lunatics, and one symptom of their malady consists in their being possessed of the idea that all seclusion is a grievance. A canal is soon to join Loch Tarbert to Loch Fyne, destroying my little Virgilian harbour.

To-morrow to Glasgow. Hech! hech! The poetry of the Circuit is over. The sow that hath been washed returneth to its

185

wallowing in the mire.

But I have forgot to mention a defence that was made for Argyle by a true Campbell when the chief was said to have got Ardshiel killed, though innocent: "Ay, to be shure, that's the very thing. Onybody can get a man hanget that's guilty, but it's only 'Lummore (Macallum More) can hang a man wha's guilty ava."

Bonaly, Saturday Night, 27th September 1845. — After four days of trials at Glasgow, I came here to-day.

The cases were mere dirt; thirty-nine, of which above thirty were thefts. Such common-places might almost be tried by steam. Only two things curious. One of them was the striking tact of a blind woman, a witness, who identified a considerable number of articles of dress and furniture, solely by the touch. She generally mentioned the colours, and distinguished her own from others readily and accurately. The other was a poor Irishman convicted of bigamy. He pleaded guilty, and consequently could have no speech in his defence. But this he ascribed to his poverty, but for which his innocence, he flattered himself, would have been clear. His phrase for this struck me. After Moncreiff had given him a very good address, "Please your honour," said he, "if I had only had money to buy a tongue, your honour would not have had all that to say."

It was the first time I was in the new Court. An immeasureable improvement on the old cave. Except that the old one, being a cave, was good for hearing in, for which the new square is very bad. The Judge's head is too high set, and his lordship is his own echo; not unnatural defects, since the internal arrangements were all usurped by our worthy chief, my Lord Justice-Clerk, John Hope. The imperfections of the room, however, curable.

David Mure was our Depute.

My books were both American — Rush, the Ambassador's, *Residence in London,* and Prescott's *Essays,* or rather Reviews. Rush seems to have looked at London intelligently. But I can't understand how an ambassador, or his family, can publish, or be allowed to publish, his official proceedings. I thought that the interviews, schemes, instructions, and plots of such men, had been all secret, and sacred. Everything that Prescott writes is sensible and candid. His criticism is so. Without any pretension to genius, originality, or learning, all he executes is made pleasing by judgement, industry, and amiable impartiality.

SOUTH CIRCUIT
1846

Bonaly, Thursday, 23d April 1846. — I left Edinburgh on this

Spring Circuit last Thursday, the 16th, and here I am again. I have — and can have — nothing to say.

My companions were my two daughters, Elizabeth and Johanna. We went to Jedburgh on the 16th. In Court all Friday, and till two on Saturday, the 17th and 18th; went to Borthwickbrae to dinner on Saturday; stayed there till the morning of Monday the 20th; went that day, by Langholm and Lockerbie, to Dumfries; met Moncreiff there; in Court till nine at night on Tuesday the 21st; and returned to Edinburgh yesterday, the 22d, leaving Moncreiff to take Ayr alone. Rainy, cold weather.

Very few cases. The people are all employed, either on railways, or in consequence of them. There was a child murder at Dumfries, where doctors differed as to their scientific "tests" of the child having been born alive. But its throat was found crammed full of bits of coal, and there were the marks of a thumb and two fingers on the outside of the neck. These practical tests had little effect upon medical opinion; but as mothers don't generally throttle children that are dead, they were quite satisfactory to the jury. This was said to have been the fourth illegitimate that she had disposed of by violence. A tall, strong, dour, ogress. Still, hanging is at such a discontent now, that, clear though it was, the prosecutor would have got no conviction unless he had restricted. Whenever any of the murderous appearances, such as finger-marks on the neck, was put to one of the doctors in defence, the scientific gentleman, after parading his vast experience, always stated that however these things might startle the ignorant, they were of no consequence to a person of great practice, and that he had seen hundreds of children born with these very marks. "Ay, but, doctor", said an agrestic-looking juryman, "did ye ever see ony o' them born wi' coals i' their mooth?"

NORTH CIRCUIT

Stewart's Inn, Trossachs, Tuesday Night, 8th September 1846. — Mrs. Cockburn, my daughter Elizabeth, and Elizabeth Richardson, embarked with me on a northern voyage, in a carriage on the Falkirk railway, at eight this morning. The carriage had been sent forward last night, and met us at Falkirk a little after nine. We breakfasted at Stirling, after which Lizzie Richardson and I explored the castle and the city under a torrent of rain. We set off about one; and after leaving our cards for David Dundas, the new Solicitor-General of England, at Ochtertyre, his seat, we got here about half-past six. The two Lizzies and I walked, and just saw this end of Loch Katrine under a still, grave, peaceful evening. The day brightened before we got to Ochtertyre, and has continued steadily fine ever since.

Comrie House, Wednesday Night, 9th September 1846. —
We passed a couple of hours yesterday on Loch Katrine; then
went to Callander; renewed my acquaintance with the Falls of
Brackland, which I saw last in March 1811; left Callander about
two; and gliding along Loch Lubnaig and Loch Earn, got here at
seven, amidst the blaze of a glorious sunset. All excellent; but
too common, even to myself, for reflections worth recording.

The world is still paying homage to the genius of Scott at the
Lake of his Lady. I find that Stewart's inn can accommodate
about a dozen of people comfortably, and about twice that
number with some decency. But there is now a small steamer
on the loch, which goes three times down and three times up
daily, and generally loaded. There are omnibuses to carry them
on to Callander, besides gigs, cars, and private carriages. But
they all arrive from Loch Lomond, Callander, and other
quarters, expecting accommodation at the wonderful and
expansive place called Stewart's inn, and, except the twelve or
the twenty-four, are all daily, or rather hourly, destined to be
disappointed. On our way from Callander to that place we
counted about fifty people returning from Stewart's inn in
vehicles. There had been above one hundred people at that inn
that day. Yet the two peers, Willoughby and Montrose, have
not sense either to shut up the loch altogether, or spirit to build
a proper house.

Montrose's side of the loch is still bare. It was cut, or rather
grubbed out, I don't remember how long ago, but certainly after
the publication of the poem; for I remember Scott, in his indignation, threatening to save the trees, and to disgrace their
owner, by getting up a penny subscription, and paying the £200
(this I believe, was the sum) for which they were to be sold. But
we observed one of the very finest weeping birches, on the
right-hand side of the road going towards Loch Katrine, which
we were told that Lady Willoughby had given five guineas to
save. I trust, and have no reason to doubt, that she has in store
the treasure of many as good deeds.

Loch Lubnaig, it is supposed, is going into Glasgow, — to
cleanse faces and be made into punch. I believe that an Act has
been obtained for the supply of what the inhabitants delight to
call the Metropolis of the West, with water from this lake.

Comrie House, Thursday Night, 10th September 1846. —
Another fine day, passed in roving, in an open carriage, through
the exhaustless glories of this portion of Strathearn.

This Comrie House, tenanted by my nephew Robert
Whigham, the Sheriff of the county, is the very perfection of a
small Highland retreat. What can hills, trees, water, rocks,
home scenery, distant prospects, and a sensible house, do
more?'

Comrie House, Friday Night, 11th September 1846. — Ditto

to-day.

Dunkeld, Saturday Night, 12th September 1846. — This has been a day!

We left Comrie about seven; breakfasted at Killin; went through the grounds at Taymouth; and were here a little after eight P.M.

Of the space between Comrie and Killin I say nothing, except that from the day of its creation, it was never more lovely.

I have not been at Killin and Kenmore since, I think, 1823, when I loitered through the district with Richardson and his now deceased wife, and Lady Bell and her now deceased Sir Charles. Nor had I ever before come down, or gone up, the right bank of the river, so that all this was now nearly new to me. I pity the man to whom it can ever become hackneyed.

The day was perfect. The clear blue sky, diversified by rich white clouds, sailing slowly along, as if freighted with angels enjoying the surface of this beautiful world, and everything breathed upon by airs fresh from Paradise. A finer day never was, or ever can be, in Scotland.

The peculiarity of Killin is in its assemblage of such a variety of picturesque objects in so small a space. All the sketchers in Britain might sketch there for their whole lives, and not exhaust it. I had never gone over to Finlarig before. Besides its own interest, it is a platform for many views. But the burial-place of the Macnabs is more singular, and like the final resting-place of a race of savage chiefs. It looks as if they had expected to be obliged to stand a siege even in the grave. It is needless to speak of our country parish churchyards. Some of the new town cemeteries are decent, and some even beautiful. But our country ones! The one at Killin is in a situation fit to inspire any human creature, except a Scotch Calvinist, with proper sentiments, and a proper cinerary taste. But what an abomination! It makes death horrid. Yet lairds, kirk-sessions, ministers, and people, all submit, contentedly from generation to generation. It sinks them lower in the scale of animals than any fact of their history.

If seeing Ben lawers be the only object, those are right who say that the south side of the Loch Tay is the best to take. For the general scene, I am confident that the north is better; were it merely because it runs on a higher level, and makes everything be better seen. Oh, how the lake shone to-day! Bright and unruffled, save when a whisper of breath played with bits of the surface, or the fishes, looking up, left little widening rings when they sunk again, or the progress of a fly rippled the surface crystal; every object mirrored in the water. Much of the hills, on both sides would in any other situation, be tame, for they are often without rock, or peak, or gully, or corry, or any roughness. But, as placed, they all harmonise. The peculiarity of the whole scene seems to me to lie in the absence of seats or

189

villages, and in the profusion of little farms and toons, with their irregular patches of bright grain, their blue smoke, bits of mills, and hamlet trees; the boat, the bleaching of the homespun linen, the peat stack, and all the other appearances of happy and simple rural life. It seems to be a population over the enjoyments and virtue of which a great landowner might be proud to preside. I am thankful that I have beheld the scene once more, before it be polluted by the smoke, and noise, and bustle of a railway. But Tay! thou art doomed! We passed the surveyors' flags — the scientific upas, — twice this forenoon. I wonder how many millions it would take to make me, if it were mine, send the Gallowgate, ten times a day, along the loch.

Lizzie Richardson and I walked through the grounds, and looked into the hall of Taymouth Castle, — a noble place, admirably kept. The house much improved, because broken in its outline, by the addition of the library; but still one can't help regretting that out of so much work and cost, so very little of real architecture has been produced. The central and chief part of the edifice is a mere copy of Inveraray, the worst-looking Bridewell in this country. Yet old Grandtully Castle still stands, for hints, but a few miles off, We looked at it as we passed. A good old mass, — maintaining a feudal atmosphere around itself.

A passage down the Tay is glorious. We lost a few of the last miles in the dark, but all the rest were seen in the splendour of the very finest evening. Independently of this accidental charm, Strath Tay is the glory of Scotch straths. Where have we a rival valley to that which begins at Killin and ends at Dundee? The lake, the river and its tributaries; Killin, Kenmore, Dunkeld, and Perth; the mountains, the wood, the rock, the culture, the seats, and the villages, — I admit no equal competitor for this rich and unbroken assemblage of well-composed materials of the best class. It is especially the mixed cultivation and wildness that delights me. The people continued out to-night to the latest seeing hour, securing the bright stooks that contrasted so well with the dark wood; women sitting at the doors mending the Sunday's clothes, children playing with young calves, whose ribs brightened in the sun; the ferry and other boats secured in their little creeks, and always protected beneath some great sheltering branch; the trout rising; we almost the only travellers. Though brilliant, everything was still. And a deeper serenity was diffused by its being a Saturday evening. The repose of the coming day seemed to touch the close of the preceding one. And well did the sun do his duty! How he kindled Ben More and Ben Lawers, turning every speck of cloud that dared to interfere with him into instant fire, and after dazzling everything, except the cool recesses of the Tay, and the shadows he himself produced, with the softest splendour, died gracefully away into grey tranquillity! No week of rural happiness and industry could be brought to a more impressive close. There was more truth, as well as poetry, than she probably was aware of, in the expression by Miss Richardson, that "everything seemed soaked in gold."

Arbroath, Sunday Night, 13th September 1846. — We left Dunkeld to-day at about ten, and came here, by Cupar-Angus and Forfar, by about five. A very fine day, and a very fine country; more English-looking than any such long stretch (about fifty miles) that I know in Scotland. It is full of seats, good trees, respectable old spires, and excellent agriculture. The stages from Dunkeld to Cupar, and from Forfar to this, make it far better than the ordinary Strathmore road.

Castleton, Friday Morning, 18th September 1846. — We got to Aberdeen, after showing Lizzie Richardson the usual sights, on Monday to dinner; were in Court all Tuesday and part of Wednesday, on the evening of which day we had another Aberdeen ball at our steady friend Mrs. Milne's, and yesterday came here, with Archibald Davidson, our depute, in his own carriage.

I forget what I have already said of this Deeside, and I have not the volume here. But if I have not raved, I have been stupid and unjust; for I now see that it is a fit rival of Strath Tay, not in soft beauty, but in varied grandeur. The whole sixty miles are most noble, at least from the moment that the suburbs of Aberdeen are shaken off, and the Dee is seen glittering under the birch. At first one is afraid that it is going to be too agricultural, but before reaching Banchory this alarm goes off, and the character of a wild though cultivated valley is secured. This impression is gradually increased as we go on, the valley narrowing, the corn-bright haughs lessening, the hills getting more into each other's company, the Scotch fir maintaining a more equal part with the birch; till at last, on approaching this city of Castleton, it is all pure, striking, Highland scenery. The profusion of birch is beautiful, and of good old birch, with thick, honest, rough stems, such as I thought were only to be seen along Loch Ness; and weeping, not like poor contemptible solitary creatures, cultivated just in order to weep in a garden, but pouring and waving miles of tears, as if they thought the Dee could not flow without them. And the Scotch fir! profuse, dark, large, with arms tossed about as if defying even the oak, and looking as eternal as the rocks they have taken possession of. It is a glorious firth of wood. The hills are seldom, if ever, peaky; but their massiveness is grand; and they all disclose the truth of the great extent of their region.

The strath is not peopled with nearly so many hamlets and villages as smile along Strath Tay; but it has enough — with all their accompaniments of mills, dyke-riding children, colts, peat stacks, and broken carts. And the poor people's houses are, in general, excellent. I did not see a mud one the whole day. They are built houses; and in building, it is not difficult to have doors and windows and chimneys, the absence of which is generally owing to the edifice being made of turf, which admits of little beyond mere wall. And the four capitals of the valley — Banchory, Aboyne, Ballater, and this Castleton — are all delightful. In Switzerland, each of these would be the metropolis of a Canton. The houses are comfortable, and, for Scotland, tidy; and there is no appearance of street, or of any parsimony of space. Nor has each merely its own neighbour-rejecting, fenced portion, but they are all scattered and tossed about without order or plan, as if each person had been allowed to squat as he chose. This has produced wide, irregular, open-greened villages, a thousand times better than any design could have made. Ballater is the most striking of the three lower ones; but even Ballater is utterly superseded by Castleton, — the most curious and picturesque of Scotch villages. The approach to it, past the noble place of Invercauld, and the strange Castle of Braemar, till at last it is seen standing on its mountain-circled knolls, with its straggling houses, rival spires, and blue peat-smoke, — it is like coming upon some long-heard-of, and first-seen, place in a far-away country. For it has no apparent connection with any place else, but seems to have been formed just because people had got to the head of the Dee, and were obliged to rest there because they could get no further. This impression of solitude is very strong; and it is increased rather than lessened by the little capital seeming to have everything, though in a very humble way, within itself. I found the coachmaker to be the carpenter, and the haberdasher the bookseller. It stands above, and aside from, the Dee, and is dashed through by the rocky Cluny, the banks of which are of themselves sufficient to give a place reputation. The prospects both down the valley and up to the hills are grand, and vary at every step. But neither the valley nor the hills are nearly so interesting as the Castleton itself, which is a very curious place. Were the hills more peaked it would have a very Swissish air. The impression of its peculiarity, too, is increased by the number of strangers, who, besides the professional slayers of wild beasts, come here merely to wonder at Castleton. The little, nice, clean hostel we are in has one party of nine, and another party of seven, delicate ladies and gentlemen, some with titles, besides our party of five, and sundry individual "heads without name", most of whom seem to have nothing to do but stare and lounge about this spot; and who look as if adventure and community of purpose gave them a sort of right to confer with each other as fellow-pilgrims.

In addition to its former Catholic and Establishment temples, there is now a Free Kirk. I am told that, with true religious spirit, according as religion is too often practised, each sect lives in orthodox hatred of its brother. One would think that the sight of these peaceful and seemingly eternal mountains — gilded as at this moment they are by cloudless morning sun, private drive several miles up the glen, and although he was by far the greatest deer-killer in Scotland, he not only permitted, but encouraged strangers to use it freely. His son, the duke who died last week, had been confined as a lunatic above forty years in England; the estate was managed after his succession, by his brother Lord Glenlyon, and on his death it fell under the despotism of his son, who has, by the lunatic's recent death, become the duke within the last six days. It pleased him and his father to keep Glen Tilt to themselves and their game-keepers; and, ever since, it has required a ducal ukase to see this portion of God's creation. This is not easily obtained. I had fortified myself by a letter from Whigham, who had also spoken to his lordship; and whenever I arrived I wrote a note with respectful compliments, etc., and re-duking and re-gracing him, and humbly begging that such a worm might be permitted to set its base wheels on this once free drive. The great man was engaged, but I got a gracious answer from his brother, enclosing a regular, partly printed pass.

But the day is bad, and in as bad a style, for what we want, as is possible; heavy, misty rain, hiding the hills, covering everything with one dull hue, wetting one's skin, and, worse than all, printing a wheel-mark in the mud of the drive. But having got the pass we must use it; else the beast would roar.

The view from this window recalls the established feud between the Atholls and the owners of Lude, whoever these may be. Their kingdoms are too near to let the rival sovereigns be on good terms. But, besides that, the last (sane) duke, a man not to be rubbed against the hair, succeeded in establishing his strange claim to a right to shoot over Lude. As soon as he obtained his decree, his Grace, instead of declining to exercise so offensive a privilege, which his own boundless forests made unnecessary for his own sport, proceeded to annoy General Robertson, his neighbour and legal antagonist, by a grand, ostentatious day's deer-shooting over the lands of Lude. But the general out-manoeuvred him by a move which everybody admired. His lawn was ornamented by eight or ten cannons. These were distributed conveniently, and wherever the great man and his tail appeared, off went the guns, startling every hill and glen by their echoes, of course off went the deer, and his grace had nothing for it but to retire, cursing, with every ball in his rifles.

Bridge of Tilt, Sunday Night, 20th September 1846. — We got up the Tilt, to a mean-like place called the Forest Lodge, eight miles up. The magic of sunshine would, of course, have made it a different sort of thing; but still, in so far as mere seeing was concerned, we saw it all distinctly enough.

It is not the least like what I supposed. Ever since the days of Playfair and Seymour, I have heard so much of the geological treasures of Glen Tilt, that I fancied it to be all a bare, gullied,

193

rocky valley. Whereas superficially, and to the ungeological eye, there is almost no rock, except in the very bed of the stream, which is all rock together; the lower part of the glen is all wood, and the upper part, especially on the left bank, is softened by the purest and the finest turf I ever saw at such an elevation.

In order to see the wooded part, which reached, I should suppose, about three or four miles above Blair, it would be necessary to get down to near the very river, which we, with a carriage, could not do. Because the drive road is high above it; so high that the existence of the torrent is only known by its roar, and by a few occasional glimpses that have been secured artificially. And though there be a profusion of excellent wood for the scene, particularly a great deal of admirable birch, it is all nearly superseded by the abominable larch poles with which the whole of Atholl is defaced. The bed, and the near banks of the river, must be full, every step, of striking picturesque beauty; but from our position we could not make its acquaintance; and if there be no made footpath below, nobody, except a splash-defying geologist, can.

To us, therefore, Glen Tilt, properly speaking, only began where the planted and preserved wood ceased. A carriage-borne visitor knows, indeed feels, that he is in a glen while the wood lasts, but he sees few particulars, and does not understand the thing till he escapes into the free valley. He then finds himself in the liveliest of glens. It is very narrow; the stream dashes through curious plates of edge-placed rocks, and tumbles over innumerable little precipices; it is sprinkled along its sides by birches and mountain ashes, standing sometimes in groups, but most singly; and, while the remote summits are heathered to the entire satisfaction of stags and moorfowl, the lower sides of the hills are covered, especially on the left bank, with beautiful turf. If my soul ever goes into the body of a sheep, I trust that the south side of Glen Tilt may be my pasture. I could nibble there for ever. It is all vegetable emerald.

We fed our horses at the lodge, where we blew up a good peat fire, saw a number of deer on the horizon of the hill nearest us, and had much talk, inside with a little girl, who seemed to be left in charge of the establishment, including Sandy, an infant, while all the rest were at church at Blair, and outside with an old, clear, grey-eyed, telescoped keeper, who surprised us by his low and freely expressed opinion of his ducal master.

There is a carriage drive for about twelve miles from Braemar, so that there is only a space of about eight or ten miles between that and the Atholl drive. Through this space there is at present only a footpath, and this closed. It is very natural for these Grafs to keep their strath within their own power, and to protect their deer-stalking, the most manly of British sports. But nothing would exalt dignity, as the lords of such scenes, so diffusing its blessings equally on them all — might teach them the insignificance of many of their follies.

The only blot on the strath is Aboyne, which still exhibits all the signs of dilapidation and insolvency. But while his woods are falling, and railways are waiting to sleep upon them, the contemptible old monkey-faced wretch of a beau, who danced at Versailles with Marie Antoinette about sixty years ago, is still grinning and dancing somewhere abroad, at the expense of creditors who can't afford to let him die. Every other place seems in happy and respectable order. And there are several of them. I thought Abergeldie the best.

I should like to explore the many grand and lovely glens that stream down and lose themselves in what an engineer monster would call the trunk valley. I saw something in Aberdeen papers about the incredible advantages of the Deeside line. I never see a scene of Scotch beauty, without being thankful that I have beheld it before it has been breathed over by the angel of mechanical destruction.

Kindrogan, Saturday Morning, 19th September 1846. — We lingered about Castleton till near twelve yesterday, and then came here about five. The two stages are the Spittal of Glenshee, fifteen miles, and Kindrogan, seventeen. Soon after leaving the Spittal, the Highland appearances abate, and we could somtimes almost imagine that we are degraded again into Lowlandism. But all the first part of the way is admirable. The instant that Castleton disappears, which it does in a mile or so after it is left, we are in a new world. From being surrounded by wood, there is not a single leaf. No villages, no travellers, no Dee, — nothing but great heavy mountains, with tops powdered with grey broken granite, a few large stone-streaked corries, solitude, and game. This continues about ten miles up Glen Cluny. And then comes a glorious plunge down Glenbeg. It is literally a plunge — a long, deep, rapid descent, faced at first by a towering and splintered rock, and requiring a mile or two to lay us on the level below. And so we come to the hospice of Glenshee, where we found a very nice inn, — excellent eggs, butter, and oatcakes and milk, which the flocks of Abraham could not have surpassed. A party of five Irishmen went away last week, after being there since the 12th of August, and killing nearly 1600 brace of grouse. This autumnal influx of sporting strangers is a very recent occurrence in Scotch economy. Almost every moor has its English tenant. They are not to be counted by ones, or pairs, or coveys, but by droves or flocks. On the whole, these birds of passage are useful. They are kind to the people, they increase rents, they spend money, and they diffuse a knowledge of, and a taste for, this country. The only misfortune is, that though some of them try to imitate Celticism, on the whole, the general tendency is to accelerate the obliteration of everything peculiarly Highland.

I spent part of the hour that we gave to the Spittal in examining its small and very lonely burying-ground. The chapel of ease is quite new; but one or two tombstones showed that here dust had been long rendered unto dust. I found the following inscription. It refers only to mortal and natural feelings, and is composed with singular simplicity; and its affection is rather deepened by recency.

"1845

"Erected by Peter Macgregor, in memory of his John, who died at Inverherothy, June 1844, aged 22. Low he lies here in the dust; and his memory fills his parents, sister, and brother with grief. Silent is the tongue that used to cheer them."

The sheep are evidently getting the better of the grouse throughout all the lower part of Glenshee, and even of Glenbeg, and there cannot be better hill pasture. This has been a grassy season, moist and warm in summer, and the verdure generally has been remarkable. All over the whole of these straths and glens the heather and the nut-brown ferns have been beautifully mixed, and contrasted not only with bright gleams, but with large vivid fields of the very finest green.

Bridge of Tilt, Sunday Morning, 20th September 1846. — We left nice, kindly Kindrogan yesterday about twelve, and came here by three or four, amidst dull, drizzling, foggy rain. The wild and secluded Eden of Fascally, which we went through, looked as well as it could; and so did the bridge in the pass, which we went down to.

My object in coming here is to show the district to Lizzie Richardson, and Glen Tilt to myself, which I have never seen. But it is not easy to see it now. I wanted to go direct from Castleton by the glen or glens to this. But there is no road for any carriage, or even car, which is very unfortunate, as my equestrian, and thirty-mile-a-day pedestrian, days are over. But had they been in their ancient vigour, the traveller, though even in quest of such innocent things as botany, geology, or scenery, is now stopped by his Grace the Duke of Leeds, the tacksman of the Mar Lodge shootings, who says that he has a right to protect the deer from disturbance. The public says he has no such right; but as there is no town at hand with its contemptuous citizens, of course the steady perseverence and the long purse of the single nobleman will soon get the better of the poor Celtic slave, the irritated tourist, the sulky drover, and even the London newspapers, who, in this slack season, have taken up the case. And then, at this lower end of the glen, another Grand Duke — he of Atholl — has been pleased to set his gates and his keepers, and for the same reason, that he may get more deer to shoot easily. His grandfather, the last sane duke, who died about twelve or fifteen years ago, made a much as to lay them open, by a private road, to the eyes of such passengers as they can trust. A general authority might be given to the innkeepers, whose houses would be ruined by being deprived of the power, if it was abused, to send strangers through; for the necessity of always making a personal application to the proprietor is a virtual prohibition.

We afterwards went and saw the falls of the Bruar; and to-morrow for Perth.

Perth, Monday Night, 21st September 1846. — Came here to-day; a beautiful day. Walked through Fascally; and took Liz Richardson into Dunkeld. The interior of the cathedral thoroughly Scotch, being most beastly. The square tower will certainly be down, because "the great dukes," as Perthshire delights to call those of Atholl, can't afford £20 to pin it up.

Tulliebole, Saturday Morning, 26th September. — The Court occupied us in Perth all Tuesday, Wednesday, and Thursday, and about an hour yesterday. The only interesting case — a murder, by poisoning — went off, on a doubt of the relevancy of part of the charge,

We then came here. Miss Richardson and I visited Lochleven Castle by the way. A mean and melancholy residence Mary must have had of it, especially considering her habits and folly. Her friend Elizabeth would have swum ashore every forenoon, or would have consoled herself by Greek, or by successful plots.

Often as I have been invited, both by Sir Harry and his son, I was never at Tulliebole before, and am much surprised at it. I had fancied it a tall keep, standing nearly treeless, on a black moor. And no doubt it, like all Kinross, was black enough a few years ago. But now industry has transformed it into a good grassy and oaty country; and I find some most respectable old trees round the house, and an admirable small castle. A delightful castle, inside and out. The date, 2d April 1608, and two inscriptional texts carved above the door, a tower, walls seven feet thick, turrets, odd, small windows, queer irregular little up-and-down bits of stairs, and a general air of quaint solidity and primitive awkwardness, give it all the charm of ancient habits, which, in this instance, is not disturbed by the slightest attempt at modern innovation. The dining-room alone seems, from its size and its height, to be too good for an old edifice. But it is as old as the rest. The castle's recent history was rather curious. When Lord Moncreiff's father, Sir Harry, succeeded, the property was worth less than even the living of Blackford, which he held. He was therefore very poor, with several brothers and sisters to educate, The family chateau was in very bad order, and instead of trying to keep it up, it was decided that the best way was to take the roof off and sell its materials, and to let the whole concern go down. This was done; many of the best trees were cut, and the castle stood as an abandoned ruin from 1771 till 1801, when Sir Harry was able to put on a new roof and windows, and to turn out Aeolus and the crows. The error of the place is in not cutting trees and letting in light and air. Its misfortune is, that it is in Kinross-shire, the most oozy and melancholy of Scotch surfaces. We were treated to the novelty of a fair day at Kinross yesterday; but the weather is making up for this absurdity to-day.

So we proceeded to town, minus my Lizzy, who has remained in Perth on a visit, and this Circuit is over.

I have read nothing in particular, and very little in general. The only entire book has been *Cyril Thornton,* by the late Captain Hamilton, the brother of the learned Sir William and the Ensign O'Doherty of the Noctes Ambrosiance. There is not a word of the novel good, except the Scotch scenes, which are all excellent.

GLASGOW CIRCUIT

Bonaly, 28th December 1846. — Lord Mackenzie and I performed the Glasgow Winter Circuit last week — a very insignificant affair. About thirty-seven cases, of which about thirty were vulgar thefts. We went on the morning of Monday the 21st, and were done on the evening of Wednesday the 23d.

Only two things struck me. One was that the ladies who expected transportation had all, quite plainly, concerted that they were to enact a faint when the reality of that doom was announced. Accordingly, each, in her turn, cast up her eyes, clasped her hands, screamed a very ill-acted scream, and then pretended to fall back into the arms of a female who sat behind apparently for the very purpose of receiving them; after all which she stumped downstairs cursing, and the sound of a battle with the officers closed each one's scene. The misfortune was that their teacher had made them all do it in the very same way.

The other was the remark of a Glasgow thief, who had been often imprisoned in vain, and on having his trade destroyed, by our sentence, for ten years in this country, expressed his feelings in the language of the commercial place he belonged to. On being told that his trial had ended in transportation, he first looked at the judges with a stare and an exclamation of surprise: "Ay!" and then turned round to the gallery, and remarked with the greatest coolness, "There's a wind-up for you!"

WEST CIRCUIT
1847

Bonaly, 2d May 1847. — The Spring Circuit now over was so expeditionless and commonplace, that I merely record the dates.

On the evening of the 7th of April I went alone to Stirling, where I joined Moncreiff. The business kept us there till the evening of Saturday the 10th, when I came home, leaving Moncreiff, who wished to remain for some visits. But he signalised the Circuit by tumbling downstairs; an alarming fall, attended with severe bruises and a good many cuts, and much bleeding. However, two days of bed and a week's repose made him all right.

On Monday the 12th Mrs. Cockburn and I went from Bonaly to Edinburgh, where after being joined by Miss K. Thomson, we went at ten o'clock, on rails, to Glasgow. We there got into a respectable hired carriage, and went to Luss, where we stayed all night. Next day we went to Inveraray. The horses stuck in trying to haul us up to Rest-and-be-Thankful; which obliged us to wait till we got other horses from Cairndow; and gave us an excellent opportunity of treasuring the beauties of Glencroe.

All the guilt of Argyle and Bute was disposed of on Wednesday the 14th.

On Thursday the 15th we departed at eight in the morning; and going by Dalmally, Tyndrum, and Glenfalloch, reached Tarbet about seven in the evening. Next day (Friday the 16th) we got to Glasgow for the half-past three train, and were at home again by about seven.

The weather, though cold to the skin, was most beautiful to the eye. I won't soon forget the evening from Glenfalloch to Tarbet, and the unwillingness of the sun to quit the top of Ben Lomond.

On Monday the 19th Mrs. Cockburn and I and Elizabeth went to Glasgow. These two returned here on Friday the 23d. I remained in Court all day, till Saturday at ten at night, when the horrors of a Glasgow Sunday drove me here, which I reached between one and two in the morning. After a delicious pech among my ribuses, hyacinths, and primroses, I returned by ten on Monday morning (26th), and continued till Thursday the 29th, when we were finally liberated, and got here (to find my hyacinths nearly all smashed by a hurricane) in the evening.

There were ninety-six indictments, the greatest number ever served for one Circuit at Glasgow. Of these, I should suppose, nearly ninety were tried, — a most effectual clearing out. Nor was it all mere paltry common thefts. There were murders, and large forgeries, and railways and steamboat mismanagements, and fire-raising, and abundance of bad robberies, and, in short, a respectable infusion of dignified crime. Thirteen of the culprits had been previously convicted in the Justiciary, i.e. had defied long imprisonment to frighten or reform them. And there were probably twice thirteen whose conduct had proclaimed the same fact after sentences by Sheriffs.

Dumfries, 20th September 1847, Monday Night. — The old round, so I shall say nothing about it. Musing along in the carriage to-day, I thought I had better try to recall some of the features of our ancient Circuits, which time has effaced. I have known Scotland, Circuitously, for above forty years. Many curious recollections arise on looking back on such a travelled road. The shades of many old lords, famous barristers, notorious provosts, sonorous macers, formal clerks, odd culprits, and queer witnesses reappear. But like wayside objects that we cast behind us on a journey, they cannot all be retained, and many must be let die. Some things, however, may be worth preserving.

Those who are born to railroads, or even to modern mail-coaches can scarcely be made to understand how we, of the previous age, got on. The state of the roads may be judged of from two or three facts. There was no bridge over the Tay at Dunkeld, or over the Spey at Fochabers, or over the Findhorn at Forres, nothing but wretched, pierless ferries, let to poor cottars, who rowed, or hauled, or pushed a crazy boat across, or more commonly got their wives to do it. There used to be no mail-coach north of Aberdeen, till, I think, after the battle of Waterloo. It consisted of a sort of chaise, drawn by two horses, and held three persons, two of them placed as usual in a chaise, and the third stuck into a kind of sentry-box opposite, with his back to the horses, and, of course, there were no front windows. To reach Inverness by the mail thirty or even twenty-five years ago took only about nine hours short of the time required to get to London. If the direct Highland road was preferred, then there was neither public conveyance nor post-horses. It was necessary to take the same horses all the way from Perth, and then the journey occupied three entire days from Perth and four from Edinburgh. I once came from Inverness to Perth with the Justice-Clerk, Charles Hope, who was always very kind to me, and used to take me about with him; and our days' work, with his four horses, were these: The first day we got to Kinrara, where we dined with the famous, clever, agreeable, profligate old Duchess of Gordon, who gathered all the neighbours within many miles for a ball. The second day brought us, towards its close, to Dalnacardoch; the third to Perth. Of course we had to rest and feed the steeds every stage. Even the public coach, when set agoing, delighted the lieges by making them sleep only two nights by the way. They could only reach Perth (the Queensferry very bad) the first day. Starting next morning at five, Pitmain was accomplished about nine at night, and Inverness appeared on the evening of the third day. The ark of a vehicle was generally moved by three horses, but for the stage between Dalnacardoch and Dalwhinnie it had four, and sometimes it had only two; and no set ever escaped with a single stage.

It was not just so bad on other Circuits, bit it was bad enough. Dumfries and Ayr were both unattainable in one day; and Inveraray was out of the world. Even Glasgow was a good day's work; and hence the inns next it, and next Edinburgh, were excellent, for Scotch inns of that day, and were generally crowded every night. The fact is incredible now — but it is a fact — that there were few hostels more resorted to by newly married pairs than those of Midcalder, Uphall, Holytown, Noblehouse, and Blackshiels. These now mean ruins were then bowers of Hymen. It was not distances or bad roads that were the obstacles to progress, so much as the want of horses.

What it must have been a few years before my time may be judged of from Bozzy's *Letter to Lord Braxfield,* published in 1780. He thinks that besides a carriage and his own carriage horses, every judge ought to have his sumpter horse; and ought not to travel faster than the waggon which carried "the baggage of the Circuit". I understood from Hope that after 1784, when he came to the bar, he and Braxfield rode a whole North Circuit; and that, from the Findhorn being in flood, they were obliged to go up its banks for about twenty-eight miles, to the Bridge of Dulsie, before they could cross. I myself rode Circuits, when I was Advocate-Depute, between 1807 and 1810. The fashion of every depute carrying his own shell on his back, in the form of his own carriage, is a piece of modern dignity.

This slowness of movement, and badness of up-putting, prevented ladies from accompanying lords so habitually as they do now. But to make up for this, every judge carried about a lately fledged advocate as his humble friend. To be seen travelling Circuit with my lord, was thought such a feather in a youth's cap, that his friends never allowed him to decline the honour. Decline being aide-de-camp to the general! But, Lord, it was dull! I never knew one victim that enjoyed the sacrifice. There could, for weeks alone together, be no cordiality between age and youth, patronage and dependence, levity and dignity. Even Hope's kindness, and cumbrous efforts to be jolly, could not save it from oppressiveness. With most others, it was the *peine forte et dure.* The sedate driving, the two-hours pauses every stage, the disrespect of taking refuge in a book, the positive insult of walking off alone, the condescending remark of my lord, only so much the worse when it was intended to be gay, the respectful acquiescence of "the young man." Och! och! it was dreadful. Nearly fifty years have not yet effaced the Lord Mackenzie's sufferings under Lord Craig.

There is nothing in which the old Circuits differed more from the modern than in the paucity of their business and the excess of their politics. Little as the business is now, it is at least five-fold what it was formerly. To be sure, being in no want of time, they wasted it freely. I have heard Jeffrey say that if there was only one cause in the world, it would never be done at all. It is only necessity that produces judicial expedition. The old debates on relevancy on every indictment, the technical objections to witnesses, the long harrangues to juries in every case, the written verdicts, the parents of endless additional objections and discussions, these, and much more other useless and teasing weft with which the woof of our old practice was crossed, made every trial, however clear and insignificant, a matter of keenness, pertinacity, eloquence and sweat. That fifteen cases may be disposed of in eight hours, and that a Depute-Advocate may do his duty well, and yet not address a jury once in fifty trials and that prisoners' counsels may decline addressing in the great majority of cases — these facts, with which we are not quite familiar, would certainly be discredited if they were told to Braxfield in Elysium.

To make up for want of business, our predecessors exerted themselves powerfully as political trumpets. What harangues! about innovation, Jacobinism, and the peculiar excellence of every abuse. No judge could preserve his character, and scarcely even his place, for a month, who was to indulge in such exhibitions now. But that time applauded him. For example, when I was Advocate-Depute, with Hope as Justice-Clerk, at Aberdeen (1808 or 1809, I think), his lordship, after leaving the bench early, went and reviewed the volunteers! Yes, the Judge of Assize doffed his wig, mounted a charger, and reviewed a regiment; and went forward next day on his Circuit. After the display on the field, he entertained the officers and the military authorities of the place at dinner. There probably never was so much scarlet or so many epaulettes at a judge's assize banquet before. It was a grand military day in Aberdeen, and entirely extinguished the poor glory of the Court.

All this seems odd now. But the wonder will abate when we recollect that the reviewing judge was an actual and most active Lieutenant-Colonel, and that though the judicious lamented this, the period permitted it. And indeed the judges, as representing the sovereign, had, and I fancy still have, a right to take the command of the whole military within the Circuit town. This is not practised now, but it was uniformly practised since I remember. The judge was formally waited upon by the commanding officer, or by some officer representing him, and asked for orders, and to give the password for the day. I never knew the judge give any orders, but he very generally gave the word; and the daily military report was frequently made to him by an officer lowering his sword.

There is one change for the worse. Magistrates and gentry are positively ordered by old royal proclamations, I believe, to testify their respect for the law by attending the Circuit Courts. Long after this had become a mere piece of antiquarianism, the gentry did attend the Courts, from a sense of propriety partly; but hardly one of them does so, voluntarily, now. This is wrong, but it is a mistake to think that it proceeds from the modern rise

202

of popular vulgarity, or disrespect of authority. On the contrary, its chief cause, is, that people respect the law so much, and so habitually, that they don't think that it needs any extra aid. The very decline of political interest contributes greatly to the absence of the aristocracy. But nothing contributes so much as the change of the law, which took the nomination of the jury from the judge. While this power lasted, the judge took care to secure the presence of gentlemen and friends, who would grace the procession and the banquet. A good diner was sure to be paid the compliment of being summoned.

After opening the Court with all attainable splendour, the best modern practice is for the judges to go to and from the court-house as quietly as possible. But the fashion, till lately, was never to move but in procession, — always fully tailed, and on foot, that the tail might be seen the better. It is not very long since there was a foot procession to and from every meeting and rising of the Court; even in Glasgow, where, whatever sneers it produced, it could produce no village awe. Yet twice every day did we walk, horn-blown, about a mile, through that contemning mob; ay, and with torches if it was at night. The last Glasgow foot procession I remember being in was about 1820. It was a wet day; and I have often regretted having lost a caricature which John Lockhart, a master in that art, drew of Lord Pitmilly, with his umbrella over his wig, and his gown tucked up out of the mud, to the exposure of his lordship's odd and well-known legs. We have taken to carriages and cavalry at Glasgow now. I hope to see the neighing steeds dispensed with soon; but as to this I am at present solitary. (I have since found this picture.)

It carries me far back into my fresh-hood, to recollect the time when I thought the Circuit dinner an imposing affair.

Cumpston, Friday, 24th September 1847. — But this was during the revolutionary war, when there was some aristocracy and red cloth at them. The frivolous smile at the horns now; but when they croaked forth God save the king, a tune that no one could safely treat even with jocular levity then, — they were listened to with proud and decorous respect. A poor creature, whose case was not capital, cut his throat in jail (at Ayr, I believe), as soon as he heard the brazen sound which announced the approach of Eskgrove. At which his lordship rubbed his hands with delight, and explained, chuckling, how gratifying a sign it was of the wholesome terrors of the Circuit Judge. The first Circuit dinner I was at (Perth), I happened to say to a person beside me that a whole Circuit must surely be tiresome. "This is my sixty-third, sir" (or some such enormous number). I stared at him as a midge might at an elephant. It was Henry Johnstone Wyllie, the clerk, who lived to go about, or above, one hundred. He was a good man, and a stiff, correct clerk, famous in his day. When he at last retired he was compliment-

Robert MacQueen, Lord Braxfield

ed by a grand Circuit bar dinner.

At Edinburgh, the old judges had a practice, at which even their barbaric age used to shake its head; they had always wine and biscuits on the bench when the business was to be plainly protracted beyond the usual dinner hour. The modern judges — those I mean who were made after 1800, — never gave in to this; but with those of the preceding generation, some of whom lasted several years after 1800, it was quite familiar. Black bottles of strong port were set down beside them on the bench, with glasses, carafes of water, tumblers, and biscuits; and this without the slightest shame of attempt at concealment. The refreshment was generally allowed to stand untouched, and as if despised, for a short while, during which their lordships seemed to be intent only on their notes. But in a little some water was poured into the tumbler, and sipped quietly, as if merely to sustain nature. Then a few drops of wine were ventured upon, but only with water. Till at last patience could refrain no longer, and a full bumper of the pure black element was tossed over, after which the thing went on regularly, and there was a comfortable munching and quaffing, to the great envy of the parched throats in the gallery. The strong-headed ones stood tolerably well. Baachus had never an easy victory over Braxfield. But it told, plainly enough, upon the feeble or the twaddling, such as Eskgrove and Craig. Not that the ermine was absolutely intoxicated. But it was certainly very muzzy. This, however, was so ordinary with these sages, that it really made little apparent odds upon them. Their noses got a little redder, and their speech somewhat thicker, and they became drowsier. But these changes were not very perceptible at a distance; and they all acquired the habit of sitting and looking judicial enough, even when their bottles had reached the lowest ebb.

This open-court refection never prevailed, so far as I ever saw, at Circuits. It took a different form there. The temptation of the inn frequently produced a total stoppage of business; during which all concerned — judges, and counsel, and clerks, and jurymen, and provosts — had a jolly dinner; after which they returned again to the transportations and hangings. I have seen this done often. It was a common remark that the step of the evening procession was far less true to the music than that of the morning. The excitement and indecorum once produced a scene of violence at Jedburgh (after 1807) which it was miraculous did not, in due time, place the judge at the bar.

Nothing was so much disliked in those days as the appeals, which it was the fashion to treat as intrusions, and almost to smother under impatience and disdain. Besides other indecencies, they were generally heard after dinner, and at the inn. The dining-room, still fragrant, was cleared, or half-cleared, and, after tea, my lord reappeared wigless, gownless, regardless; flustered, and with an obvious impatience for supper.

Circuit balls, now totally given up, were then quite established, but only at certain towns. There was always one at
Dumfries and at Ayr, and frequently at Glasgow. And very nice
balls they used to be; easy and merry. The judge was always
expected to attend, and generally did so.

Aberdeen used to be distinguished by "The Entertainment",
which was an evening party given to the Court by the magistrates. It was not exactly a supper, for it had little of the true
supper solidity. It was a refection, — as slight, elegant, and
intellectual as a municipal banquet could be. It took place on
any convenient Circuit night, at nine or ten o'clock, in a handsome civic hall, and lasted about two hours. There seemed to be
from eighty to one hundred persons present — the city's cream.
The ailments consisted of nothing but fruits, dried or fresh, all
manner of cakes and biscuits, and a bottle of claret between
each two persons. There being thus no need of changing plates,
or sending for distant dishes, and various drinks, servants were
superseded, and there were none in the room unless rung for.
The Provost presided. But he was above the vulgarity of toasts.
This duty was devolved on a city officer, who stood, in uniform,
behind the Provost, with a list of the toasts, which he proclaimed on getting a sign, in a loud voice. There were very few,
and very short, speeches, and scarcely any cheering. But there
was a competency of mirth, and some songs, and a homely
species of kind, and not very difficult, wit. On the whole, it was
the most civilised magisterial festival I have ever seen. Why, or
when, it ceased. I don't exactly know.

Of the old picturesque Lords, none can hold up their heads
against Eskgrove and Hermand. The whole of this volume
would not contain one-half of the diverting, and now incredible,
sayings and doings, of these two judicial men, who shone in
quite different spheres. No outrageousness of originality could
ever make Hermand cease to be a warm-hearted gentleman of
the olden time. Eskgrove was a personified compound of
avarice, indecency, official insolence and personal cowardice,
great law, and practical imbecility. He cannot be thought of,
in the Circuit days I refer to, except in connection with
Brougham, who, during the four years he was at our bar, laid
himself out, and with triumphant success, to make fun of this
creature, by torturing and exposing it. I can describe neither at
present, nor give any of the countless anecdotes that signalised
their peregrinations. It is difficult to say whether spectators
laughed most at the ludicrous and contemptible absurdities of
the mean and testy judges, or at the able and audacious
extravagances of the counsel. Paired, they were perfect.

Cumpston, Saturday, 25th September 1847. — There being
little criminal, and no civil business, the more eminent counsel
were rarely seen at Circuits. But every Circuit town had its own
great barrister, generally connected with it personally. James

Fergusson, afterwards a consistorial judge and a principal Clerk of Session, one of the best-natured and most absent of men, predominated at Ayr. Dumfries boasted of Robert Corbet, subsequently Crown counsel in the matter of tithes, and keeper of something in the General Register House; also an excellent and able, but vulgar and illiterate man. Aberdeen rung with the empty eloquence of James Gordon of Craig, the only Aberdonian I ever knew at the bar who had not a particle of granite in his head, or his discourse; all sputter, and froth, and declamation. Perth was the dunghill of _____, the patron of blackguardism, yet who never had a client equal to himself in that quality.

Wordiness was the peculiarity of all these men; as it ever must be of the local class, which must suit itself to the taste of the local market, where zeal is the prized virtue, and loud loquacity is the clearest mark of zeal. I am not aware that there is any district barrister now, except my friend Mr. Logan, who charms Stirling. Increase of business has abridged speeches, and when a case occurs that can pay for a speech, facility of travelling secures a better tongue than the provincial one.

The last generation was not rich in curious Sheriffs. Fraser of Ferraline at Inverness, Gordon of Culvennan at Kirkcudbright, and Edward McCormick at Ayr, were perhaps the least common; but even they are insignificant. Walter Scott, to be sure, gave justice to Selkirkshire, and always cheered the Circuit at Jedburgh. His talk and mirth drove even the Abbey out of our heads.

Of all my old Circuit companions, there is none it is so delightful to recollect as Jeffrey. I have been with him often, at every Circuit town except Inveraray, and we generally travelled together. Every court-house and every inn is associated with him. Striking as his professional displays used to be, they were always effaced by his personal worth and his rich and playful conversation. Whether walking through beautiful scenery, or shivering in a state of half-nausea in a crazy Kinghorn passage-boat, or toasting himself over the kitchen fire of a bad inn, in the grey of a spring morning, till the ostler could be roused, he never failed to enliven the scene by his speculations and his discussions with anybody, however humble, who came in his way. Would that he were on the Justiciary bench. But it may not be.

Craigie House, Sunday Night, 26th September 1847. — The facts as to this Circuit are these:-

My daughter Elizabeth and Joanna Richardson are with me. We left Edinburgh last Monday, and dined at Dumfries, where we joined Moncreiff, who had taken Jedburgh. We were in Court at Dumfries all Tuesday the 21st and part of Wednesday the 22d; on which last day we got to Cumpston in the evening, with Moncreiff. He left it for Brougham Hall on Friday. We stayed there till this morning, when we came here, by Carsphairn and Dalmellington.

A most beautiful day; worthy of such a drive. The Glenkens part of it — from Cumpston to Carsphairn, — about thirty miles, is really admirable. I grieve for Dalmellington. It has the appearance, and the reputation of being a singularly virtuous and happy village; and I am told is perhaps the last place in Ayrshire where, with a good deal of old primitive manufacture, rural simplicity and contentment still linger. But it is now to taste of manufactures in an improved state. The devil has disclosed his iron, and speculation has begun to work it. There seemed to be about a dozen of pits sinking within half a mile of the village, and before another year is out those now solitary and peaceful hills will be blazing with furnaces, and blighted by the presence and the vices of a new population of black scoundrels. They were already lying snoring, and, I presume, drunk, on many indignant knolls.

Bonaly, 30th September 1847. — I was in Court at Ayr all Monday and Tuesday, and till near one yesterday; after which we railed to Edinburgh, and were here in the evening. I lived entirely at Craigie with my old friend James Campbell, who was my companion on many a Circuit in the days of yore. Escape into country air, or into any air but that of a steamy, noisey fetid, obscene public-house, was so agreeable, that it revived my scheme of having the abominable Circuit dinner abolished, and the judges let alone in their private lodgings.

The only curious case on this Circuit was that of a worthy husband at Jedburgh, who wanted to get his spouse killed; but instead of resorting to commonplace violence by himself, tried to make the law do it. For this purpose he fell upon the device of making it appear that she had poisoned him; for which she was committed for trial, and was very nearly being tried. But suspicion being excited, it was discovered that his whole statements on precognition were false, and all his dexterous imitations of being poisoned were utter fabrications. The result was that he was brought to trial himself for fraud, and was transported for seven years.

NORTH CIRCUIT
1848

Stonehaven, Sunday Night, 9th April 1848. — I left Edinburgh yesterday morning with my son George and my daughter Elizabeth, who has now become a part of the Circuit.

Our route and conveyance were new; I sent the carriage across to Burntisland on the evening of Friday the 7th; and we got on the railway yesterday at 8.17; were at Granton in a few minutes; crossed in less than half-an-hour; re-railed to Cupar, where we found the carriage and horses waiting for us; drove to the Dundee ferry; crossed; railwayed again from Dundee to Montrose; posted here, where we arrived at six; doing in ten hours that it had taken Moncreiff, who preferred the old way of horses and Perth, two days to achieve.

We did this on Saturday, because, as yet, there is no railway travelling on Sunday; and therefore we were obliged to pass this whole day here, with Moncreiff and his daughter.

I passed two hours or so loitering round the point opposite the harbour, and along the shore, to very near Dunnottar; a way I never took before. It is a most glorious walk, with a good foot-worn path along the edge of the beach all along. Most pictur-esque rocks, — black, water-carved into strange forms, inter-spersed by delicious little bays, as to which it is impossible to avoid always doubting whether the velvet of the soft bank turf, or the pure stones glittering before and under the bright fresh ocean, be the most beautiful. And what an ocean, as seen to-day! Blue-blue, calm, shipless, boundless, gazed over in silence by the ruin. I have seldom passed two hours of more useful solitude.

Inverness, Sunday Evening, 16th April 1848. — We meant to have begun business at Aberdeen on Monday the 10th. But after the Circuit had been fixed for that day, it was discovered that it was their Sacramental Monday; and we were obliged to give up the entering procession and to adjourn till two. But we went there to breakfast.

We were in Court that day till seven; all Tuesday, all Wednesday, and part of Thursday. There was nothing curious in the business. But I took a note on the spot of a thing that struck me as very curious in the Circuit prayer. It shows the extent to which some people's faith in the reformation of criminals goes. The reverend gentleman, after praying for the judges and the jurors, and the witnesses, and the Advocate-Depute, and the counsel — on each of whom he bestowed a separate aspiration — came to the prisoners. And as to them, he expressed his hope and his belief that they would all come to consider their detection, and their conviction, and their punish-ment, and "their very crime", as so many kindnesses or Providence to lead them into the right way; and that if they did so, they might be assured that "at last they would shine as the brightest gems in the Redeemer's crown." These were his very words.

Moncreiff returned southwards, and I came on here, after Aberdeen. We got to Elgin on the evening of Thursday the 13th, and stayed there (bad inn) that night. Next morning we breakfasted at Knockomie and remained there till six in the evening. I again visited what, to me, was once the paradise of Relugas. My friend Sir Thomas Lauder, under whose domestic sunshine I used to know it, is dying, and I felt it a very sad visit. Believing his recovery impossible, I hope never to see it again.

The worthy lady of Knockomie made her hospitality include both an excellent breakfast and an excellent dinner. But we at last prevailed upon ourselves to take to the road, and we got here about nine in the face of a magnificent sunset.

Our business was over yesterday, in one short day; and then came the dinner.

This morning, as on the morning of yesterday, I walked up to the island, by the left bank of the river. Then went in gowned procession, and heard a very bad, noisy sermon. After which I went to the canal basin, along this side of the canal, till it nearly touches Craigphadrick, up to the top of that hill of Patrick; down, and across fields to the river-side opposite the island; and so home. And now, after a quiet repast, with Edward Maitland, Francis Russell, and Burnet, and a night view of the river from the bridge, I am "bedward ruminating".

Every place I revisit is improving. The increase of religious and educational buildings is very striking. Huntly, Keith, Fochabers, and Forres, are each dignified by new edifices in a style certainly not below the importance of the places; and the people here, having got some funds, are beginning to discover that the capital of the north requires a college. The vanity of Bell, who has ordered all his charity schools to be called Madras Colleges — one of which is at Inverness — has vulgarised this once respectable title all over the country. The new jail, now erecting, willbe a very great improvement in the composition of this already beautiful place. But it is melancholy to see a new house building even in little old Forres. Jails and schools, and such things, necessary, like railways and post offices, for modern accommodation, must be submitted to; but a new private dwelling-house introduced into Forres! with its insolent front to the street, its ostentatious windows, its brass knocker, and a plate announcing the scoundrel's name!

Aviemore, Tuesday Morning, 18th April 1848. — We left Inverness yesterday about ten, and were here by three. A good, clear day, though certainly not sultry. I walked till six, trying to find the way to the house of Rothiemurchus which, often as I have been here, I had never gone to; and after going nearly two miles wrong, I succeeded in getting within hail of it, but there was no boat to take me across. In the evening we went to see a little loch within less than a mile of the inn, which I never even heard of till now, when two gentlemen at Inverness were loud in its praise. It is well set, in a hollow — amidst birches — at the base of a respectable rock. But the water is too shallow and too small; a mere saucerful. The mountains were in great splendour, with their perpetual darkness, relieved by much bright snow, and all their forms, and valleys, and gullies, and corries, palpably near us. And, before bedding, their silent regions were looked upon by an excellent moon. But our Scotch moon is a cold creature.

And there they are again this morning; in a still finer day. O ye Cairngorms, how have ye never produced a poet of your own? Had I been born among ye, no doubt every one of your summits and your valleys would have been sung. I cannot look upon you, and doubt that your bard is rearing.

Bridge of Tilt, Tuesday Night, 18th April 1848. — Left Aviemore at nine and were here by five. The day cold but bright, and the long, silent range in an excellent state. There is no better drive for a contemplative man. We revisited the Bruar Falls; the ducal monster being in London, George and I dared to walk to his castle. Outside — which is all that we saw — it is all in a wretched condition, — mean, comfortless, squalid.

When I left home, I thought of devoting these pages to anecdotes connected with famous trials, chiefly those in which I have been professionally engaged. But I find that it would not do, without far more detail than anybody would care to follow. Let me therefore just tell three stories, which are all simple and curious.

In July 1800 a person of the name of Elliot was convicted of a capital offence — either horse-stealing or forgery — and was doomed to die. Owing to some legal doubt he was pardoned, only a day or two before he was to have suffered; but another man, who had been condemned to be executed on the same day, was not so fortunate. Lord Medwyn (who is my informer) was caught, by accident, on the Lawnmarket of Edinburgh, and could not escape from the crowd which he found assembling to witness the execution of the law's remaining victim, but he got into a remote spot at the upper end of the street. A man came there hurriedly, and in intense agitation, and stood out most part of the scene. His eyes were strained towards the scaffold, as if they would burst, his hands clenched in agony, his chest heaving, the very picture of horror. It was Elliot. Medwyn had seen him in court, and knew him. Instead of flying, he felt it irresistible to witness the proceeding in which he himself had so nearly been an actor; and probably suffered far more in seeing the position of his associate, and in sympathising with himself, than he would have done if he had been the spectacle, and not the spectator. It was a strange feeling that forced him there, yet not an incomprehensible one.

I had a client called David Haggart, who was hanged at Edinburgh for murdering his jailor in Dumfries. He was young, good looking, gay, and amiable to the eye; but there never was a riper scoundrel, a most perfect and inveterate miscreant in all the darker walks of crime. Nevertheless, his youth (about twenty-five) and apparent gentleness, joined to an open confession of sins, procured him considerable commiseration, particularly among the pious and the female. He employed the last days of his existence in dictating memoirs of his own life to his agent, with a view to publication. The book was published, and my copy contains a drawing of himself in the condemned cell, by his own hand, with a set of verses, his own composition, which he desired to be given to me in token of his gratitude for my exertions at his trial. Well, the confessions, and the whole book, were a tissue of absolute lies, — not of mistakes, or of exaggerations, or of fancies, but of sheer and intended lies. And they all had one object, to make him appear a greater villain than he really was. Having taken to the profession of crime, he wished to be at the head of it. He wanted to die a great man. He therefore made himself commit crimes of all sorts; none of which, as was ascertained by inquiry, were ever committed at all. His guilt in these deathbed inventions was established by as good evidence as his guilt in the act for which he suffered was. A strange pride. Yet not without precedent; and in nobler walks of criminal ambition.

Mrs. Mackinnon was convicted of murder on the 13th of March 1823. Jeffrey and I were her counsel. Her family had been respectable. It was sworn, by a person who had served with him, that her deceased father was a captain in the army. But by misfortune after misfortune, or more probably by successive acts of misconduct, she was at last, when not much, if at all, above thirty, reduced to the condition of being the mistress of a disorderly house in Edinburgh. But still she was not all bad; for a strong and lofty generosity, by which she had been distinguished before she fell, neither the corruptions, nor the habits of her subsequent life could extinguish. She had stabbed a man with a knife, in a brawl in her house, and it was for taking his life that her own was forfeited. If some circumstances which were established in a precognition, taken by orders of Sir Robert Peel, then Home Secretary, after her conviction, had transpired on the trial, it is more than probable that Jeffrey, whose beautiful speech, on the bad elements in his hands, is remembered to this hour, would have prevailed on the jury to restrict their conviction to culpable homicide. But, in law, it was a murder, and Peel, though moved, was advised that she could not be spared.

So she died publicly, but gracefully and bravely; and her last moment was marked by a proceeding so singular, that it is on its account that I mention her case. She had an early attachment to an English Jew, who looked like a gentleman, on the outside at least; and this passion had never been extinguished. She asked him to come and see her before her fatal day. He did so; and on parting, finally, on her last evening, she cut an orange in two, and giving him one half, and keeping the other herself, directed him to go to some window opposite the scaffold, at which she could see him, and to apply his half to his lips when she applied her half to hers. All this was done! she saw her only earthly friend, and making the sign, died, cheered by this affection.

Here the anecdote ought to have ended; and if it had been an invention, it would have ended here. But see how nature's wonders exceed those of art. She had left everything she had, amounting to four or five thousand pounds, to her friend. He took the legacy, but refused to pay the costs of her defence, which her agent only screwed out of him by an action.

Perth, Wednesday Night, 19th April 1848. — We came here to-day, amidst ceaseless and heavy rain.

Perth, Sunday Night, 23d April 1848. — Getting on slowly, and dull, commonplace work. The audience was relieved yesterday by a murder. But it was a poor one. An infant suffocated in its clothes by its natural father. He was condemned, but won't be hanged.

We went to church to-day in state. A grand oration, from the same mouthy declaimer we had on the 27th of April 1845. His fancy goods are of a bad pattern, and want body.

After church Whigham and I had a beautiful walk over Kinnoul Hill, down to Kinfauns, and home by the road; all glorious. There are few finer scenes in this country. Were I a Perth residenter, my morning and evening meditations should be inspired by the quiet beauty of the North Inch; my forenoon exercise ennobled by the rich magnificence of the prospects from the hill of Kinnoul.

Bonaly, Thursday, 27th April 1848. — We only got quit of Perth yesterday about two.

George had left us on Saturday. The first one who ever ran off from one of my Circuits before it was finished. He has the misfortune to be an Episcopalian, and talked of being home on Easter Sunday. But he is also married, and his young wife was not with him.

My books were the last numbers of the *Edinburgh* and *Quarterly Reviews*. Both dullish. I then took to *Grantley Manor,* a novel which I could not get on with. And then, for the fiftieth time, I discovered new beauties in the *Fair Maid of Perth.*

Mr. Edward Maitland shed his first odours, as public accuser, over this Circuit. Hard and grim outside; but inwardly, soft enough; calm, firm, sensible, pious, and honest. He had a little friend called Francis Russell, advocate, with him, — a self-thinking fellow, as to whom I would not be surprised if he were to become some one.

WEST CIRCUIT

Comrie House, Sunday, before dinner, 3d September 1848. — My route this Circuit will be nearly the very same as it was in this month 1845; so I shall literally just keep the log.

Thursday, 31st August 1848. — Left Edinburgh at seven A.M., by the Stirling train, with my son George, his wife, my daughter Johanna, and Marion Thomson of London. Reached Stirling (the carriage with us) at nine. Breakfasted; saw the castle and everything; departed at half-past eleven; passed one hour and a half with Sir David Dundas at Ochtertyre; got to the Trossachs at five; loitered by the lochside till six; returned, dined, snored. The whole day bright, calm and warm.

Friday, 1st September 1848. — Went to Loch at eight A.M.; boated; returned at ten; breakfasted; got to Callander at twelve; went to the Brig of Bracklin; set off at 2.30; reached this via Loch Lubnaig and Lochearn at 6.30; a party to dinner; a sort of a dance in the evening. Day bad at Callander; otherwise excusable.

Saturday, 2d September 1848. — Drove and walked about all day; lunched at Dunira; dined here with two Strowan Stirlings and Dr. Malcolm. Day good.

Sunday, 3d September 1848. — Went to Comrie Established Church; walked to Lawers; impatient for dinner. Got it. To bed.

Monday, 4th September 1848, 9.30 P.M. — Left Comrie to-day at eight; and got here (King's House) at six. Such a track! and such a day! A day to be remembered almost in the grave.

Tuesday Night, 5th September 1848. — Left King's House to-day at eleven, and was here, at Ballachulish, at three; a beautiful day till about five, when the rain began. We met John Stuart, M.P. and chancery barrister, here, and arranged to sail up to his retreat at the head of Loch Leven with him to-morrow. Meanwhile we all dined at his brother's, the Laird of Ballachulish.

Wednesday Night, 6th September 1848. — A day of unceasing torrents of rain, and of furious wind. No Loch Leven possible. We have scarcely got our noses out. The glories of this place all veiled in black fog.

Thursday Night, 7th September 1848. — Ditto nearly. I never saw rain before. However, in desperation I went, with Charlotte and Marion, seven miles up Glencoe, to see and hear the torrents roaring down the sides of the hills. It was grand, but not so much as I expected.

No two worse days could be contrived for this place.

Saturday, 9th September 1848, Noon, Oban. — Yesterday

morning promised so well, that Marion and I went, before breakfast, in a boat, that she might make a sketch of the Episcopal chapel, — the grandest and the most beautifully placed chapel in Britain. While she was so occupied on an island, I loitered about, and saw many glorious gleams of glorious scenes.

We left Ballachulish yesterday at eleven, and got to Oban at half-past six. A torrent of rain, and thick fog, with high wind, the whole way. We just saw enough to show us what we were losing. A drive of singular magnificence. This distance — which I record because I got such opposite accounts of it — is twenty-six miles, exclusive of the two ferries, of which Shean is above a mile across, and Connel, about a quarter of a mile. The north side of Shean is sixteen miles from Ballachulish, the south side ten from Oban. We had horses waiting us at the south side of Shean from Oban.

Our carriage was heavy, and the pair of horses from Ballachulish so light (or so sensible), that they stood stock still till we got out at every hill; so that from our walks, and the two ferries, we were wet the whole day. And, like an idiot, I let us be put into the same open boat with the carriage at Shean, though the sea was as rough as a violent head wind could make it in a space one and a quarter mile wide, and we had only two oars, each with two rowers. It took them above an hour to get us, inch by inch, across; the carriage, heavily laden, swung; the nine Celts who had charge of us jabbered and roared, all gesticulating opposite directions; and in spite of their assurances that there was no danger, yet we were all alarmed, and I know one who was in a genuine fright. I had my cloak unbuttoned, a plank which was at my feet secured, and my mind made up as to the point I was to try for. My chief fear was for Johanna, who chose to remain in the carriage. For our real danger lay in its swinging over, in which case she was gone. The boat would have been upset; but we, who were free, had some chances from spars and the keel, but she would to a certainty, have been drowned in a box. Mrs. George was in dreadful agitation. Marion resolutely composed, though in great alarm. George sensible and quiet, and, like myself, had his thoughts on the keel, and his eye on the best spot to make for, should the keel fail. It was a very dangerous, and a culpably foolish proceeding. We should have waited for a small boat for ourselves, though we had waited a year. They are disgraceful ferries, having too few boats, and none of them good; no landing places; no planks, or gangways, or cranes; no men, excepting such as can be withdrawn for the occasion from their proper land occupations; no master; no system, or skill, or power either of speaking or of hearing intelligently. Passengers, cattle, and carriages are just lifted and thrown into clumsy, crazy boats, and jerked by bad rowers, with unsafe oars, amidst a disorderly tumult of loud, discordant, half-naked, and very hairy Celts, who, however, expecting whisky, are at least civil, hearty, and strong. Bad though all this be, it is perhaps as good as the smallness of the traffic and the insolvency of the lairds admit of.

To-day the weather is as bad as ever. How it roars and pours! I begin to consider the spectacular part of the Circuit as over.

Nevertheless, my four companions set sail, in the steamer Dolphin, this morning, at seven, for Iona and Staffa. Poor wretches! I don't believe they will land at either.

Sunday Night, 10th September 1848, Taynuilt. — But they landed at both, and describe even the sail, the gleam-broken clouds, and the dun hills of Mull as preferable to the quiet brilliance of a fine day. Right to make the most of things.

This day has been beautiful. At eleven A.M. we all went to the Episcopal room in Oban, and heard an English stranger read prayers, very ill; and a young Oxford tutor who has been there for two months with pupils, preach very gently and elegantly, and quite uselessly. There were above seventy persons present, all strangers, as the landlord of the hotel told me, except about twenty or twenty-five.

A Free Church has been erected in Oban since I last saw it. It is beautifully placed, and better in its structure than most of them. They are also beginning to make a few villas. No sea place has better or more varied sites than Oban, insomuch that under the wealth of England it would be a beautiful marine village. But with the poverty of Scotland, and the untidy habits of the people, the positions and the prospects are lost. At Ballachulish, the paradise of Scotland, the inn is exquisitely placed, within a few feet of the water's edge; but the paradise is only to be seen over the dunghill, which is spread out between the windows and the clearest water in nature.

To-day we left Oban about three; went in a boat to Dunstaffnage, and got here about half-past six. A good bad inn. To-morrow for Loch Etive.

Monday Night, 11th September 1848, Dalmally. — A very successful expedition up Loch Etive. The day is excellent, a capital boat, and four good and sensible rowers, one of whom renewed his acquaintance with me, having been in the same capacity in 1845. It is a magnificent piece of solitude, not improved since 1845 by the opening of two granite quarries, and with more pasture than I formerly supposed.

We left Taynuilt about four, and came here. A glorious stage.

Tuesday Night, 12th September 1848, Inveraray. — Came here this forenoon. A day worthy of Loch Awe.

Wednesday Night, Inveraray, 13th September 1848. — Moncreiff joined us here yesterday. In Court till six P.M., and then the degrading dinner, which some of my brethren think essential for the preservation of the constitution.

Tarbet, Thursday Night, 14th September 1848. — Came here to-day at four P.M. A beautiful day. Stopped and saw reformed Ardkinglas. A delightful Highland spot. The flower-garden is excellent; and the piece of water saved from the usual offensiveness of artificial ponds by the neatness with which it and its adjuncts are kept. Noble ash-trees, and silver firs; but I doubt if there be two of the latter that are not suffering from the competition of paltry enemies. The axe should spare nothing that touches, or even shades, a leaf of these magnificent pines.

Glasgow, Friday Night, 15th September 1848. — Left Tarbet to-day after breakfast; loitered, by land and by water, for some hours at Luss, and were here about seven P.M. As perfect a day for Loch Lomond as there can be without bright sunshine.

Bonaly, Saturday Night, 16th September 1848. — After inspecting the beautiful and well restored Cathedral of Glasgow, and the striking but spoiled burial-ground, affectedly styled the Necropolis, and the venerable but doomed college, we came here to-day to dinner.

I return to Glasgow part of the business on Monday night. Too much time was allowed between Inveraray and Glasgow, and I have resorted to this home pause from economical necessity.

My book during the last fortnight has been *Ivanhoe* once more. But I grieve to say that I read it with diminished admiration. Probably nobody else could have written that work; but his genius seems never to find profusion of matter except in Scotland. See how the figures rush up into living life in any of his good Scotch novels. Take *Waverley* with MacIvor, Flora, Macwheeble, Davie Gellatley, Bradwardine, Evan Dhu, Maccombish, etc. Or *Guy Mannering* with the Dominie, Meg Merrilees, Dandy Dinmont, the old Laird, Dirk Hatteraick, etc. Or *Rob Roy*, with Rob, Helen MacGregor, the Bailie, Andrew Fairservice, the Dougal Cratur, etc. And so many go on with nearly the whole works, each teeming with original life, exhibited in fresh, natural scenes. Rebecca is almost the solitary figure in *Ivanhoe*; the passage at arms, and the glorious night between Richard and the Clerk of Copmanhurst, almost its two great scenes. The revival of Athelstane from the supposed dead, though such an incident may have occurred, is an absurdity and a trick, and unworthy of the work and of its author. There are other scenes, such as the storming of Torquilstone Castle, and the two interviews of the Templar and Rebecca — in the one of which he tries to make her become his mistress, and in the other to escape with him as his wife — that are admirable, but they are of inferior importance. On the whole, *Ivanhoe* is a great prose epic, but it wants the varied, natural originality which signalises the works drawn from Scotch life and scenery.

Bonaly, 27th September 1848. — On the night of Monday the 18th my daughter Elizabeth and I returned to Glasgow, where we remained till Saturday the 23d, when we came here to dinner. And on the morning of Monday the 25th I went back to Glasgow, but got finally free on the evening of Tuesday the 26th.

There were only about 71 cases, and as we cleared off 36 in the two first days, we deluded ourselves by the hope of a speedy liberation. But the pleas of guilty always come first. These were succeeded by some tough trials, including one bad murder. The bad nature of the cases may be judged of from the results. There were only 71 cases, involving 100 prisoners, of whom about eight or ten prisoners, owing to the illness of witnesses, etc., were not disposed of, and one had the solitary good luck to be acquitted, leaving about eighty individuals to be dealt with. Now of these —

1 was imprisoned	... ...	6 months
2 was imprisoned	... ...	9 "
9 was imprisoned	... ...	12 "
10 was imprisoned	... ...	15 "
4 was imprisoned	... ...	18 "
31 were transported	... ...	7 years
20 were transported	... ...	10 "
2 were transported	... ...	14 "
1		death
80		

The murderer was John McLuskie, a miner or collier, and Irish by nativity, who relieved the tedium of a quiet Sunday by stabbing James Macbride, his next door neighbour, four times, once mortally, with such a total absence of all provocation, defence, or mitigation, that except upon the principle of the brutal disregard of other peoples' lives which sometimes operates on stupid savages, the proceeding was altogether unintelligible. The jury recommended him to mercy on the ground that there had been no previous malice, — a ground equally applicable wherever a man murders a stranger, and triumphantly where he murders a friend. Nevertheless this nonsense of the want of previous malice saved the beast's life.

NORTH CIRCUIT
1849

Bridge of Tilt, Monday Night, 10th September 1849. — On the

old round, with my daughter Johanna and my niece Mary Fullerton. Her sister Elphy was to have been with us, but being smitten with a hurly-thrumbo, her doctor, at the last moment, forbade her, to my great sorrow.

We left Edinburgh by the Northern Railway at ten A.M., and in spite of the ferry, got to Perth at about a quarter before one. We then made the agreeable change to posting, and got here about half-past six.

A dull day; and heavy rain from Dunkeld to this, with great fog. As bad a day for the scene as possible.

I again went into the grounds of Dunkeld; and think it a duty to record another execration against the almost swindling extortion and offensive insensibility of its noble and most contemptible owner. I cannot understand how a duke can degrade himself by such pecuniary exaction and nauseate the lieges by keeping the cathedral in so loathsome a state.

I had at different times planned different expeditions for this Circuit. They have all failed, chiefly from the impossibility of trusting this summer for two days together of good weather. But I may record them, for future guidance.

One was, to take the mail from Inverness to Wick; the steamer from Wick to Kirkwall, a six-hours' sail; to see Orkney, and to return by steam to Wick. The steamer at present leaves Wick on Saturday forenoon, and returns there on Tuesday forenoon; and two days are quite enough for Orkney. So that one week would suffice for this Circuit parenthesis.

Another was to stop in the hackneyed Highland road at Dalwhinnie, and to go from Dalwhinnie by Loch Laggan to Fort William, a distance of about fifty miles; and from Fort William by the steamer, through the lochs and the Caledonian Canal, to Inverness. The road from Dalwhinnie to Fort William I understand to be excellent; and the country, especially if Loch Treig be turned aside for, beautiful. The inns are not to be depended upon in this season, and still less the horses. But the Dalwhinnie horses, by sending a pair on, do the job easily. Besides the weather, I was deterred from this by the chance of finding the steamer crowded by jurymen, witnesses, tourists, and other injudicial accompaniments.

A third was to give eight days to an exploration of Sutherland. I was much bent on this, and would have done it had the weather not frowned. I had a good route from Mr. St. John, the author of the excellent works on Highland sports. And as few people know how to see this out of the way county, I shall preserve his stages here.. The whole journey was to have been performed by the same pair of horses, taken from Inverness.

First day. — From Inverness to the Bridge of Alness, twenty-one miles; from this to Ardguy (or Ardgye) fifteen miles.

Second day. — From Ardguy, by Bonar, along the shore of the firth, to Invershin, five miles; from this Altnagach Inn, where the horses rest; then to Inchnadamph.

Third day. — Inchnadamph to Loch Inver, twelve miles, and back to Inchnadamph, because no road further. But all this may be omitted without deranging the route.

Fourth day. — From Inchnadamph to Scourie, by the base of Quinigan, "the grandest of hills". The picturesque ferry of Kylesku to be crossed.

Fifth day. — From Scourie to Durness.

Sixth day. — From Durness by the head of Loch Eriboll and Loch Hope, through Strathmore, to Altnahara.

Seventh day. — To Lairg, eighteen miles; and by head of Loch Shin to Ardguy. Or from Lairg to Golspie, eighteen miles, i.e. to Dunrobin, which is twenty miles from Tain.

If the third day's work be given up, a day is left for going from Scourie to Tongue, and to Ben Loyal.

The whole road is excellent; and all the inns, particularly at the proposed sleeping-places, are most comfortable. I did not always get the miles, but no day's journey is at all excessive, and, in general, they are rather moderate.

This is the thing to do. Unless one were to go both to Orkney and to Shetland, the rock scenery of which I believe is well worth any trouble or any suffering, except being torn inside out by the tossing of one hundred miles of restless water.

Aviemore, Tuesday Night, 11th September 1849. — A dull, but fair day.

I shall probably never see this noble tract again. They talk of continuing the Aberdeen railway to Inverness. This will destroy the posting and the inns on what has hitherto been called the Highland road, and will compel us to be conveyed like parcels — speed alone considered, and seeing excluded.

Cairngorm was mistified.

The Highland coach going south was overset within a mile of this this forenoon. Nobody killed, but several hurt. There being no doctors here, they were all obliged to go on. One English gentleman, whom we saw sitting in a carriage, had a very uncomfortable-looking cheek.

Inverness, Wednesday Night, 12th September 1849. — Here to-day, through a ceaseless torrent, and a world of wet grey fog. What a scrape it would have been to have gone, as I was nearly doing, from Dalwhinnie to Fort William, and to have either received all the splash of this day on the deck of a steamer, or to have escaped it by the far worse horrors of a small cabin crowded by wet men stinking of tobacco.

Knockomie, Saturday Morning, 15th September 1849. — The Inverness criminal business was finished on Thursday night.

But I must not forget the mail-coach. It was the one from Edinburgh to Inverness, by the Highland road. It was due at Inverness about nine or ten on Wednesday night, but was upset on the north side of Moy into a swollen stream, and the whole insides were very nearly drowned. They had, after being saved, to shiver, in their drenched garments, and without fire, though in a sort of mud toll-house, for six or seven hours, after which they were got on. Mr. Aitken, the Clerk of Court, and two counsel, were three of the drooked. The clerk's papers all went down the stream, but were recovered, though well steeped.

The only thing memorable in our business was a case of rioting, deforcement, etc., charged against four poor respectable men, who had been active in resisting a Highland clearing in North Uist. The popular feeling is so strong against these (as I think necessary, but) odious operations, that I was afraid of an acquittal, which would have been unjust and mischievous. On the other hand even the law has no sympathy with the exercise of legal rights in a cruel way. The jury solved the difficulty by first convicting, by a majority, and then giving this written, and therefore well-considered recommendation, "The jury unanimously recommend the pannels to the utmost leniency and mercy of the Court, in consideration of the cruel, though it may be legal, proceedings adopted in ejecting the whole people of Solas from their houses and crops, without the prospect of shelter or a footing in their fatherland, or even the means of expatriating them to a foreign one," a statement that will ring over all the country. We shall not soon cease to hear of this calm and judicial censure of incredible but proved facts. For it was established (1) that warrants of ejection, that is, of dismantling hovels, had been issued against about sixty tenants, being nearly the whole tenantry in the district of Solas, comprehending probably three hundred persons, warrants which the agents of Lord Macdonald, had certainly a right to demand, and the Sheriff was bound to grant; (2) that the people had sown, and were entitled to reap their crops; (3) that there were no houses provided for them to take shelter in, no poor house, no ship. They had nothing but the bare ground, or rather the hard, wet beach, to lie down upon. It was said or rather insinuated, that "arrangements" had been made for them, and in particular that a ship was to have been soon on the coast. But, in the meantime, the peoples' hereditary roofs were to be pulled down, and the mother and her children had only the shore to sleep on, fireless, foodless, hopeless. Resistance was surely not unnatural, and it was very slight. No life was taken, or blood lost. It was a mere noisy and threatening deforcement.

I am sorry for Lord Macdonald, whose name, he being the landlord, was used, but who personally was quite innocent. He was in the hands of his creditors, and they of their doer, a Mr. Cooper, their factor. But his lordship will get all the abuse.

The slightness of the punishment, four months' imprisonment, will probably abate the public fury.

Inverness, since I last saw it, has been injured in its beauty in two ways. One is by the erection, on a conspicuous position, of a very ugly Free Kirk school. The other by the total destruction of the old stone bridge, which was carried off by a flood last winter. No loss could be greater. It was a most picturesque bridge, with pointed, ribbed arches, of a brown stone, and narrow. We shall have a far better new one, wider and flatter, and of a harder material; but Inverness won't look half so well.

I had to go to Court yesterday for about an hour, after which we set off, and got here about half-past two. We instantly proceeded; and after having seen the Sand Hills of Forres for above fifty years, I at last stood upon them. They form a very curious world of fine sand. On our way home we visited the garden of Dalvey, a place near Forres, belonging to a Mr. Macleod, a lover of horticulture. It is a very excellent shrubb-eried garden, prettily placed on a bit of haugh, with his comfort-able-looking house on a bank above it, and a good stream below. His deodars are the best I have seen in Scotland. When his roses are out, it must be splendid; but at present his gardens, like all others, are crushed and dissolved by the pitiless torrents of this drenchy 1849.

Knockomie, Saturday Night, 15th September 1849. — This day, which was pleased to fair, was given to Pluscarden, nine miles off, and reached by a coach filled inside and out, and two saddle horses. We loitered about the ruin for some hours, and had a turf refection, and a good deal of calotyping, conducted by my friend Cosmo Innes, the Sheriff of the county.

The abbey is larger, and its fragments better, than I supposed. The colour of the walls, when the sun is on them, is singularly beautiful. It is far better kept than most Scotch ruins are, but still is kept very ill. And in ten or twenty years more, little, if anything, will be visible except a mass of ivy. It is really distressing to see so much architectural ornament given entirely up in so many places, to this insinuating and insatiable usurper. But what is to be expected where a great part of a religious ruin has been half converted into a modern dwelling-house, and another has been converted entirely into a modern kirk! The said kirk, a little paltry Free Kirk Chapel of Ease, amidst the greatest Presbyterian meanness, has a beautiful pulpit of dark, massive carved wood, dated 1684. The wise men of Elgin in rebuilding their church a few years ago, rejected this relic as unworthy of their novelties, and this chapel got it.

We were home by half-past six, and had a party to dinner. And now for the land of Nod.

Fochabers, Sunday Night, 16th September 1849. — Innes and I revisited the unmatched Findhorn to-day, and called at Altyre. It is long since I became acquainted with the woods and glorious river scenery of this place (Altyre), but till to-day I had never resisted my aversion to go near the house. It is a beautiful garden, especially the lawny part of it. The Portugal laurels are

222

the largest, except at Broomhall, I have ever seen in Scotland.

We dined at Knockomie at three, left it at four, were at Elgin at six, saw the cathedral, and were here by eight. And now, Nod again.

Aberdeen, Monday Night, 17th September 1849. — Came here to-day where Moncreiff joined me.

Castleton, Saturday Night, 22d September 1849. — The Aberdeen criminal business exhausted four days, Tuesday, Wednesday, Thursday, and yesterday. There were not more cases than usual; but they happened to be of a worse description. In particular, there were four capital cases, viz. two murders, one murder combined with raptus, and one raptus alone. One of the murders ended in an acquittal, and very properly, because though the guilt was certain and savage, the evidence was not satisfactory. In another murder, a plea of culpable homicide produced twenty years' transportation. The simple raptus ended in a conviction, and in transportation for life. The murder and raptus combined caused a sentence of death. This last was a horrid crime.

The prisoner was James Robb, a country labourer of about twenty-five, a known reprobate, and stout. His victim was Mary Smith, a quiet woman of sixty-two, never married, or a mother, who lived by herself in a lonely house by the wayside. There was a fair held at a village in Aberdeenshire called Badenscoth, which sometimes, though in no eminent degree, produced some of the disorderly scenes natural to fairs.

Mary Smith, though not the least alarmed, happened to observe casually that "she was not afraid of anybody, except that lad Jamie Robb". That very night Robb left the fair (9th April 1849) about ten, avowing that he was determined to gratify his passion on somebody before he slept. He had then no thought of this old woman; but, unfortunately, her house lay in his way. He asked admittance, upon pretence of lighting his pipe. She refused. On this he got upon the roof and went down the chimney, which consisted of a square wooden box about 5 feet long by 2½ wide, placed about 6 feet above the fire. Its soot was streaked by his corduroy dress, which helped to identify him. Having got in, the beast fell upon its prey. She was thought in good health, but after death was discovered to have an incipient disease in the heart, which agitation made dangerous, but which might have lain long dormant. The violence of the brute, and the alarm, proved fatal. She was found dead in the morning, and the bed broken, and in the utmost confusion. A remarkable composite metal button, broken from its eye, was found twisted in what the witness called "a lurk", or fold, of the sheet. Buttons of exactly the same kind, and with the same words and figures engraved on them, were found on his jacket, all complete except that one was awanting. But its eye remained; and this eye, with its bright recent fracture, exactly fitted the part of the button that had been found. These circumstances would have been sufficient to have established his having been in the house. But his declaration admitted the fact. Consent was excluded by its being obvious that it was the energy of her resistance that had killed her.

It is difficult to drive the horrors of that scene out of one's imagination. The solitary old woman in the solitary house, the descent through the chimney, the beastly attack, the death struggle, — all that was going on within this lonely room, amidst silent fields, and under a still, dark sky. It is a fragment of hell, which it is both difficult to endure and to quit.

Yet a jury, though clear of both crimes, recommended the brute to mercy! because he did not intend to commit the murder! Neither does the highwayman, who only means to wound, in order to get the purse, but kills.

Within a few hours after he was convicted he confessed, and explained that the poor woman had died in his very grip. (He was executed, solemnly denying his guilt, quoad raptus!)

We left Aberdeen this morning, and breakfasted at Drum, the seat, in Strath Dee, of my college acquaintance, A. Forbes Irvine. The house is one of the noble old castles of Aberdeenshire. But I saw no beauty about the place. He has two dollies close beside the mansion, the largest I have ever seen. They are forest trees, very nearly 8 feet in circumference.

The day was excellent, and the whole drive up here still more glorious than I formerly thought it.

The Queen is living at Balmoral, and therefore I expected to be obstructed by some of the usual bustle of royalty. But it is reputable for the royalty of this nation that, except by a paltry flag set up before his door by the innkeeper of Ballater, there was not a vestige of Majesty in any part of the strath. We did not encounter a single carriage, nor a single rider, nor one soldier, nor a police officer, nor anything to mark a distinguished presence. The inns were rather less crowded than usual, the post-houses as fresh, the strath as natural. The sheep, the stots, and even the barelegged children, all went off exactly as before. Balmoral itself was silent; flagless; apparently unguarded; calm; beautiful. I think this very respectable in her Majesty and family. It seems to show sense and taste. And the fact that such enjoyment of such virtuous pleasures is not merely possible. but easy and habitual, demonstrates how deep the monarchical principle is in the mind of the country, and how much better it is promoted by rational conduct, than by the common follies of royalty. The once resolute sovereigns of Europe have often thought that the limited monarch of Britain was no monarch at all. Which of them could now live for an autumn only the more safely that they lived in an unguarded wilderness?

Perth, Sunday Night, 23d September 1849. — Came here to-day by the Spittal from Castleton. All beautiful. What a delightful contrast between the glorious green valleyed and blue summited hills of Glenshee, sublime in their treelessness, and the flush of picturesque richness that begins in Stratheric, and continues, through the splendid culture of domains and farms, till it be crowned in Perth.

Bonaly, Thursday Night, 27th September 1849. — We got free from Court to-day at one, and into the Scottish Central Railway at about four, and after a pause in Edinburgh were here by nine. Her Majesty passed through the Perth station while we were there, on her way home. She left Balmoral by the highway this forenoon; got on the railway at Cupar-Angus, and was in Edinburgh, by Stirling, in two and a half hours. All the stations were crowded with people, panting for a sight of her; and her gracious condescension was expressed by whisking past them at the rate of about thirty miles per hour, with all her windows shut. Immense folly! When I'm a queen, I shall hold it to be my dignity to go slow.

I was absorbed during our journey by Sir Charles Lyell's *Second Visit to the United States.* I had no idea that my geological friend could write such a book. It is the most manly, the most candid, the most sensible, and the most gentlemanly book existing on America, within his limited range.

Edward Maitland was the depute. Excellent.

GLASGOW CIRCUIT
1850

Edinburgh, 17th January 1850. — On Tuesday, the 8th inst., Lord Ivory and I began the Glasgow Winter Circuit. It was not over till the night of Tuesday the 15th, being seven Court days.

It was an unusually black tribunal, there being 79 cases, involving about 125 culprits; among whom six (seven?) were charged with murder, and many with other serious crimes. Of the murders, one, a female prisoner, was doomed to die; two were transported for life, and one for seven years, one was acquitted, one escaped, and one was imprisoned. The prisoner had first stolen a bank deposit-receipt, and then finding that she could not get the money without the owner's signature, she forged it, and then, having committed these two offences, she murdered the victim in order to hide them. She was tried for the whole three crimes. The forgery, and the administration of arsenic were very clearly proved. But there was a doubt about the theft, and therefore the jury found it not proved. Yet upon this fact a majority of them grounded by far the most nonsensical recommendation to mercy that any jury, known to me, ever made themselves ludicrous by. They first recommended

without stating any reason, and on being asked what their reason was, they retired, and after consultation, returned with these written words, viz.: that they gave the recommendation "in consequence of the first charge, of theft, not having been proved, which they believe in a great measure led to the commission of the subsequent crime!" Grammatically, this means that it was their acquittal of the theft that did the mischief, but what they meant was, that the murder was caused by a theft not proved to have existed. It is the most Hibernian recommendation I have ever seen.

The preceding recommendation, though backed by the whole force of the very active party opposed to capital punishment, failed, and the poor wretch died.

Of the 125 accused, about 122 were tried, and of these only six were acquitted, a fact honourable to the criminal practice of Scotland. Eighty-five were transported.

The peculiarity of this Circuit was that, for the first time at any Circuit in this country, the two judges sat, generally, each in a separate court, of course doing double work. A statute was passed to sanction this, about two years ago, but it had never been acted upon. Ivory and I were glad to set the example. It was very popular with everybody, as it saved time and expense.

This was the first time I had seen Ivory as a criminal judge. He is excellent. His law, and agreeable manner could not be doubted. But, like other good lawyers, he is apt to be beset by nice doubts, and loves them in civil adjudication; and many people were afraid that he might be troubled by this infirmity on the criminal bench. But if he was, which, however, I saw no symptom of, necessity made him shake it off. He was as decided and hardy as needed to be. A most excellent man.

WEST CIRCUIT

Tarbet, Loch Lomond, Saturday Night, 14th April 1850. — I am here with Mrs. Cockburn and my niece Elphy Fullerton, on the usual distribution of Argyleshire justice.

If the people who call themselves "the friends of Sabbath observance" had been possessed of common-sense, I would have been enabled to have attended church, and to have performed all domestic Sunday duties at home to-day, and would then have gone to Glasgow by an evening train to-night, and would have easily reached Inveraray from Glasgow to-morrow. But, being idiots, they allow no Sunday trains on the Edinburgh and Glasgow railway; one consequence of which has been, that I was forced to come here yesterday, and to pass the whole of this Sunday in a public house. This is what they call Sabbath keeping.

I have never seen a worse Loch Lomond, and hope never to see it again under heavy, vulgar clouds, a surly north wind, and a late spring.

The monsters are far on with a railway from about Bowling Bay to Balloch. The great benefit of which is, that henceforth the public can steam from Glasgow to Bowling in less than an hour, and railway from Bowling to Balloch in ten minutes, and steam again all over Loch Lomond at pleasure; for which pleasure there are now three Loch Lomond steamers ready. I am told that the owners of Killarney have been so insensible, or so abstemious, as to resist this luxury for their lake.

Tarbet. Monday, near Noon, 15th April 1850. — A horrible day of rain and wind. The very mason can't work. But we are off for Inveraray.

Tarbet, Wednesday Night, 17th April 1850. — We were at Inveraray from Monday at four till to-day at one.

All yesterday, till near eleven at night, was passed in Court trying one case. And a peculiarly villainous one it was. The accused was a tall, well-looking scoundrel of twenty-one, originally an Ayrshire farmer, but who last Whitsunday had taken a farm near Campbeltown. His affairs got desperate; and having ascertained that this was fact, and that a declaration of bankruptcy was necessary, he closed his last ten free days by the following achievements. He first, by fraudulent conceal-ment of his circumstances, got a very respectable gentlewoman to marry him. He then insured his stock and crop at above four times its true value, and then he set fire to it, having first made a collection of straw among the couples of his byre, which secured the burning alive of thirty cattle. All within ten days. It was for the fire-raising that he was tried; and being convicted, I must confess that the torture of the poor cattle gave me great pleasure in transporting him for twenty years.

Home to-morrow.

Bonaly, Friday Night, 19th April 1850. — We left Tarbet yesterday at nine, got to Glasgow at half-past two, left Glasgow at four, were in Edinburgh at half-past five, and here by seven. This gives me a peck of three days amidst my hyacinths and primroses, and on Monday I breakfast at Glasgow.

Bonaly, Wednesday, 1st May 1850. — After that breakfast, Moncreiff and I went to Court, and worked away dilligently, and with a total abstinence of all unnecessary speech, yet we could not finish our 74 cases in that week. I therefore came home by the train that leaves Glasgow at four, and passed Saturday evening and all Sunday here. On Monday the 29th I returned to Glasgow by ten o'clock, and was kept there till next day (yester-day) at three. This was far too long for 74 cases, of which not, I should suppose, above 65 were actually tried. But there were three long ones, each of which usurped a whole day.

SOUTH CIRCUIT

Edinburgh, 5th November 1850. — Moncreiff did Ayr; we met at Dumfries; after which I meant to have done Jedburgh.

But on my way by rail from Bonaly to Dumfries, on Monday, 15th September, I was seized with what from its frequency seems to be an attack generated by railways, and reached Dumfries in great torture and great danger. I lay in the inn there (the King's Arms) twenty-three days before I could be brought back to Edinburgh and never can forget the horrors, or the mercies, of the visitation. Of course, it was a blank and bitter Circuit. I am not myself yet, and sometimes wonder if it be true that I am still alive?

It is but justice to the King's Arms to record that, if any one should have to be severely ill in a Scotch inn, he should select this one, which, though in a noisy position, was quiet inside, and contained a household of the most devoted attention and apparently affectionate kindness.

WEST CIRCUIT
1851

Tarbet, Tuesday, 8th April 1851. — Mrs. Cockburn, my daughter Johanna, and my granddaughter Lily, left Edinburgh yesterday at four P.M., and stayed at Glasgow all night. To-day we came here. A beautiful day it has been.

I little fancied, last September, when Moncreiff took leave of me, two-thirds dead, at Dumfries, to do my work at Jedburgh, that he, and not I, was to be first removed from these scenes. But, alas! he died a few days ago (30th March 1851). I shall try to do justice to his character in some other place. Meanwhile, a Circuit without him seems to me a left-handed affair. Ivory, whom I am to meet at Glasgow, is my colleague now.

Luss, Friday, 11th April 1851, Night. — We went to Inveraray on Wednesday the 9th; I was in Court there yesterday till six; left it to-day, and were here by four, where we repose all night.

The weather has been perfect, and if I had not prosed enough about scenery too often already, I would feel particularly compelled to do it now. The three lochs were never more glorious. But the two salt ones have no chance with the fresh.

I think it was when I was on this Circuit in spring 1850 that I observed that the marble slab on Smollett's monument in the village now called Renton was falling out, and that it had been gradually doing so for years. The whole monument, indeed, was in a disgraceful state, going to ruin on the spot of his birth, and near the dwellings of his descendants, and in one of the richest districts of Scotland. In my indignation I wrote a statement of the case, and sent it to my old Outer House friend, Mr.

Outram, who now conducts the most widely spread newspaper in Glasgow. He published this, and powerfully appealed to the proper feelings of all concerned himself.

Well, when I came this way again last Tuesday, I expected to find it all right. Brutes! it is worse than ever! Nothing has been done except by time, and a few months more must see the tablet fall and break. I shall renew my exposure; and I am strongly inclined to do it openly and in my own name. One pound would do it probably, and certainly five would. Yet to save this sum, and a little care, nativity, nationality, and pedigree all stand by and see it fall into gradual, but rapid and certain ruin. It is inconceivable, and would justify any terms of abuse.

Bonaly, Saturday Night, 12th April 1851. — We came here to-day from Luss. Stirling — which Ivory takes — comes next, and Glasgow on the 22d.

Bonaly, Saturday, Noon, 26th April 1851. — On Thursday the 17th Mrs. Cockburn and I went from this to Thornton, Ayrshire, to visit her sister and spouse, the Cunninghams, and stayed there till the evening of Monday the 22d, when we went to Glasgow.

Next day Ivory and I went to hold the two Courts, a sensible innovation first begun by him and me there in January 1850. Luckily there was no cavalry in the town, and so we got quit of the absurdity of always going to do justice surrounded by red-coats, sabres, and clattering hoofs, which, however, some of my brethren still love. The business lasted four days, and we came home last night.

No ferlies to tell. Yes, I saw Outram, who told me that Smollett's representative, whose estate is near the monuments, holds that since the family erected it, nobody else shall inter-fere, and that he himself shall have the sole honour of repairing it. But then there are two considerations which obstruct him. One is that he has been blamed for not doing it. The other that it will cost a few pounds, perhaps even four or five; a monstrous sum, considering that he has laid out several pounds already. And thus I suppose it will be allowed to disappear under the joint action of touchiness and penury. He should put the inscription on a metal tablet, and add £2 a year to the salary of the schoolmaster beside it, provided its preservations shall show that his taws have done their duty. At present it is, as the inscription says, "Amoris, eheu! inane Monumentum."

SOUTH CIRCUIT

Bonaly, 5th October 1851. — This Circuit Journal has become so insignificant that I had forgotten to make any entry in it till this volume, when I happened to open the desk that contained it, seemed to reproach me.

But this is all I have to say —

I went to Kirklands, alone, on Friday the 12th of September, and stayed there till the morning of Monday the 15th, when I went to Jethart, and did justice there, from ten to half-past three, on six paltry villains. George Dundas and I then walked up the Jed, in the sweetest of evenings. At six that beastly Circuit dinner was held. It was described in the papers next day as "an elegant entertainment". Elegance and the Spread Eagle at Jedburgh never came together before; and the only elegance that I am aware of, was, that nineteen persons drank thirty-five bottles of wine. At night George and I returned to Kirklands, so that the eagle had me in his claws scarcely at all.

I came home on Wednesday the 17th.

On Friday the 19th Mrs. Cockburn and I, and my daughter Johanna, and my granddaughter Lily, went to Thornton, near Kilmarnock, where my brother-in-law, Mr. Cunningham, was living; and on Monday the 22d, I, leaving the test there, went to Doonholm, the hired seat of my Lord Justice-Clerk, where I dined, and stayed all night. Lord Ivory was there, and he and I processed into Ayr next morning to breakfast, after which we judicially dittoed eight dittos, and then had a glorious walk along the beach, from four to near six. Then came the banquet. And then, that night, I drove back to Thornton.

Ivory did Dumfries alone. I had no desire to excite the recollection of the sufferings there of last autumn.

And so ends the South Circuit of autumn 1851. Twenty-four cases in all, out of a population of nearly half a million.

An accident occurred at Ayr worth recording for the edification of the idolaters of Form. A few hours before the Court was to open, the clerk came to me with his hair on end, and announced that, by some blunder, none of the proper technical papers had arrived from Edinburgh. There were no original indictments, declarations, or productions, no executions, consequently no evidence that any accused, or juryman, or prisoner, had been cited to attend — no anything. I bade him hold his tongue, and proceed as if everything was right, and explained to all the counsel who were present for prisoners what had happened, and that their objecting could only end in the trials being put off, and their clients suffering longer imprisonment. In this state we proceeded to business. What communication took place between them and the prisoners I do not know, but everything went on as usual. Jurors and witnesses attended and acted, copies were read instead of originals, and nobody could have suspected that there was any flaw. No Circuit could proceed more quietly, or more effectively; nor was any attempt ever made to raise any doubt afterwards. A valuable precedent against nonsense.

Aberdeen, Thursday Night, 8th April 1852. — I left Bonaly this morning at eight, with my daughter Johanna. At half-past nine Miss Susan Lauder joined us at the station, and we dived into the tunnel for Granton, crossed to Burntisland in less than half an hour, and in three hours from our first moving, were at Broughty. We stayed there two and a half hours, and at 3.15 set out again by the rails, and in about three hours were here.

My object in selecting this track was to avoid the long round by Stirling and Perth, and to get the rest at Broughty; Dumfries having taught me, in September 1850, that too much railery is an unbecoming thing for an aged judge.

I never was in Broughty before. It is the Portobello of Dundee. And, except in one particular, it is decidedly superior to the Portobello of Edinburgh. It is backed by high rising ground, and of uneven surface, on which are perched an increasing variety of good gardened houses, some of which are obviously excellent mansions; and it had a visible and near coast opposite, instead of the boundless sea. But it wants the glorious Portobello sands; and it seems to me that its marine ablutions must be greatly interfered with by the intervention of the railway between the houses and the sea. The want of shore-line makes Portobello the least marine of any sea-place I know.

The day was beautiful. But except the ocean and perfect farming, there is nothing to attract from Burntisland to Aberdeen. The sea was dead calm, under a sleepy haze, the fields all dressed like gardens, and all in a dry, weedless purity.

Westhall, Saturday Afternoon, 10th April 1852. — We left Aberdeen yesterday forenoon, and came here.

This place is about nine miles from Inverurie, and one from Pitmachie, and about one mile off the high-road to the West. My excellent friend Lord Ivory took it on lease last year, and has it till next May. He has a very odd custom of going to the country every year, but of changing his quarters every two, or at most three, seasons. I have known him in I should suppose at least a dozen of ruralities, including Mid-Lothian, West Lothian, Peeblesshire, Argyle, Aberdeen, etc., and this summer he honours Perthshire. It is a good way to see districts, but not to enjoy the country. A man's taste for nature must be very abstract which attaches itself to no particular scene, which has no alliances with its known fields, or trees, or flowers, no associations with the effects of the sun as it revisits his chosen haunts or prospects. Accordingly, it is fishing that he is chiefly hooked by; and, to be sure, a lover of the angle is very apt to love angling alone.

This was the portion of earth from which the judge called Lord Westhall took his official title. He reigned on the bench from

1777-74. It is a very enjoyable place, at least in the splendid weather of yesterday and to-day. The old portion of the house, though very small, is worthy of Aberdeenshire. The original tower, and the secondary structure, are both very curious. The tower very picturesque. A modern addition has been recently made, much to the inward comfort of the domicile, but of the most necessary abominableness outside. It is nearly surrounded by hills, which, however, are not so near as to form parts of the home scenery. One of these, and the nearest — about two miles off — is the famous Benachie, at the back of which the Gawdie runs — the said Gawdie being within three or four hundred yards of the house I am sorry to be obliged to confess that there is as little poetry in the stream (but plenty trout) as in any poetised stream I ever saw. It flows through an open, and bare, and rockless country, and has not pebbles enough to keep itself always pure. Bennachie is a very respectable range of mountain, with one towering summit, and one or two of lesser pretensions, — no rocky accompaniments that are apparent, and no ravines or corries, but a very respectable long line of hill.

To-day we drove round it — a drive of about twenty miles. On this side of it is the Gawdie, on the other side the Don. This side is generally woodless; the other all wooded. We went through Castle Forbes and a good deal of Monymusk, through both of which the Don flows. Lord Forbes (who forsakes the Scotch Don for the society of an English priest) has lately built a new house, in as bad taste as possible. It seemed to me like a copy of the house at Johnstone, near Paisley; only what may be excusable in one place may be inexcusable in the other. Castle Forbes is on the Don, and in Aberdeenshire! I wonder that the builder did not tremble lest the true old castles of this most architectural shire should step out and tread his base tower and contemptible bright freestone under their feet. I saw no ornamental attempt about the grounds; but Nature has done as much as she can ever do for the river scenery with no rock, and with only young wood. But the hills, the stream, the cultivated haughs, and the profusion of wood scarcely middle-aged, made miles of the valley delightful, even though the trees, including the very larches, were all leafless. In summer it must be beautiful.

The Monymusk forests seem to me much older, and the whole character of the ground consequently much superior.

But, in every respect, the strath of the Don is greatly inferior to the strath of the Dee.

Industry can point to no greater triumph than to this part of Scotland called Garioch. The people's slow victory over obstacles that would have seemed insuperable even to a Dutchman, is perfectly astonishing. The result is, large districts of cleared open fields, treeless and hedgeless, fenced by mounds of great granite blocks, and all admirably cultivated, though with almost no sheep pasture. Every manageable portion seems to have been given up, to be subdued, to one or to a few families, which seem to have become the tenants of what their toil had created. One pleasing effect of this system has been the scattering of small farmers and "toons" all over the reclaimed regions, with their simple but comfortable establishments of little barn-yards, peat-stacks, and hoary splashing mills. I saw in one village, of about a dozen one-storied houses, this sign:- "Entertainment for men and horses, clothier, and grocer". And another announcing "Lodgings and small Beer".

Knockomie, Friday Night, 16th April 1852. — On the 11th of April we went from Westhall to this very agreeable next, which took us from about nine to five. Next day, till five o'clock, was passed on the Findhorn, and at dear Relugas. No such river scenery in Scotland.

At five we set out for Inverness.

Next day, being Tuesday the 13th, the Court opened there, and the business lasted till Thursday (yesterday) about two.

The only interesting case was that of Mrs. and Mr. Fraser, a mother and her son (a lad), who had chosen to poison their father, a shopkeeper in Ross-shire. They thought him a useless creature, and that they would be better without him, especially as the wife had forged his name to bills, in reference to which his removal, before they became due, would be convenient. I never saw a couple of less amiable devils. The mother especially, had a cold, hard eye, and a pair of thin resolute lips, producing an expression very fit for a remorseless and steady murderess. She saw her daughter, a little girl, brought in as a witness, and heard her swear that there were no rats in the house, and that her father's sufferings were very severe, with a look of calm, severe ferocity, which would have done no discredit to the worst woman in hell. They were both convicted, but I fear that the gallows won't get its due. A legal doubt occurred, on which we held ourselves bound to consult the Court before pronouncing sentence; and if this doubt be resolved in the prisoners' favour, they will escape altogether; and even if it be decided against them, the delay will probably save their lives, which will be a pity.

We came here again yesterday evening. This day was spent in paying visits in Forres, at Dalvey, and at Altyre. At Dalvey I saw the Victoria Lily for the first time, not in flower, but living, and in leaf. I was taken to visit an old lady in Forres, called Miss Macpherson, certainly a person well worth seeing. She called herself eighty, but is said to be eighty-four, and has a face which must have once been beautiful, and is still very handsome. She is in perfect preservation, and in great talk; has known, and recollects every person and every event in the north of Scotland in her day; is always in excellent spirits, and has a delightful northern accent and dialect, with a willing flow of strong sense and acute observation, generally of a cheerful character. A most enviable specimen of old age. She twice made use of an expression which struck me as very descriptive. I had asked who a particular Grant and a particular Fraser were, and she, meaning to describe them as just of their respective clans, said of each, "Hoot, he's just the growth of the ground". She goes to Edinburgh in a few days to get her tusks repaired. "Not from vanity, but because I can't eat well."

I went to Altyre to see Sir William Cumming, but missed him, a far more curious creature than any that his son Roualeyn encountered in Africa.

Aberdeen, Monday Night, 19th April 1852. — We went from Knockomie to Westhall last Saturday, the 17th, and stayed there till this forenoon. Yesterday I walked with Archibald Davidson, the Sheriff of Aberdeenshire, to very nearly the top of Benachie. Fog made it needless to go on. It is a very easy, and for prospect a very useless exploit.

Perth, Thursday Night, 22d April 1852. — We left Aberdeen to-day at 2.30, after two contemptible and very tiresome days in Court.

While there I heard of the deaths of two locally great men.

One was James Gordon of Craig, whom I have mentioned already, the most splutteratious of orators, but who seeded in his old age into a very kind and respectable country gentleman.

The other was William, Baron Panmure, who was buried last Tuesday, aged above eighty, of whose virtues and grand funeral the district rings. The funeral, no doubt, was as grand as a mob of tenants and dependants, and police officers, and military pensioners and magistrates, and all manner of burgh feculence, could make it. He had lived all his life among them, and had always made himself popular with those who chose to be submissive, and, to such, was never close in the fist. But the virtues were a different matter. To his unfriends — and he made many — he was insanely brutal. His wife, his daughters, and at least two of his three sons, he compelled to fly from his house — his daughters at midnight, and ever after shut his door and his heart against them; neither time not their worth ever abating his mad and savage hatred. And so it was with every one who incurred the ineffaceable guilt of daring to resist the capricious and intolerant despotism of his will. He would have roasted every soul of them, and their bodies too. A spoiled beast from its infancy.

His oldest son, who presumed to save his sisters by helping them out of the house, was the object of his peculiar hatred; a hatred which the public eminence of the son rather aggravated than lessened. About two years ago the monster celebrated his survivance from a dangerous illness by a dinner to some of his tenants. His health, of course, was drunk, after which he gave "The Disappointed one", meaning his son; upon which a farmer quietly observed that "he had never heard the Deil drunk before".

My plan, on leaving Aberdeen, was to have been to-night at Birnam, and to have passed the next three days there. For this purpose I had written to the Birnam host to send a carriage for me to the Dunkeld road station. But on reaching that station, no carriage appeared; and while we were wondering and speculating, the train that had taken us there was allowed to proceed; and we were left, ten miles from Birnam, and four from Perth, on the road at six P.M. It looked, for some time, as if we should have had to walk here. But at last we got a car for our three selves, and a cart for the luggage, and made for this harbour of refuge. But this misadventure, joined to our first bad weather, has extinguished our Birnam visions, and reconciled me to the unnatural idea of returning home to-morrow and passing the two next days at Bonaly, before opening the criminal fire here on Monday. This is a sad break in a North Circuit. But I shall see my too soon blown, and too rapidly dying, hyacinths.

Steell's magnificent bust of old Panmure, which has been erected, I believe, in the Town Hall of one of his parasite burghs, will transmit to any posterity that may inquire about him, an idea of his outer man. As a work of art, it is admirable; and though those who never saw the original must suppose it to be colossal, it is rather a miniature of one who was nearly as monstrous in coarse bodily structure as in the composition of his mind. It has already transpired by his settlement that the wretch maintained his domestic fiendism to the last. He is understood to have left a considerable personal residue to a domestic captain, and only about £2000 to one of his three poor daughters, and a sort of curse to a son. If it be so, the pleasure of anticipating the posthumous effect of this living heartlessness, was, next to predominating over a jovial crew of low flatterers, probably his greatest living luxury.

Perth, Thursday Night, 29th April 1852. — I enjoyed the hyacinths for two days, having gone to Bonaly on Friday the 23d, and stayed there on Saturday and Sunday, and returned here to breakfast on Monday last the 26th, where Ivory rejoined me.

There was one buff hyacinth that, of itself, was worth the whole journey. It shone, amidst its fellows, like a speech by Logan at Stirling. I was just in time to catch their dying odours.

We are here still, but shall return to peace and Eden to-morrow.

This has been the most murderous Circuit I have ever known. Besides the two Frasers at Inverness, we have had three Cains here — viz., Thoms Lyneham, who beat his sister-in-law so as to cause her to die; Mrs. Blyth, who broke her old mother's head with the tongs; and Charles Fancoat, who plunged a butcher's knife literally through the body of a fellow-workman who had

237

struck him with the fist some time before. However, there was only one capital sentence. The sister-in-law was in such bad health, that this raised one of the doubts, at which juries are, justly, so apt to catch, and he was treated as an assaulter. Mrs. Blyth was proved to have been insane when she did her deed, and was disposed of accordingly. She was a hard, sensible-like woman, who lived in a village in Fife with her mother, to whom she was much attached. But the daughter's reason had been gradually leaving her for two years, till at last it was gone, and she passed her time in visionary misery in bed. One of her prevailing alarms was for her nose, which seemed a very respectable article; but she was convinced that it had got black, and was going to fall off. When told that she had killed her mother, she said, "Weel, had she no lived lang eneuch." Nevertheless, she was clearly of the opinion that she herself ought to be hanged, and was disappointed when the ceremony was avoided. Fancoat, though strongly recommended to mercy by the jury, will probably suffer. His was a clear murder. He and his victim had been quarrelling throughout the day, and in these half-drunken conflicts he had been ill-used. But at last they had parted, and he was safe, when, instead of being quiet, he went and borrowed a long and mortal knife, and proceeded apparently in quest of the other man, and meeting him, gave him a strong stab, which produced death in a few minutes. He is a young Englishman, of excellent character, whose good feelings were evinced to those who, like me, observed his emotion when some of his native villagers came forward to attest his peaceableness and humanity of disposition. I cannot help wishing that his life may be spared. It was whisky and groundless fear that, for the moment, overthrew his better nature.

My excellent friend A.S. Logan was counsel, both in this case and in that of the Frasers, for the prisoners, and shone in neither. He is a very curious man. To talent, sense, and a considerable power of speaking, he joines great kindliness, perfect honesty, and a more comfortable predominance of professional candour than generally is, or can be reduced to practice amidst legal conflicts. His father was a dissenting minister at St. Ninians, and if his son could have got out of the manse a little in his youth, especially to England, he might perhaps have refined himself out of some of his defects. For he has the misfortunes of a homely, good-natured vulgarity, a bad, loud, voice, a taste for bad jokes, which owe all their effect to their resolving into Loganisms, and a propensity, always dangerous, towards stories about himself. These things, which he thinks his excellences, keep him in a lower sphere than his talent, his honesty, and his worth belong to. I have a great regard for him, and mean to adventure on an admonition some day. But I fear that his skin has now become too Ethiopian.

Bonaly, Saturday Night, 1st May 1852. — Ivory, who was panting for his two last weeks of Westhall (for he goes this year to Rossie Ochil) left me yesterday morning, and would dine in Garioch. Only one case, but a most brutal one, remained, and in a couple of hours it ended in a transportation for life.

I need scarcely say that it came from Dundee, certainly now, and for many years past, the most blackguard place in Scotland. Perth and its shire are always remarkably innocent. Nearly the whole guilt at this place proceeds from the two counties of Fife and Forfarshire, and, of course, chiefly from their towns. Of these towns, Kirkcaldy, Cupar, and Montrose seem well behaved enough. Arbroath is not good enough; Dunfermline (always meaning the district) very bad; Dundee a sink of atrocity, which no moral flushing seems capable of cleansing. A Dundee criminal, especially if a lady, may be known, without any evidence about character, by the intensity of the crime, the audacious bar air, and the parting curses. What a set of she-devils were before us! Mercy on us! if a tithe of the subterranean execration that they launched against us, after being sentenced, was to be as effective as they wished it, commination never was more cordial.

Our weather could not have been better for our purposes, if we ourselves had had the choice of it. How beautifully Inverness and Perth lay, in the mornings, amidst their calm rising smoke, their bursting verdure, and their soft, glorious rivers.

Our accusing spirit was David Mure, of whom eight years more of acquaintance enables me to confirm all that I have already said.

I never owed so little to books on any Circuit. My friend Susan Lauder, when left to herself, was steadily busy with an Italian work which professed to make Astronomy clear to the simple; and Johanna turned over the leaves of a variety of circulating library trash. No relief for me there. For myself I had *Adam Grahame of Mossgray,* a new novel by the young authoress (whose name I forget) who has written some other excellent Scotch fictitious stories. This seems to me to be a considerable descent, for her. I could only yawn and nod over it. But when I had in the 194th number another of the sound and learned, but heavy opiates of the reverenced *Edinburgh Review;* and this generally made the nod sink into slumber.

WEST CIRCUIT

Bonaly, 25th October 1852. — What a date for a Circuit! But last July the Richardsons were idle enough, or kind enough, to wish to read this journal, and I sent it to them, and only brought it back from Kirklands to-day.

However, I have nothing but dates to tell about my western Circuit of September.

I went alone(!) to Stirling on Wednesday, the 15th, in the forenoon, and had rather an alarming entry into that historical city. The magistrates met me at the station, from whence we processed to the hotel, they on foot, and my lord in his four-horsed carriage. But no sooner had my lord got near the hotel, than the band of the 42d Regiment, a company of which was posted at the door, struck up a sudden crash of drums and pipes, whereupon the unmilitary steeds made a furious and sharp counter-march, and were flying down the steep street, to the horror of the spectators, when, after throwing off the drivers, they were brought to a halt by one of them falling on its side, on which his lordship whisked out, by the aid of a bailie, who said, "Gude God! the like o' this never happened in the toon o' Stirling before."

Leonard Horner, Mrs. and Miss Joanna Horner, Mr. John Tait, Sheriff of Clackmannan, and his brother Archibald, now Dean of Carlisle (but to be a bishop), dined with me. A pleasant evening.

Next day, the 16th was for the Court, which was dissolved about four, and then followed the tiresome and disreputable dinner.

On the 17th I came home, with the Horners.

Stirling was never more glorious than during these two days.

I remained at home from the 17th till Friday the 24th, when, with my daughter-in-law Mary, I went to Thornton in Ayrshire to visit my sister-in-law Mrs. Cunninghame; and on the morning of Monday the 27th I went to Glasgow. I was there joined by Ivory, who had been at Inverness, and we opened the Court at twelve. The business there lasted till the evening of Friday the 1st October, and I returned home on Saturday the 2d.

A shabby affair.

The Depute was Edward Gordon. He is agreeable, modest, and able; one of the very best specimens of our Celts. His talent, industry and power of pleasing distinct speaking, I predict will raise him high in his profession. He is one of the few counsel who can be calm without feebleness, and argumentative with vehemence. Listening to Edward Gordon arguing law is like listening to a piece of what is meant to be mathematics. The demonstration may often fail, the demonstration tone never.

GLASGOW CIRCUIT
1853

Edinburgh, 2 Manor Place, 19th January 1853. — I had nearly forgotten the late Glasgow Circuit, — the last winter one I shall last to go.

I went to Glasgow alone(!) on the morning of Monday, 3d January 1853, and, after the usual proceedings, I got home in the forenoon of Thursday the 6th. Ivory's cases detained him in Court for some hours upon that day; but he was domestically housed that night.

I have little else to record.

The whole four days and nights were one ceaseless torrent of rain, which fell through one unbroken mass of cold, thick, wet, palpable fog, through which carts, cabs, vans, drays, and all sorts of manufacturing conveyances roared, as usual, without above two hours' cessation in the twenty-four. These two hours of truce were, and in Glasgow are, between two and four in the morning, before and after which neither London nor hell contain any vehicular roar more accursedly magnificent. Indeed, even these two hours are not always safe. For whence I was deluding myself, in my second night watch, with the hope of silence and Elysium, the roar went on till four o'clock roused the whole host of labour to the toil and the noise of the day. And what caused this exception? A ball, in the college, at the professors of divinity! The least offensive sort of theological turmoil.

There were two cases of murder, with convictions in both. One was a mere commonplace affair of a woman drowning her illegitimate infant. About 2500 decent women have petitioned the Crown for a commutation. The other was a case of a fellow who, in hatred of his stepmother, intimated his determination to kill the child which she was soon to be delivered of, and kept his word by cutting off its head. His defence was insanity. And no doubt he was as mad as gusts of passion could make him, but not nearly mad enough to cut off heads with impunity. However, I did not discourage the jury from convicting him, and thus avoiding the usual dangerous verdict, but recommending him to mercy on the ground of his intellect being defective. This they did, and his life has been allowed to proceed. But as the public reason on this question has been returning of late, the next half-crazy murderer will probably fare worse.

SOUTH CIRCUIT

Bonaly, 16th April 1853, Saturday. — On the evening of Wednesday last, the 13th, I went alone, by rail, to Melrose, took horses there, and got under the wings of the Spread Eagle at nine. Was in Court next day till four, then up the Jed with George Dundas, — a walk I never willingly miss. There is something in that valley that never fails to move me. The lateness of this season deprived it of its due of leaves, but it was rich in buds and mavises; its haugh, where grassy, was so green, and where under crop, so clean and so evenly harrowed, its stream so pure, and all so soft and peaceful, that it felt like an amiable heart. He must be very prosaic indeed whom the softness of that glen, especially in the evening, does not touch with some poetical emotion.

After a beastly dinner, and another night of the Bird of Jove, I drove yesterday to Melrose to breakfast, and feel bound to record the unrivalled excellence of fried eggs and bacon. Melrose and its associates were most beautiful. But on the whole I think Jedburgh the better place of the two; not perhaps in its actual and present state, for it is squalid in daily increasing poverty, but in its possibilities. It has a deeper feeling of old repose. The ruin, though less beautiful than that of Melrose, is grander. For enjoyment and personal affection, the little Jed is not inferior to the large and guarded historic Tweed. Jedburgh nestles better into its hidden nook. All that it needs is the summer attraction of visitors and families to put some life and some pence into it. Melrose is greatly improving itself in this way, owing to its having a railway at its door. If Jedburgh cannot get its dotage stopped somehow, the abbey will soon be the loveliest thing in it.

Whoever wishes to see the contrast between the Scotch past and the Scotch present, should look on Melrose and Galashiels, and on Jedburgh and Hawick. Mouldering ruins, attesting the predominance of a single worship, and that the papal, and connected with great national occurrences, solitude, poverty, and silence, on the one side, and, but a few miles off, manufactures, bustle, wealth, population, and newness, on the other; the solitary ruins sink the modern vulgarities into contempt. Both are best, but each in its place. Trade cannot mix itself with the sacred haunts of visible antiquity without profaning or destroying them, and should therefore keep to its own place. And I suppose it is from conscious shame that it generally does so.

I left Melrose at 11.15, and was here — in my natural grey jacket attire — by two.

In one case I added hard labour to imprisonment — a thing I never did, or saw done, in our Justiciary before. It is only now that we are enabled to do it by Government, through the Prison Board having prescribed what the hardness should consist in. It ought to be part of the punishment of male incorrigibles in almost all cases.

Ivory goes in a few days to Dumfries, after which the waters meet at Ayr.

Thornton, Sunday Forenoon, 24th April 1853. — My daughter Johanna and I came here from Bonaly the day before yesterday; from hence I go to Craigie House to-morrow, and we hoist the Bloody Flag on Tuesday the 26th.

One of my youthful acquaintances was Robert Kennedy, eldest son of the then John Kennedy of Underwood. He came to the bar a year or two after me, and died in 1805. We were very intimate for about six years, and had a kindred ardour in the pursuit of all things becoming ambitious youths. We read and discoursed about literature and philosophy — wrote essays and

242

made orations in the Speculative Society; dined, and quaffed, and recited verse, and walked for ever — the sea, Roslin, and Arthur Seat being our favourite haunts. I went twice to see him at Underwood, which is within about five or six miles from Ayr, and on one of these occasions (in 1802 I think) remained about six weeks. None of the family were there except his father — a very kind and excellent man, whose only defect consisted in an intense, and somewhat fantastic, desire not only to be a gentleman, which he really was in his conduct and feelings, but to appear like one in his manners and talk. So Robert and I had six weeks of Ayrshire rusticity, in July and August, to ourselves; and we enjoyed it greatly. We walked, and coach-topped, all over the country, got deep in the then perpetual balls and dinners and flirtations of Ayr, and as the gentleman was never from home, and was very kind and social with us, we were always sure of a good plain dinner, and any quantity of wine and of punch, with him. They were very happy days. Our most ambitious labour was in the construction of a bathing-place in a small burn near the house. We were tempted to it by the excessive heat of the season, the umbrage of two or three respectable beeches, and the pleasure of toiling, especially as the toil provoked the dinner goblets of porter, and the evening cups of wine. We worked more than half-naked, and were bitten as red as partans by the horse-flies and midges, which, however, produced refreshing contrasts by perpetual plunges into the pool. I left it all finished when I came home, the model, as we thought, of a rustic open air, burn bath, and our names cut, for immortality, into the bark of a beech.

Well, I never again beheld the scene of all this till yesterday. John Kennedy, Robert's brother, who is now laird, was obliged to leave Edinburgh from bad health about three years ago, and retired to Underwood; hearing that I was to be in the neighbourhood, he invited me to go and see him and the place. I said that I would, and yesterday did so.

The place, which is a mere farm, and has very little beauty, either natural or artificial, is nearly quite unchanged. A recent porch has improved the house, and the adjoining steading is modernised. The burn trickles as of yore. But of the bath, though long protected, after Robert's death, by the affection of his father, not a vestige remains, not a particle or a trace. I fancied that I could plausibly refer to a few marks as showing that it still owned fragments of us, but was conscious that the truth was that it did not, successions of other names, down apparently to last year, have followed ours, and are all passing into our oblivion. Such is vanity, or glory, or the aversion to be forgotten.

Few things are more fallacious than anticipations as to how young men are, or are not, to turn out. But, though his manner was good, I still think that if poor Robert's life had been prolonged, he would have been distinguished; for his abilities were superior, and they were combined with great industry, ardent ambition, and excellent affections. His poor father survived him many years, but his spirit was always hovering about his son's grave.

I saw a journal yesterday which it seems that Robert had been in the practice of keeping. It contained this entry: "7th June 1803. Dined with Cockburn, sate till four" (he means next morning), "walked" (i.e. both of us) "to Arthur's Seat, and returned at five in the morning." Thus summed up. "Study, 6½ hours; company, 15½, exercise, 2; sleep, 0."

He and Richardson and I were insatiable of Arthur Seat and sun's rising. It was our Parnassus. And this was a common way of enjoying it. First to dine about four, to be sociable for a few hours, then a walk, then more sociality from about ten till the sun's hour was approaching, then up the hill, and then down to a few hours' sleep, or, as on this day with Kennedy, to feverish study. Yet, TAKE NOTICE, there never was the slightest drunkenness. Elevation there was; but it stopped far, very far, below the intoxication mark. Excess in wine was never the habit of any set of friends into which I have been thrown.

Bonaly, 29th April 1853. — I left Thornton on Monday the 25th; dined and stayed all night at Craigie House; was in Court on Tuesday and Wednesday the 26th and 27th; got off on the 27th in time to dine at Thornton; stayed there all night; left it on 28th (yesterday), and was here to dinner.

I expected to be kept much longer at Ayr; but a friendly witness favoured a bad murderer by staying away, a culpably negligent railway guard had the sense to prefer outlawry to conviction; and an apothecary weaver, who slew a child by a wrong dose, professed penitence and pleaded guilty, and these "Providences", as some religious pedants call such things, freed us.

Our Depute was Andrew Clark, a youth of whom I augur very favourably.

NORTH CIRCUIT

Castleton, Braemar, Wednesday Night, 28th September 1853. — Ivory took Inverness, which I escaped.

But on the day before yesterday — being Monday the 26th instant — my daughter Johanna and I left Edinburgh at 6.30, and got to Perth, by Stirling, by ten. After remaining there three hours, we set off for Aberdeen, but had to wait for three-quarters of an hour at Forfar, — an excellent arrangement, which all railways should be compelled to adopt, because pauses are good for the health and for looking about. At 5.15 we were at Aberdeen, and were borne into the granite city in a blaze of Circuit glory.

The only thing that I observed along that dull Strathmore, was the little village of Dubton, near Montrose. I was not in it, but it seemed to be an unusually nice Scotch village. It is common for inlanders to go to the seaside in summer; and it seems to be as common for seasiders to go in summer inland. Each wants change. Dubton, I understand, is the summer retreat of the Montrosers; and their need of respectable houses has made this an unusually comfortable city of little villas.

The business at Aberdeen was finished yesterday by three o'clock. Another unlicensed doctor had poisoned a child by an absurd dose. This Circuit is the first occasion on which we had to expound and apply the recently introduced punishment of "Penal Servitude" in place of short transportations. I augur no good of it.

After getting out, Ivory, Archibald Davidson the Sheriff, and I spent two hours on the harbour and the pier. We went over a very fine new ship, which was nearly finished, and means, in four months, to be dashing aside the waves of Australia. But, as in all British traders, the place for the crew was disgracefully small, dark, and airless. We also saw a ship on the stocks, which (though only about 1500 tons), is the largest sailing vessel ever built in Scotland. It, and another ship beside it, were building in a yard entirely covered over.

A part of the wreck of the Duchess of Sutherland, a large passenger steamer, which was dashed to pieces upon the point of the pier a few months ago, with great loss of life, is still unremoved, and fixed in the sand. I was much struck by the appearance of two gentlewomen, who were leaning on the rail at the pierhead. One I could swear had had her heart broken by that wreck, and was gazing on the fragments amidst which some dear one had perished. The other was standing aside, not obtruding, but visibly watching the emotion of her friend.

We had a beastly Circuit dinner, on a sanded floor, and came eagerly away this morning from the stinking Royal Hotel, and breakfasting at Banchory, were here about five — Ivory, his daughter, and daughter-in-law, being with us. I have nothing more to say about beautiful Deeside. But below Ballater it is not improving. Up to Banchory it is polluted by a railway; the wood is disappearing, and agriculture encroaching. Above Ballater it is unchanged, and I hope unchangeable, and the whole eighteen miles are glorious. The new house building for the Queen at Balmoral may be better than the old one for residence, but I don't anticipate that it will equal the old one in picturesque beauty. The day was not very good, and yet not very bad. It was excessively cold, with too much wind, and some surly showers. But on the whole there was a prevalence of bright light, and Lochnagar never shone in greater splendour.

I think it my duty to record the unmatched merits of a leg of mutton which we had today at dinner. It was a leg which stands out even amidst all the legs of my long and steadily muttonised life. It was glorious. A leg of which the fat flats of England can have no idea, and which even Wales, in its most favoured circumstances, could only approach. It was a leg which told how it had strayed among the mountains from its lambhood to its death. It spoke of winter straths and summer heights, of tender heather, Alpine airs, cold springs, and that short sweet grass which corries alone can cherish. These were the mettle of its pasture. It left its savour on the palate, like the savour of a good deed on the heart. And then the room was so breezy, and our cloak devices so diverting, and we were always heaping so much wood on the fire, and had so much true wit with an old body of a waiter, who said his name was Malcolm, and who was pleased by being dubbed the king, and the brandy and hot-water were so satisfactory, and the evening closed by such a comfortable drowsiness, that, joined to the leg, it was a worthy close of a worthy day.

Perth, Thursday Night, 29th September 1853. — We left Castleton this morning at nine, and were here about six. A brilliant, though cold day. But a glorious district. I think I have tried to describe it somewhere already. I am not sure but that the descent on this side is as good as the rise on the other. O these large, heathery, silent hills! Treeless, peakless, and nearly rockless! Great masses of solitary silence, broken only by high rills, tumbling into raging and sparkling torrents in the valley! And the gradual opening of the rich low country, ending in the beauty of Perth! Were I to see it yearly for a thousand years, I cannot conceive that its impression would ever fade.

Rossie Ochil, Sunday Night, 2d October 1853. — In Court all Friday and Saturday. And we must go back — like the sow that hath been washed — to our mire to-morrow. Meanwhile Ivory and I came here from Perth to breakfast this morning.

On Friday the sad and unexpected tidings of the death of Lord Anderson reached us. He was to have opened the Circuit at Glasgow to-morrow. His judicial life was only about a single year long. A good lawyer, a good judge, and a good and agreeable man, his sudden extinction makes one think. The few remaining old targets must be struck soon.

I was never at this spot before. Ivory has it on lease. The ten or twelve miles between it and Perth are all beautiful, and pass through several very desirable places. No sensible man would object to take either Moncreiffe, or Kilgraston, or Freeland, or Rossie, or Invermay, even under the necessity of living at them. This Rossie Ochil is an aeolian residence on the eastern end of the Ochil range. It is a small, sensible house, standing on the very top of an almost treeless hill, in the midst of a wide amphitheatre of much higher hills, the inner circle all varied by many heights, and masses of wood, and farms, and deeply engraved into countless valleys and gullies, gurgling with countless

246

bright little streams, all falling into the May, which, after becoming a river, yields itself up to the Earn, and thus goes, like thousands of other rivers, to swell the majestic Tay. The elevation and openness of this farmhouse kind of a spot secures its being smote by every gale that blows, and therefore I should suppose that it would seldom be too hot. But its views, and freedom, and fresh air, make it a place that I am certain I would like.

We had a long saunter through the countries, and found a profusion of clear and rocky waters, green old turfy haughs, respectable trees, and good agriculture, with decent children coming from the Sunday school, and old hinds lying on the grass, playing with infants. But even these were less interesting than Ivory's more early walk and mine to the top of Kinteuchar Hill. What a prospect! Nothing inland could be nobler! But amidst all its splendours, there was nothing on which my eye rested with more pleasure than on the very humble farmhouse of Kinteuchar. It was formerly tenanted by a poor farmer called Deas, whose son is now a judge, a man of fortune, and of great worth, and born in that place. What is more refreshing than the sight of the lowly cradles of eminent men? What is so luxurious as the delight of a poor father in the public elevation of an affectionate son?

And so I go to bed, but I first must add that from Braemar to this higher ground have been richly sprinkled with snow.

Bonaly, Wednesday Night, 5th October 1853. — We came from Rossie Ochil to Perth on the morning of Monday the 3d, and were in Court till eight that night. Next morning Ivory went to Glasgow to do what would have been done by poor Lord Anderson. I stayed at Perth, and got the business concluded by one. We left, Perth, by Fife, at three, and were here by seven in the evening.

The cases throughout the Circuit were commonplace. There were no fewer than twelve attacks by masculine brutes on women and feminine children. Mary Mackenzie, an incorrigible thief, was almost the handsomest figure I ever saw at a criminal bar. Young, stately, intelligent looking, and with a calm manner, she looked like one who, under favourable circumstances, might have shone on the stage, or in a high drawing-room; but trained, as she had been, in iniquity, a steady eye, and a resolute lip showed that defiance of society had become a necessity to her position, and that little more was wanted to make her an excellent devil. I wanted her counsel to marry her, but the paltry fellow had not the courage.

I am confident that this new-fangled "Penal Servitude" won't do, even if strictly enforced. But it is plain by the establishment of "Tickets of Leave," that Government means, or will be tempted, to save expense by emptying the jails upon the public, which will be drenching us, instead of our colonies, with tolerated villains.

I see that my Lord Justice-Clerk, John Hope, has been lecturing the authorities on his Circuit from the Bench, on the duties and the details of the stink removing precautions against cholera. No other judge has thought this matter within his province. And clearly neither it is. It recalls the days, now about forty-five years gone, when the Circuit judgment-seat was regularly converted into a platform from which Tory judges preached Toryism to the Tory authorities beneath them. A discourse upon drains from the Bench! Instructions to inspectors of nuisances by my lord the judge! And the absurdity of the thing is, that as the scavengers are not bound to obey the wig, and know much more of their own business than the ermine does, they hear the obtrusive address and inwardly laugh at it. O John, John! when will you be modest?

I heard a Scotch proverb, from a witness at Perth, which to me was new. A young woman had told her mother that she was afraid to return to the mill, because a man who worked there had said to her that he meant to wrong her. The mother, a decent-like body, presumed that, since he had announced it, he must have been in joke, and advised her girl to go back to her work, saying "It's no aye the cart that rumbles maist that gangs first ower the brae".

SOUTH CIRCUIT
1854

Bonaly, 22d April 1854. — A most contemptible Circuit; short solitary, expeditionless.

It has been the South. Ivory was again fixed for Dumfries, and I hoped to soothe myself under the pensive silence of venerable and fading Jedburgh. But a cold prevented me; so Ivory, with his usual kindness took that too, and I went to Ayr, where he joined me.

I left this last Saturday the 15th, alone. Yes, for the second time alone. Which at least shows that I am not deemed to be yet quite doited. It may be said to testify my increasing moroseness, but my-self-conceit doubts even this, for I see no other symptom of it. The truth is that she, who for above forty-three years has been, and still is, my second and better self, is no longer able for journeys beyond her own flowers, and that my only travellable daughter had occupations with stronger claims at home. So I braved the perils of a pilgrimage to Ayr by myself.

I went to Thornton on the 15th, where I remained till the evening of Monday the 17th, when I went to Ayr.

We were in Court all the 18th and 19th, and a part of the 20th.

The only interesting case was that of Alexander Cunninghame, charged with murdering his wife, and convicted on the clearest possible circumstantial evidence. It was a singularly atrocious proceeding. He was about thirty-five, a strong, resolute-looking, dogged scoundrel. She had been a well-conditioned, good woman, whom he had been twice punished for assaulting, and who was obliged, for the preservation of herself and her four children, to cease living with him. She was twice or thrice persuaded to go back, but was always obliged to fly again, and they had been entirely parted for about a year. During all this time, the children were maintained solely by her labour. He often said that he would like to kill her, and that he would shoot her as easily as he would "that gull". An acquaintance to whom he once disclosed this inclination, warned him against "letting such thoughts enter his heart", as they would certainly lead to his being hanged. No intimation of these threats, or rather indications, was ever made to the authorities, because they were believed to be mere sulky words.

Though they were both in so small a place as Girvan, he for nine months did not know where she was working. At last he found this out, and next day borrowed a gun, powder, and shot. That evening about seven, — a calm, dark evening last December — he got into the garden behind the house she was working in, and saw her sitting, with a candle, at her loom. She was not sitting quite right for receiving the full effect of his shot. He therefore threw a little gravel against the window. This made her look up. He fired and she was dead.

Yet, though the evidence was quite clear, and the jury said nothing of lenity, I expect an exertion to be made by the idiots who have got into a habit of distinguishing themselves on such occasions, to save the life even of this miscreant. They have luckily made their efforts somewhat ridiculous of late, not so much by the folly of their reasons, as by their shameless fecundity in the creation of false evidence.

The prisoner was very attentive to the proceedings, and understood everything that was going on. But he got into a very odd speculation. I observed him make a sign to his counsel to come to him. The counsel did so, and resumed his seat, with a look in which I thought I saw some horror and a little mirth. I afterwards asked him what his client had said. It was this, "If they hang me, what will they do wi' ma claes?"

This was our last criminal case. It was over about two P.M. of Thursday the 20th. I left Ivory to try a civil cause, and, passing by the back of the Court, found myself on the seashore. It was one of the finest days even of this unsurpassed spring. The beautiful bay of Ary could scarcely have been more beautiful. The advancing sea was insinuating its clear waters irresistibly, yet gently, into the innumerable little hollows and channels of the dry sand. Few people were out, but plenty sea-fowls playing on the beach, and in the air, and with the long soft waves. Three white-skinned boys were bathing. No ship, not even a boat, was visible. There was no sound, except of an occasional hammer by a few lazy masons who were pretending to be repairing the point of the pier, the ring of whose implements only deepened the silence. The picture of repose was completed on reaching the pier, every projecting point of which was occupied by one or two old bodies of rod fishers, who were watching the bobbing of their corks as attentively as slumber would allow. They caught nothing, and said that they would not till it should rain, which it had not done for six weeks. So the very fishes were at rest too. It was all a refreshing contrast to the heat and the crowd of that horrid Court.

I went to Glasgow that evening, stayed there all night, and came here yesterday forenoon.

(Next day Lord Cockburn was seized with a serious illness, and died on Wednesday the 26th April, in his seventy-fifth year.)